California 2025: Taking on the Future

• • •

Editors:
Ellen Hanak
Mark Baldassare

2005

Library of Congress Cataloging-in-Publication Data
    California 2025: taking on the future / Ellen Hanak and Mark
Baldassare, editors.
        p. cm.
    Includes bibliographical references.
    ISBN: 1-58213-110-4
    1. California—Economic conditions. 2. Infrastructure
(Economics) I. Hanak, Ellen. II. Baldassare, Mark.
    HC107.C23C33 2005
    330.9794—dc22

                                                    2005004054

Foreword

In the late 1990s, PPIC began a systematic assessment of growth, development, and infrastructure issues in California. The first report looked at metropolitan planning organizations and the implementation of federal transportation policy. The second focused on redevelopment as a form of subsidy to local governments. Subsequent reports covered topics as diverse as local growth controls; infrastructure planning, budgeting, and financing; housing supply; the regulation of electricity; and the future of water markets in California. It would be hazardous to identify a single, simple theme in all of these studies, but they all do conclude that building for the future of California will not be "business as usual." In the past, California relied on increased spending to meet its needs. The future will increasingly require improved efficiency—making better use of existing facilities rather than the wholesale construction of new ones. Moreover, the state's growth plans are, and will probably continue to be, heavily constrained by a combination of local and state policies that regulate everything from the environment to affordable housing.

By 2003, PPIC had a much better understanding of infrastructure supply, including the options for putting new capacity in place and the process for implementing plans. We were less certain about future demands and what the future will bring in terms of population growth and composition. Is our current system of infrastructure planning and investment up to the job?

We approached the William and Flora Hewlett Foundation with an ambitious plan—mobilize resources from both institutions to take a look out to the year 2025. PPIC was in the unique position of having a research team that had just completed ten years of research on the changing population, economy, and governance issues facing the state. We had also just completed five years of work on infrastructure. Our proposed project identified a wide range of relevant issues—population and economic forecasts, systems of governance, the financing and requirements for infrastructure, the equity of alternative solutions, and statewide public opinion about the need for new infrastructure investments. The Hewlett Foundation had a strong interest in bringing the state's future requirements to public attention and highlighting the kinds of solutions necessary to bring demand in line with supply. With substantial support from the foundation, PPIC launched the project in the fall of 2003. *California 2025: Taking on the Future* is the result of that effort.

This project draws some remarkable conclusions. The contributors see a future of slowing population growth and a shift in economic growth trends that will put less pressure on infrastructure. They also conclude that major strides have been made in the planning and financing of infrastructure and that many of the demand-management options once politically unattractive are entering into the process of balancing supply and demand. Rather than facing a crisis, California seems to be at a critical point—looking at a future that could be managed with a set of policy options that fall short of budget-breaking solutions.

Ironically, the major concern raised in the report relates to the supply of high-skill labor. Providing sufficient human capital, rather than more physical capital, could well be California's biggest challenge in the year 2025 and beyond. California has always drawn on a national and international labor market to help meet its needs for high-skill labor. However, those born in California who do not get a four-year college degree might well find themselves left out in future growth cycles. The relative supply of jobs for high school graduates will shrink while jobs for higher-skill workers expand. The authors conclude that this shift, coupled with some demographic trends, could create a state with increasing numbers of workers without the skills to make significant gains in lifetime earnings. Their conclusions point once again to the importance of education to the state's economic growth and especially to the integration and well-being of individuals from second and third generation immigrant families.

This report provides a unique profile of California's future. From population and economic growth to the supply of infrastructure. From physical capital to human capital. From "hard" solutions to "soft" solutions to our infrastructure challenges. And from importing our future labor supply to growing our own. These are the challenges facing the state today. *California 2025: Taking on the Future* provides the facts and clarifies the options.

David W. Lyon
President and CEO
Public Policy Institute of California

Contents

Figures

Tables

Acknowledgments

We wish to thank the William and Flora Hewlett Foundation for their generous support for the "California 2025" research project that resulted in this edited volume. We appreciate the continuing interest of foundation President Paul Brest in this topic and the attention to this project by program staff, Terry Amsler and Malka Kopell. We also benefited from the Hewlett Foundation grants that provided funding for related research projects carried out by the Center for Collaborative Regional Leadership, PolicyLink, and Viewpoint Learning that informed some of the research reported here. We thank our colleagues at those three institutions for sharing their knowledge with our staff. The topics and policy questions addressed in this research project, and the content and editing of this volume, were solely determined by the Public Policy Institute of California. The editors and authors would also like to thank Peter Richardson for his careful editing of each chapter in the volume and Joyce Peterson and Abby Cook for their comments and suggestions on the substance of the research, Lisa Cole for her efforts in coordinating the California 2025 project activities, Madhavi Katikaneni for her administrative and editorial assistance on the project, and Vanessa Merina for her assistance in the report's production.

The authors of each chapter would like to acknowledge the following people who contributed to their work at various stages:

For Chapter 2, "California's Population in 2025," Hans Johnson would like to thank Ellen Hanak, Dowell Myers, and Tim Miller for their helpful reviews of an earlier draft. Mary Heim of the California Department of Finance was generous with her time, expertise, and population projections model. John Pitkin and Dowell Myers graciously provided preliminary information from their population projections model. Finally, Joseph Hayes provided valuable research assistance.

For Chapter 3, "Trends and Patterns in California's Economic Future," David Neumark would like to thank Stephen Ciccarella, Jon

Norman, and Douglas Symes for outstanding research assistance and Ellen Hanak, Doug Henton, Manuel Pastor, Deborah Reed, and Chris Thornberg for helpful comments.

For Chapter 4, "Infrastructure Financing in California," Shelley de Alth and Kim Rueben wish to thank Dana Curry, Mark Newton, and Mac Taylor from the Legislative Analyst's Office; Henry Wulf, Donna Hirsch, Jeffrey Little, and Steve Poyta of the U.S. Census Bureau; Alice Fong and Anita Tomasovitch of the State Controller's Office; and Ellen Hanak.

For Chapter 5, "Sizing Up the Challenge: California's Infrastructure Needs and Tradeoffs," Elisa Barbour and Ellen Hanak would like to thank Richard Howitt, Kim Rueben, and Martin Wachs for guidance on the overall analysis. Thanks also to reviewers who provided feedback in areas of subject-matter expertise, including Kim Rueben for K–12 education; Pat Callan and C. Judson King for higher education; Norman King and Martin Wachs for transportation and integrated approaches; and Robin Hook, Richard Howitt, Darrin Polhemus, and Al Wanger for water. Jon Norman provided valuable research assistance.

For Chapter 6, "California Comes of Age: Governing Institutions, Planning and Public Investment," Elisa Barbour and Paul Lewis wish to thank Ellen Hanak, Peter Richardson, Steve Sanders, and Fred Silva for helpful comments on early drafts. Thanks also to Kim Rueben, Shelley de Alth, Michael Falcone, and other PPIC colleagues involved in the project for helpful inputs.

For Chapter 7, "Understanding Equitable Infrastructure Investment for California," Manuel Pastor, Jr., and Deborah Reed wish to thank Elisa Barbour, Jon Cohen, Ray Colmenar, Ellen Hanak, Martha Matsuoka, Robert Puentes, Stephen Raphael, Richard Raya, Peter Richardson, Victor Rubin, Kim Rueben, Nancy Shulock, Johntell Washington, and participants in California 2025 meetings for helpful comments. Amanda Bailey and Justin Scoggins provided valuable research assistance.

For Chapter 8, "Public Opinion: Californians' View of the Present, the Future, Governance, and Policy Options," Mark Baldassare and Jonathan Cohen wish to thank survey research associates Kimberly Curry, Eliana Kaimowitz, and Renatta DeFever, who contributed to the research and writing of the *PPIC Statewide Survey: Special Survey on Californians and the Future*, August 2004, on which the chapter is based.

Acronyms

AB	Assembly Bill
ABAG	Association of Bay Area Governments
BART	Bay Area Rapid Transit
BLS	Bureau of Labor Statistics
BRT	Bus Rapid Transit
BRU	Bus Riders' Union
Cal/EPA	California Environmental Protection Agency
Caltrans	California Department of Transportation
CBO	Congressional Budget Office
CCC	California Community College
CCCHE	California Citizens Commission on Higher Education
CCSCE	Center for the Continuing Study of the California Economy
CDE	California Department of Education
CHEPC	California Higher Education Policy Center
COFPHE	Capital Outlay Fund for Public Higher Education
COG	Councils of Government
CPEC	California Postsecondary Education Commission
CPS	Current Population Survey
CSU	California State University
CTC	California Transportation Commission
CVP	Central Valley Project
DHS	Department of Health Services
DOF	Department of Finance
DOT	Department of Transportation
DWR	Department of Water Resources
EDD	Employment Development Department
FTE	Full-Time-Equivalent
GO	General Obligation
HOT	High-Occupancy Toll
HOV	High-Occupancy Vehicle

ISTEA	Intermodal Surface Transportation Efficiency Act
JARC	Job Access Reverse Commute
LAO	Legislative Analyst's Office
MALDEF	Mexican American Legal Defense and Educational Fund
MTC	Metropolitan Transportation Commission
NAICS	North American Industry Classification System
RTPA	Regional Transportation Planning Agency
SACOG	Sacramento Area Council of Governments
SANDAG	San Diego Association of Governments
SCAG	Southern California Association of Governments
SIC	Standard Industrial Classification
SWP	State Water Project
SWRCB	State Water Resources Control Board
TTI	Texas Transportation Institute
UC	University of California
UCLA	University of California, Los Angeles
USBR	U.S. Bureau of Reclamation

1. Introduction and Summary

Ellen Hanak and Mark Baldassare

There has been a mounting sense of doom and gloom about the future of the Golden State. After decades of rapid population growth and repeated cycles of budget shortfalls, California appears to be drifting into a state of disrepair and voters seem to disregard the long-term consequences of ignoring its schools, roads, and other infrastructure. At least that has been the drumbeat sounded by alarmists, made up of a loose coalition that includes such unlikely allies as Republicans and Democrats, business interests and labor activists, and builders and environmentalists. Whether the growth and infrastructure crisis is as bad as some say and how to best go about planning for the future and paying for necessary repairs and expansion of infrastructure are the topics that we seek to address in this report, *California 2025*.

The project evolved out of an interest on the part of many institutions that care deeply about the future of the state and generous funding from the William and Flora Hewlett Foundation. Staff and resources of the Public Policy Institute of California were directed toward providing policymakers, interest groups, and the public with a nonpartisan, objective, independent analysis of the current state of affairs and the available policy options as California prepares to take on its uncertain future. The endeavor draws on the talents and expertise of researchers in all three of our institute's program areas—economy, governance, and population—to provide the most thorough and comprehensive investigation into the state's future to date. In areas where we lacked the depth of knowledge, or wanted second opinions on our findings, we called on outside experts from other state think tanks and research organizations.

Our choice of the year 2025 as a horizon for looking at California's future was carefully considered. The state government is required to make plans at five-year intervals, which seem too short-term for addressing long-range issues. Some population and economic projections extend 40 years or longer, but they are scarce and admittedly look into events that are well beyond the foreseeable future. The 20-year time frame provides the researcher with many data points to compare and contrast and a reasonable interval for planners and policymakers to develop policies and programs that may take years or even decades to implement.

Our focus on three elements of infrastructure—schools, water systems, and roads and transportation systems—was also considered. The large, high-impact public works projects undertaken by the state a half-century ago were in these three arenas. Prime examples include the Master Plan for Higher Education and heavy investments in public school systems, the State Water Plan's extensive network of reservoirs and aqueducts, and the massive freeway system that defines California's landscape today. These sectors continue to dominate public investment in California, receiving a significant proportion of all state and local investment dollars. There is general agreement that public education, water systems, and transportation projects will play an important part in the state's future and thus demand our attention today.

Many of the findings and conclusions offered in this volume will support the views of those who have raised serious concerns about the state's future. Certainly, it is a formidable task and complex undertaking to adequately plan for such a large and growing state as California. Moreover, this policymaker's task is critically important to the economic vitality and quality of life of state residents but, in recent years, has not received the attention that it deserves. The importance of infrastructure and the relative neglect of its upkeep and development are clearly evident themes throughout our investigation into the state's future.

Still, our research is likely to disappoint those looking for solid evidence that the state is in a downward spiral because our infrastructure needs will outstrip the available resources or those who believe that we will solve all problems by investing more funds in infrastructure. For instance, we point to many areas in which progress has been made to address shortcomings in planning and funding of state and local infrastructure. Moreover, projected demographic and economic trends will ease some of the pressures on the infrastructure base. At the same time, these trends point to some new challenges—in particular, the need for bold and unprecedented investments of public resources to ensure a brighter tomorrow for today's youth.

Although the 20th century saw progress through construction and engineering feats unprecedented for their time, the greater challenges in the 21st century are in the adaptability and effectiveness of our political institutions and system of governance. We argue that too much emphasis on how much infrastructure is needed and how much it will cost can obscure other important questions that should be part of today's policy discussions. For instance, what is the quality of the roads, school facilities, water systems, and other infrastructure that residents want for their state, and what are the most efficient ways to pay for the infrastructure systems? Moreover, how will the goals for infrastructure planning and the financing tools affect the lives of Californians? In the chapters that follow, we provide evidence that will broaden our understanding of the range of policy issues that Californians will need to confront as they take on the future.

The remainder of this introduction summarizes the major findings and conclusions of an investigation that took over one year to complete. We begin with population and economic forecasts, patterns of infrastructure financing, and the current state of knowledge regarding our infrastructure needs. We then turn to the governance and institutional challenges facing state and local policymakers as they attempt to plan for the future and the equity issues that merit careful consideration as we seek to address infrastructure challenges. Last but certainly not least, given their growing role in policymaking at the ballot box, we consider public perceptions of the state's future; their policy preferences in the realm of schools, water, and roads and transportation; and their willingness to pay higher taxes or fees to support the infrastructure they want.

California's Population in 2025

Even as the state struggles to accommodate the demands generated by the 10 million population increase of the past two decades, it is expected to add millions more residents between now and 2025. The Department of Finance projects another 10 million residents by that year, bringing the total population to 46 million. Allowing for slightly higher or lower rates of fertility and migration, our study projects a likely range of growth between 7 million and 11 million. For those concerned about meeting the infrastructure challenges of population growth, both scenarios imply some good news relative to projections made several years earlier. A decline in fertility rates, particularly among the fast-growing Latino population, has led demographers to revise their population growth figures downward. Still, most experts agree that the absolute growth facing California will be formidable, placing significant strains on public infrastructure, including educational facilities, water systems, and roads and transportation networks.

There is also general agreement about the regional patterns of growth, with much faster increases expected in the inland areas than in the state's population centers along the coast. The fast pace of growth in the Central Valley and the Inland Empire (Riverside and San Bernardino Counties) may pose particular challenges because infrastructure systems must be built from scratch or from a much smaller base. However, the Southern California coastal areas (Los Angeles, Orange, and San Diego Counties) and the San Francisco Bay Area are also likely to experience sizable population gains, putting pressure on existing systems in areas where the built-up environment makes expansion more difficult, potentially more costly, and politically controversial.

Another area of agreement is the state's shifting racial and ethnic makeup. California's transition from a majority white state to a majority-minority state, ongoing for decades, is destined to continue. Today, less than half of the state's population is white—the majority is made up mostly of Latinos but with sizable proportions of Asians, African Americans, and multiracial Californians. Almost half of all births today are to Latina mothers. Latinos are now the largest racial/ethnic group of state residents under age 30. They are expected to become the largest group in the state within a decade and eventually will account for half of the state's population.

These demographic shifts raise special concerns about how prepared we are for the future, especially when it comes to providing quality of life and economic opportunities for nonwhite and immigrant populations. For instance, young Latinos have lower rates of educational attainment

4

than the white baby boom population that now makes up a large share of the college-educated workforce. Although Latino youths have registered some progress in educational outcomes over the past decade, much more needs to be done. To ensure a better future for California, we will need to significantly improve the educational outcomes of the Latino youth who will be the state's workers in the future. Otherwise, many second-generation Californians will face low-skill, low-pay jobs or chronic unemployment. Making improvements in educational attainment in the coming decades would also benefit other racial, immigrant, and low-income groups who might otherwise also face grim prospects in the future job market.

A third area of demographic certainty is the increasing share of the state's senior population, resulting from the aging of the baby boom generation and improvements in health care. This increase will raise demands for the infrastructure serving the special needs of seniors, ranging from health care facilities to public transit.

Trends and Patterns in California's Economic Future

Population growth is likely to be the key driver of infrastructure needs, raising school and college enrollments, increasing the demand for urban water and wastewater systems, and putting pressure on transportation networks. However, the trajectory of the economy may also play a significant role, because shifts in the industrial composition and geographic location of economic activity influence the demand for both infrastructure services and a skilled workforce. To shed light on these issues, we looked at anticipated trends in the California economy. Specifically, we examined predictions about the level of future economic activity, its geographic location, its industrial composition, and the implications for the skill composition of the workforce.

California today has a large and dynamic economy rivaling that of many nations. Following the trends noted for population growth, employment growth is expected to be in the range of 30 to 40 percent in the next two decades. One threat to these forecasts, noted by experts, is that insufficient investment in the state's infrastructure could lead to a slowdown in growth over the coming decades. Although economic evidence on these linkages is inconclusive, the concern is valid and has prompted labor and business interests to call for greater attention to infrastructure financing.

The forecasts do suggest that shifts in industrial composition will alleviate growth pressures on some infrastructure services. Specifically, our analysis indicates a continuing decline in the share of manufacturing employment and a steady rise in the share of services employment over the next two decades. The industries declining in economic significance are more intensive users of water, roads, and energy than are growing industries. Agricultural water use is also likely to decline as a result of market forces. This is important because the agricultural sector now uses roughly 80 percent of the state's developed water resources. Although these shifts should reduce the relative pressures of growth, the absolute expansion level of the state's economy will put new burdens on our transportation networks, water systems, and energy.

The changing industrial composition is expected to increase demands on one infrastructure sector: the state's public educational facilities—particularly public institutions of higher learning. In the new economy, the demand for workers with a high school education or less will fall and the demand for workers with some college courses or a college degree will rise. This may seem like a surprising conclusion because the service sector is often seen as generating a preponderance of low-education and low-skill employment. However, our analysis indicates that the expected growth in service employment in California—including business, professional, entertainment, recreation, health, and educational services—will require a highly educated workforce with associate, bachelor's, and advanced college degrees. The part of the service sector expected to grow the least—personal services including household work—consists of jobs requiring less education.

These economic changes underscore the key challenge facing the state: Residents entering the workforce over the next 20 years will increasingly be Latinos—a group that now has lower levels of education. Latino immigrants and second-generation Californians, as well as other growing minority and low-income groups with low education, will have to attend college in larger proportions than today to meet the employment demands of 2025. Otherwise, the state will have to import college-educated workers in larger numbers than it does now from other states and abroad. If these college-educated migrants do not come, prospects for economic growth will suffer. That is a real possibility because we could face stiff competition with other states that offer college-educated workers a lower cost of living and more affordable housing than California can offer today and is likely to offer in the future.

If California's children and youth do not acquire a college education before they enter the workforce in the coming decades, they face the prospect of low or no employment, a lack of opportunities for high-paying jobs, and a greater likelihood of depending on public health and social services. For the state, the stakes could not be higher. California faces either a bright tomorrow with many residents in high-skill, higher-paying jobs that generate high tax revenues or a bleak future in which the jobs requiring more skills go elsewhere and its low-income residents seek public assistance.

Infrastructure Financing in California

How much have California's state and local governments been spending on infrastructure projects and where are they finding the funds? Overall spending patterns get a mixed report card, with some areas of recent success and worrisome trends in some other sectors. California's real per capita spending on public infrastructure investments declined precipitously in the 1970s and 1980s. However, by the early 1990s, it recovered to the levels of the early 1960s, California's "golden era" of public investment. The most recent figures from the U.S. Census of Governments, for 2002, show a sharp increase over the preceding five years, with real spending now considerably higher than it was in the 1960s. These overall statewide trends largely mirror trends elsewhere in the country, and California now spends about the same per person as the nation.

Nevertheless, these overall spending trends mask some important differences across the three infrastructure sectors. Like its semiarid western neighbors, California has always spent more than the national average on water resources. After decades of neglect, and thanks to the success of recent state and local school bond initiatives, the state has again caught up to the national average for educational facilities. However, California was once a national leader in road and highway investments but now invests considerably less than the national average; considerably more of its transportation budget goes for maintenance costs. In the meantime, spending on transit has increased substantially and now accounts for a fifth or more of the transportation investment budget. The low investment in roads is a major concern as the state prepares for its future population growth and increases in economic activity.

There are also troubling trends in how the state pays the bills for these investments. Federal funds have been a declining source of the state investment budget, and pay-as-you-go financing has also become less common. Correspondingly, the state government has become heavily reliant on borrowing through long-term general obligation bonds. These are paid back through the existing general fund rather than through any new revenue sources dedicated to infrastructure. In addition to the school bonds, voters have recently passed large bonds to pay for water and park projects and stem cell research and to cover outstanding state debt. As a result, the debt-service ratio—the portion of general fund revenues devoted to interest and principal payments on debt—is approaching levels that have called into question the remaining state debt capacity for taking on new infrastructure projects. This level of indebtedness also raises concerns about the state's ability to generate bond funding for unexpected developments such as response to a natural disaster.

Local revenue sources have become more important in California, and this trend may be expected to continue in an era of tight state and federal funding. As a result of Proposition 13 and related tax limitations, local governments face greater constraints than the state government does in mobilizing new resources. Whereas state bonds require a simple majority pass rate, local bonds have historically required a supermajority of two-thirds. Since the voters lowered the threshold for passing local school bonds to a 55 percent vote in November 2000, the funding for local educational facilities has become more certain.

Meanwhile, the county sales tax has become the largest revenue source for local transportation projects. Getting voter approval for these local tax increases has become more difficult since 1995, when the system shifted from a simple majority to a two-thirds vote requirement as a result of a court ruling on the state's constitutional laws. Nineteen counties currently have a local sales tax for transportation; 15 others have tried and failed to pass one. In several counties that passed taxes under the old simple majority rules, the tax is up for reauthorization under the new supermajority rules, and this has raised concerns about the ability to maintain current funding levels.

As the state looks for a stable source of funding for its roads and transportation projects, many proposals have been considered. Voters passed an initiative that earmarked a portion of the state sales tax for transportation; however, the legislature has routinely circumvented this requirement to close the budget gap. Voters defeated a measure to earmark a portion of the general fund for infrastructure spending on the same ballot that they chose to recall their governor in October 2003. Some policymakers have suggested that the vote requirement for local transportation sales taxes be lowered to 55 percent, as is now the case for local school bonds. Finally, the idea of user fees and of taxes tied more directly to infrastructure use has gained support in policy circles, particularly as planners have been rethinking the definition of "needs."

Infrastructure Needs and Tradeoffs

This brings us to the core question that has been raised by critics of state policy: Are we spending too little on our public investments, thereby compromising our economic vitality and quality of life? The conventional method for addressing this question, sometimes referred to as "gap analysis," is misleading. It begins by assessing infrastructure "needs," pricing them, and then comparing the total price tag to actual spending. The discrepancy between the price tag and actual spending is then dubbed the "funding gap."

The major problem with gap analysis arises from the way it defines and estimates infrastructure needs, that is, gauging needs by matching a targeted per capita level of services to population projections. As a result, it tends to overstate the level of needs in sectors where market mechanisms (especially prices) might shape the demand for those services. Such overestimations can be compounded by the nature of infrastructure finance, because agencies competing for public funds often have incentives to inflate their requirements.

We thus call attention to some techniques for distinguishing needs from desires—often grouped under the heading "demand management"—that have grown in importance over the last 10 to 15 years. This shifts the focus from not only asking whether we are spending enough to secure a sound economic future and quality of life but also asking whether we are making the most efficient use of our available public resources.

As noted above, state bonds and fiscal reforms have increased funding in recent years, resulting in overall investment rates much higher than in the 1960s. California is also investing at rates comparable to the national average. But is this "enough," or do we need to find ways to mobilize additional resources? Our review of education, water, and transportation provides ample evidence that there is no definitive answer to this question, if only because there is no objective measure of "needs." However, we can shed light on the areas of concern within each sector and the challenges to devising adequate public investment strategies. These challenges include striking the right balance between efficiency and equity goals and setting up appropriate funding mechanisms.

For education, the recent state and local bonds have gone a long way toward funding facilities backlogs. Bigger questions on the horizon concern the operating budgets for this sector. In particular, recent budget cuts to higher education have called into question the basic tenets of the Master Plan for Education, under which low-cost instruction is available to all California residents who can benefit from it. In light of the challenges to workforce skill development noted above, questions of both quality of and access to our public system of higher education become paramount. In facing these challenges, Californians will need to address the question of user fees (tuition) for students who can afford to pay and the relative roles of lower-cost community colleges and the four-year and graduate institutions of learning.

For water, contrary to the popular image of impending water shortages, we find that California is actually well positioned to meet the water supply challenges of growth, with many options available for making more efficient use of existing resources. Water and wastewater systems also rely on a well-developed system of user fees, enabling local governments and utilities to undertake the necessary investments. Unresolved public investment challenges in this sector include the restoration of ecosystems damaged by past water supply projects and the protection of the state's water supply from seismic activity in the San Francisco–San Joaquin River Delta.

The complexity of the transportation system makes it particularly difficult to assess whether we are spending enough in this sector. It is certain that we are now investing less in roadways, on a real per capita basis, than in the heyday of freeway building in the 1950s and 1960s. Moreover, the higher costs for rights-of-way, environmental mitigation, and modern design standards mean that these dollars do not go as far as they once did. Traffic congestion is thus a feature of life in California's metropolitan areas and, judging by public opinion polls, a source of daily consternation.

Given the costs, building enough roadway capacity to eliminate delays in peak-time travel would not be a good use of scarce public resources. Instead, it makes sense to manage congestion by investing strategically to tackle bottlenecks and by managing demand. "Demand management" can include encouraging drivers to carpool, to spread out their travel across the day, and to use transit alternatives during peak periods.

Transportation is also the sector in which the finance system is most broken. Roadways have a tradition of user fees, notably through state and federal taxes on gasoline introduced in the 1920s. But rising fuel efficiency and failures to adjust this tax for inflation have progressively eroded this revenue source. In real terms, gas taxes now raise about one-third the amount raised in 1970 per vehicle mile traveled. User fees have been progressively replaced with local sales taxes. Unlike the gas tax, these sales taxes provide no incentives to drivers to moderate car use.

Moving to more user-fee-based systems will depend on public willingness. When surveyed, Californians routinely cite traffic as one of their biggest problems. Yet they have been loath to increase transportation funding, except through local sales taxes. Legislators have not dared increase the gas tax since the early 1990s. And tolls, although promising, continue to meet with public skepticism. The alternative is a future in which we manage demand by default through longer and longer delays.

The message that emerges across all three sectors is that Californians have choices to make about their future. One part of the choice is deciding what level of public services we want to provide. Another part is deciding how to pay for them, given the range of funding options available. To the degree that we can link payments to the use of facilities, we can encourage people to use them more efficiently. The examples we provide in the realm of water show that user fees offer the potential to be robust, stable funding sources.

To be sure, there are important equity implications of more reliance on user fees—especially when it comes to education—but there are also ways to provide safety nets for low-income residents. There are also vital roles for both state and local governments in developing successful strategies to meet infrastructure demands.

Governing Institutions, Planning, and Public Investment

We next consider the institutional setting and governance structure in which policy decisions are being made about infrastructure issues. Specifically, we are interested in the ways the processes of planning, approving, and funding infrastructure projects are impeding progress in making improvements in the educational, transportation, and water systems of the state. In doing so, we consider the origins of governance challenges for public investment and the changes in the decisionmaking process for these sectors. We also examine recent examples of governance reform that may hold the key to a process in line with the political realities and infrastructure issues facing the state.

First, it is important to note that some of California's largest public projects—including the State Water Project, the Master Plan for Higher Education, and the state highway system—were passed during Governor Pat Brown's tenure about four decades ago. Democratic Governor Pat Brown had support from the state's first Democratic-controlled legislature in the 20th century. A rise in federal government aid for domestic infrastructure, notably a massive program for highway construction, helped propel Brown's efforts to expand the state's infrastructure. Brown also galvanized support for the new projects by passing the first significant tax increase since the early 1940s.

The political context of that earlier era provides a useful comparison to the current circumstances of a deep partisan divide among the state's lawmakers, a lack of federal funding for large infrastructure projects, and voters' reluctance to accept higher taxes. Today, many voters believe that their state government is inefficient, ineffective, and unresponsive; and this lack of trust adds to the political gridlock over state efforts to increase revenues or spending for roads and other infrastructure.

However, our research also concludes that Governor Brown's effectiveness ultimately rested in his ability to translate the prevailing sense of urgency for reform into pressure to force political compromises. As is true today, the state's lawmakers then were concerned about the need to expand infrastructure facilities following decades of high population growth and lagging investment. Brown's legacy suggests that a major priority for leaders at such historic turning points is to forge consensus and to prod key interest groups to negotiate so that public investments can move forward. In this respect, there are some similarities with current events: The first replacement governor through the state's recall process, Arnold Schwarzenegger, has thus far proven to be a political figure who is highly persuasive with the voters, legislators, and interest groups. He has also signaled that infrastructure planning should be a high priority for the state. However, to date he has been unable to solve the budget deficit and set a future agenda.

Although the highways, water systems, and college campuses built during the 1950s and 1960s are still with us, the confidence and consensus that launched them has waned ever since the 1970s. The investments of the postwar era helped transform the state in ways that provoked a political backlash and increasing public concerns about the environmental and quality-of-life consequences of new growth, which have ultimately led to higher costs for development. Communities protested against invasive projects such as highways, and government costs increased for mitigating the negative local impacts of these projects.

When the Proposition 13 tax limitations were passed in 1978, the "era of spending limits" had officially begun; and infrastructure investment headed into the steady decline that was not reversed until the 1990s. In recent years, the combination of record state budget deficits and political paralysis in Sacramento has once again threatened to limit investment in infrastructure and planning for the future. The monies that would otherwise flow to infrastructure have been diverted to pay for existing programs and mounting state debts. Meanwhile, the Democrats and Republicans in the legislature and the executive and legislative branches have quarreled over current fiscal priorities and have been unable to agree on a forward-thinking plan.

Further, the infrastructure policymaking process has become more and more complex. Governance today involves state, local, and regional infrastructure agencies. With a plethora of local special districts in California, often organized on a single-function basis (e.g., transportation, water, air quality), the lines of political authority and ultimate decisionmaking are often blurred. Today, when the state makes infrastructure decisions, many more private and nonprofit interest groups also seek a seat at the table—groups that range from environmentalists to neighborhood organizations to labor and business representatives. Policymaking is more contested, as community activists and interest groups have made increasing use of such tools as local and state voter initiatives and litigation to press for various causes. As a result, the approval process for both small and large infrastructure projects can be a time-consuming and difficult exercise of competing political wills.

In the current political and fiscal climate, policymakers are considering a variety of new governance strategies and different institutional goals. Planners are shifting their priority from building new physical capacity for meeting future infrastructure needs, seeking instead to encourage more efficient use of existing systems and resources. In this context, both funding and planning authority are also pushed downward from state to regional agencies and local governments—an approach that promotes greater flexibility, strategic management, and policy integration. A regional emphasis on infrastructure planning also seems appropriate in a large state with a multitude of distinct regions (e.g., Los

Angeles, Sacramento Metro, San Joaquin Valley, Inland Empire, Orange County, San Diego), each with its own large populations and geographic areas.

The institutional obstacles to a new regional approach are also formidable. The complexity of new decisionmaking structures can hamper decisionmaking. However, we have also learned that effective collaborative arrangements are possible and that the agreements reached through this type of process may actually balance state, regional, and local concerns more effectively than either imposed or top-down solutions. The state has an important role to play in creating a new governance system by providing more of a policy focus, funding mechanisms, and institutional support for local and regional decisionmaking. The state government in California still lags behind other states' efforts in this regard.

In 2004, the release of Governor Schwarzenegger's California Performance Review, with its over 1,000 specific recommendations for improving the efficiency of state government, underscores our central message that broad governance and fiscal reform are essential ingredients in today's arena of infrastructure planning. Among the proposals is the establishment of a new state Infrastructure Department with a broad mission to oversee the planning for a broad array of sectors—pointing to the importance of integrating future planning, complementary programs, and financing mechanisms.

The transition from massive statewide engineering projects to a broader consideration of the costs and effects of potential investments across metropolitan areas ultimately seems a healthy and appropriate one in such a mature and highly developed state as California. The protections now offered to environmental values, community participation, mitigation of the harms of projects, and fiscal restraint are important values to most residents. State leaders today must sometimes secure political agreements not just on how to allocate *more* services and facilities but also on how beneficiaries of state services can make do with *less*. Moreover, the priorities that are now being placed on equity issues for low-income communities in infrastructure decisions—which were not always part of institutional thinking in earlier eras—require a governance process that offers opportunities for inclusiveness and time for full debate.

Equitable Infrastructure Investment

Indeed, state law in 2002 defined the intent of infrastructure planning priorities to "promote equity, strengthen the economy, protect the environment, and promote public health and safety." However, many observers have noted that educational facilities, water supply and quality, and roads and transportation infrastructure have not been distributed equally across communities. Moreover, the negative impacts (e.g., noise, air pollution, toxic waste) that are sometimes associated with the siting of public facilities in communities also raises questions about the "environmental justice" issues that go along with new infrastructure development. The idea of promoting equity in infrastructure planning has thus taken on increasing importance over time. The concept of equity can apply to groups defined by income, gender, race, ethnicity, or age, in the context of infrastructure planning and related investment policies, but equity issues typically refer to the expected consequences for low-income and minority communities.

Our study points to three reasons for considering equitable infrastructure investment. The first reason is that it may create opportunities for communities that have been left behind by California's economic growth, since infrastructure investments may play a role in shaping economic growth. This idea takes on more relevance when we consider the patterns of income inequality in California: In 2002, incomes of low-income families were lower in real terms than incomes of similar families in 1969 whereas the incomes of middle-income families showed a 22 percent gain; and families at the high end of the distribution showed a 60 percent increase. A second reason is that such investments may help to promote broader economic growth in a cost-effective manner. A third reason for considering equity in infrastructure investments is that it may help build the political consensus required for large public projects. The latter point is consistent with a new approach to decisionmaking that involves public participation and an assessment of the benefits and costs for a large, diverse number of interest groups.

With these three rationales in mind, we examine the equity issues in the state's largest infrastructure sectors: transportation, K–12 school and higher education facilities, and water. We also discuss environmental justice issues, given their relevance as an infrastructure equity concern. We describe equity-related policies within each infrastructure sector and document major equity concerns, relying on existing studies that have recently turned attention to issues of equity and environmental justice issues.

We also argue that larger social, economic, and political forces are shaping the future of infrastructure equity and the broad policy directions that would promote more equitable investment. In particular, we point to five components of equitable infrastructure investment that we find critical in our analysis of the existing studies: an equity-based assessment of the existing infrastructure; strategies for the equitable funding of infrastructure; efforts to facilitate community participation to provide feedback for equitable decisionmaking; the need for integrated land-use, housing, and infrastructure policies; and the role of public will and leadership.

Public will is an important component of any successful major infrastructure effort. For instance, will the state's older, whiter, wealthier voters share a sense of common destiny with younger, minority, and poorer future residents as they think through future investments?

According to our recent surveys, the public today is aware of inequities in transportation and educational facilities. However, the same survey data also suggest that voters' willingness to invest more in low-income and minority communities lags behind awareness of this issue. Moreover, although a majority of California adult residents express support for redressing inequities in school facilities, just under half express support for similar attention to other infrastructure. Significantly, support for investments to overcome inequities is higher among the youngest adults and declines with age. In recent years, however, the passage of over $21 billion in new statewide bonds for K–12 school facilities seems to demonstrate that voters are willing to make large capital investments in children.

In sum, our research points to the fact that promoting equity in infrastructure investment is a growing issue. One question is whether today's state leaders will take on the task of elevating equity as a concern for future-oriented policies. Is California on a path that will lead to equitable infrastructure investments? Certainly, equity issues have emerged as major themes in infrastructure policy, but it remains to be seen how the new policies will be implemented and whether there will be cumulative effects. There remain a variety of social, political, and economic impediments to addressing equity issues. A concerted effort in this area will require public will, once again pointing to the major role of the voters and public opinion in shaping policies toward the future.

The Public's Views on Growth, Governance, and Policy Options

Does the California public realize that population growth is on the horizon? What do they see as the expected consequences of population increase? Is there any public consensus on how to address the increased demands for infrastructure that are likely to occur with growth? To answer these questions, we examine the results of a large-scale PPIC Statewide Survey, conducted in 2004, that focused on four related issues: public perceptions of present state and regional conditions; perceptions of the state's future; public attitudes toward governance; and policy preferences to address the prospects of future growth and related infrastructure demands. The extent of public consensus on conditions, predictions, governance, and policy preferences is of great importance. Voters play a key role in passing state and local funding measures at the ballot box, and they would likely be asked to approve any governance reforms proposed to deal with planning issues.

We find that Californians are evenly split about whether their state is currently headed in the right or wrong direction and deeply divided along partisan lines in their overall assessment of the state of the state. Although state residents are more upbeat about California than they were a year earlier, they were much more optimistic about their state in the late 1990s when the economy was growing at a brisk pace and the state government was accustomed to generating budget surpluses. Indeed, economic uncertainties and political distrust continue to weigh heavily on the minds of Californians even well after the latest recession has ended and the governor's recall is history. Residents say that the economy is the most serious state problem, with broad consensus across regions, racial/ethnic groups, and political groups. A lack of confidence in state government is a pervasive theme despite a popular new governor with sky-high approval ratings and support across the political spectrum.

When asked to rate the seriousness of certain conditions in their own regions of the state, problems that are related to population growth and infrastructure are the stand-out issues. Most Californians say that traffic congestion on roads and freeways and affordable housing are big problems where they live today. Many residents also cite the quality of their K–12 local public schools, the lack of well-paying jobs, and air pollution as big problems. But Californians are divided when asked if they would rather pay higher taxes and have the state government spend more money for roads and other infrastructure projects. Once again, they are deeply split along partisan lines. Only when new revenues are tied to specific projects does support emerge for new taxes, indicating again the pervasive role of government distrust.

We find that few Californians are aware of the state's current population size or its predicted size in the year 2025—this lack of awareness in itself limits a public discussion about the future. When given the current estimates, however, most Californians say that the amount of expected population growth would, overall, be a bad thing for themselves and their families. Most Californians also perceive that the state overall and their specific region will be a worse place to live in 2025 than it is now. On issues that are currently viewed as major regional problems—such as traffic congestion, affordable housing, and air pollution—most residents expect conditions to go from bad to worse in the future. Many also express pessimism about their regional economy and public educational system in the future. When asked what should be done to plan for a better future, residents focus on jobs and the economy and improvements in roads, school facilities, and water systems.

Who should be making the most important decisions today about the future of the state? Most residents say that voters should do so at the ballot box. This is because residents lack confidence in their state and local governments' abilities to plan for future growth. Few approve of the state legislature's handling of plans for the future, but most are optimistic about Governor Schwarzenegger's abilities to tackle those challenges.

The public today is largely disengaged but hardly disinterested when it comes to the state's future. Although most Californians we surveyed are not engaged in local planning discussions, many say that they want to be involved in discussions about growth and the future. When given a variety of options and tradeoffs to consider, most also have opinions about what the state must do to plan for the future.

As their top priorities for the future, most Californians name the three types of infrastructure projects that we focus on in this volume—school facilities, surface transportation, and water systems. There is also public consensus that the state government should focus on finding efficient and cost-effective solutions in all three arenas. For instance, when they are asked to consider the policy tradeoffs, they favor more efficient use of existing freeways and highways instead of building more major roads. They support efforts to use existing public educational facilities more efficiently rather than building more public schools, and they favor relying on conservation of the current water supply rather than building new dams and water storage systems. Indeed, this perspective is consistent with our other survey findings about public finance and the budget, which indicate a public belief that state government is so wasteful that the same level of services could be provided even if there are fewer resources available. The public's preferences for "demand management" rather than "bricks and mortar" also parallel many of the themes that are discussed elsewhere in this volume.

Public attitudes toward new tax increases and user fee proposals—along with an appetite for governance reform and insistence on equitable planning—will be a major force in shaping infrastructure planning for the state's future. A majority of Californians believe that their governments lack adequate funding for roads, school facilities, and other infrastructure projects, but would they support tax increases to prepare for future growth? Many voters reject the idea of increasing their taxes unless they know exactly how these tax dollars will be spent. Surprisingly, given their anti-tax reputation, many Californians say they would be willing to increase their local sales tax for roads and public transit projects and would support a 20-year bond measure to pay for local school construction projects. With certain assurances that their money will be put to appropriate uses, and especially if there are governance systems in place to make public officials accountable for their spending decisions, many voters appear willing to set aside their distrust and invest in the future. They are willing to act against their political instincts because they believe that their economic future and quality of life are at stake.

Californians also seem highly conscious of the fact that growing economic inequalities threaten the future of the state for everyone. Many are even agreeable to the idea that policies should provide for uneven investments in public schools and infrastructure that favor the least advantaged minority and low-income communities over more affluent communities. Keeping the equity perspective in the mix will be a necessary ingredient in future policymaking, given that overcoming inequities is a part of the challenge faced in achieving good educational outcomes and increasing economic opportunities in the state.

A major task ahead is finding a way to restore the public's trust and confidence in their state and local governments. To do so will require an unprecedented effort by the state's leadership. It will be a challenge to overcome the apathy, disinterest, cynicism, and pessimism that has been pervasive for decades. The public's lack of confidence cuts short any serious discussions of forward planning, which then makes it difficult to reach any consensus on goals. The solution may ultimately lie in a set of political, governance, institutional, and fiscal reforms that will make state and local government actions more transparent, accountable, efficient, and responsive to the people that they serve. Some say that the best opportunities for an overhaul of state and local governments are present in the postrecall era in California. To date, however, the focus has been reaching consensus on balancing the state budget.

In closing, despite the clear signs of success in some infrastructure sectors, and population and economic trends that will ease the growth in demand for public facilities, California faces the future without a clear mandate on how much or how to raise funds for infrastructure projects to accommodate an expected 10 million new residents. We also uncovered a "human infrastructure" issue with major implications for the future—a growing need for college-educated workers for our changing economy and a likely shortfall in highly educated adults in the fastest-growing population groups.

In the California system of public finance and governance, much will depend on the voters' willingness to raise taxes or pay higher user fees for new future-oriented proposals. The public acceptance of policies that promote socioeconomic progress in low-income and minority communities and shift from a local to a regional focus in infrastructure planning will also be critical in determining the state's future. Major political and policy shifts will no doubt require courageous leadership, but this quality has always surfaced whenever California has taken a giant step into the future.

2. California's Population in 2025

by Hans P. Johnson

Any serious discussion of California in 2025 must include some analysis of the state's changing population. Almost every area of state concern—from social services caseloads to transportation infrastructure to environmental protection—is directly affected by population growth and change. Some of California's demographic challenges are shared by other states—the aging of the baby boomers, for example, is a national phenomenon—but others are unique to California. The state's population level—36 million people in 2003 (Figure 2.1)—now exceeds that of all but 32 countries and will likely surpass Spain's in the next two decades. Moreover, California's growth rate outstrips that of any

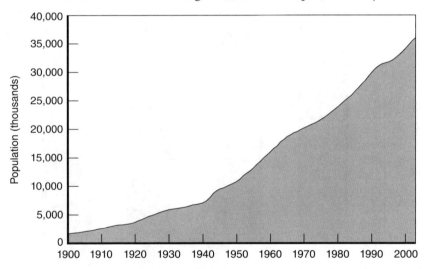

SOURCE: California Department of Finance.

Figure 2.1—California's Rapid Population Growth, 1900–2003

developed region of the world; indeed, it looks more like Mexico's than the rest of the nation's.

The state's diversity is also noteworthy. California is home to immigrant groups from over 60 countries, making its population arguably the most diverse in the world. Most of the state's recent population increase occurred among Asian and Latino populations, and much of it was due to immigration. In 1970, four of every five Californians were non-Hispanic whites; by 2000, one of every four residents was foreign-born, and no racial or ethnic group constituted a majority of the state's population (Figure 2.2).

If the 20th century brought staggering population growth and change to California, the 1990s represented a sharp departure from the usual pattern. During that time, the state's population grew only a little faster than the rest of the nation's (13.8% versus 13.1%), and for the first time since the 1850s, New York City had a faster growth rate than

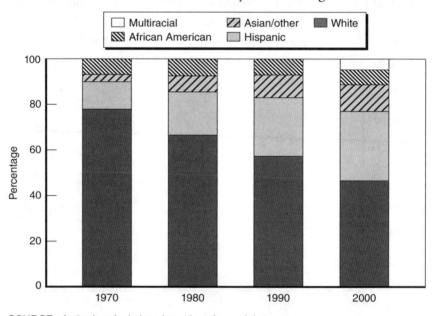

SOURCE: Author's calculations based on decennial censuses.

Figure 2.2—California's Population by Race/Ethnicity, 1970–2000

Los Angeles. The major cause of this slowdown was an exodus of Californians to other states. During the 1990s, about two million more people moved from California to other states than came from other states to California. Much of the outflow occurred in the early 1990s and originated from Los Angeles. California's population continued to grow, however, because these losses from domestic migration were more than offset by international migration and natural increase (the excess of births over deaths), both of which remained at high levels.

The domestic migration outflows of the 1990s were clearly related to the economy. The recession of the early 1990s was longer and deeper in California, especially Los Angeles, than in the rest of the nation. California's unemployment rate peaked in 1993 at 9.4 percent, compared to 6.9 percent for the nation. Domestic migration flows out of California exceeded 400,000 people in 1993 and again in 1994, when the unemployment rate differential remained large (Figure 2.3). As the state's economy improved in the late 1990s, the outflow abated. Today,

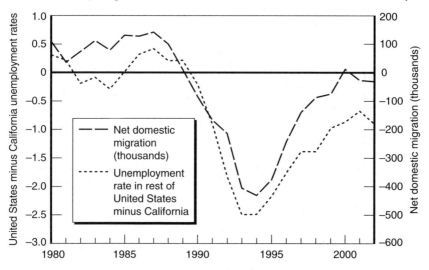

SOURCES: Author's calculations based on California Employment Development Department data and Census Bureau estimates of domestic migration.

Figure 2.3—Unemployment Rate Differences and Net Domestic Migration, 1980–2002

domestic flows out of the state are roughly offset by domestic flows into the state.

The other components of population change—births and deaths—have also contributed to a slowing in the rate of growth of California's population since the 1980s. The number of births in California has fallen substantially since its peak in 1992 (Figure 2.4).[1] This decline has occurred as the baby boomers—those born between 1945 and 1964—aged out of their prime childbearing years. In addition, the average number of children has fallen from 2.5 children per woman in 1990 to 2.2 children per woman in 2001.[2] Fertility dropped across all of California's major ethnic groups, but declines have been especially large among Hispanic and African American women (Johnson,

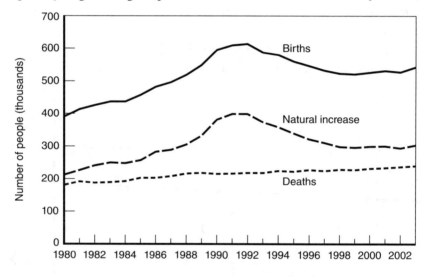

SOURCE: Author's calculations based on Department of Finance data.

Figure 2.4—Births, Deaths, and Natural Increase in California, 1980–2003

---

[1]This peak in births in the early 1990s occurred as large numbers of baby boomers reached childbearing ages and as the number and fertility rates of women in California rose with large flows of immigrants. See Hill and Johnson (2002) for a more complete discussion of fertility rates by ethnicity and nativity in California.

[2]The total fertility rate can be thought of as the average number of children a woman has in her lifetime. Specifically, we report period total fertility rates.

Hill, and Heim, 2001). By 1998, total fertility rates of Hispanics had fallen to 2.8, from a peak of 3.5, and African American fertility rates fell to 2.0, from 2.6. As birth rates were falling, the number of deaths in California was increasing as a result of the aging of the state's population (Figure 2.4). Although age-specific mortality rates have been decreasing in California, the number of older Californians has been increasing at a faster rate. The consequence of these recent trends in births and deaths has been a substantial decline in natural increase. In the early 2000s, natural increase was adding about 300,000 people to the state's population each year, compared to almost 400,000 in the early 1990s.

Alternative Population Projections

These recent trends make population projections for California especially difficult. The best forecasters rely heavily on historical patterns, and their track records are not encouraging.[3] Projections made in times of robust population growth generally overstate future growth, and those made in times of relatively slow growth generally understate it. In addition to overweighting contemporary trends, forecasters are notoriously bad at predicting fundamental demographic shifts. For example, demographers did not anticipate the large increases in fertility rates that occurred at the outset of and even during the baby boom. Similarly, most did not predict declines in fertility rates during the baby bust.

For these reasons, planners should consider alternative population scenarios. The California Department of Finance (DOF) develops only one set of projections for the state and cautions users that "these population projections depict only one possible course of future population change, i.e., the one reflecting recent trends in fertility, mortality, and migration" (California Department of Finance, 1998). The U.S. Census Bureau develops high, medium, and low projections for the nation, but the bureau's most recent state projections are outdated and provide only one alternative series. A set of California

---

[3]For more discussion of population projections for California, see PPIC working paper "A Review of Population Projections for California" (Johnson, 2005), available from the author.

projections developed by researchers at the University California (UC) Berkeley includes probability intervals, but the intervals are too wide for practical planning purposes.[4]

Working with the DOF, PPIC has developed two alternative projections for California for 2025. These alternative projections include a high growth scenario with elevated fertility and migration rates, and a low growth scenario with lowered fertility and migration rates. Specifically, the low growth scenario assumes that age-specific fertility rates will be 10 percent lower by 2025 than currently forecast by DOF and that migration will be 20 percent lower each year. The high growth scenario assumes that fertility rates will be 10 percent higher by 2025 and migration flows will be 20 percent higher throughout the projection period. These alternative assumptions represent relatively modest changes to the baseline DOF projections. Thus, we view the low and high projection series as plausible and useful alternatives for planners.

Overall Population Growth: Lower Than Previously Expected, But Still Large

The most recent projections indicate that California's population growth will not be as large as previously forecast. The latest DOF figures, for example, indicate that the state will be home to 46 million people in 2025—about three million lower than its previous projections. Projections from the University of Southern California (USC) and UC Berkeley's median projections are even lower than DOF's current series (Table 2.1). PPIC's alternatives frame all of these projections (DOF, USC, UC Berkeley median) and place the state's 2025 population at 43.9 million in the low growth scenario and 48.2 million in the high growth scenario.

---

[4]The 5th percentile projection suggests that over the next 20 years, the state's population will grow by fewer than 2 million people, whereas the 95th percentile places the growth at over 14 million. Planners could choose less extreme percentiles to develop narrower bounds.

Table 2.1

California's Projected Population (millions)

	2000	2005	2010	2015	2020	2025
California Department of Finance (2004a)	34.065	36.855	39.247	41.571	43.852	46.041
PPIC low growth scenario	34.065	36.454	38.469	40.374	42.197	43.891
PPIC high growth scenario	34.065	37.256	40.030	42.776	45.521	48.210
USC (Pitkin and Myers, 2004 preliminary)	33.872	35.744	37.794	39.950	42.151	44.344
UC Berkeley (Lee, Miller, and Edwards, 2003)						
Median	33.872	36.376	38.579	40.632	42.600	44.600
5th percentile	33.872	35.427	36.267	36.728	36.981	37.119
95th percentile	33.872	37.349	40.874	44.425	48.043	51.879
CCSCE (2003)	33.872		39.710			
UCLA Anderson Forecasting Project (2003)	34.036		39.670			
UCLA Anderson Forecasting Project (2002)	34.117		39.957		45.850	
California Department of Finance (1998)	34.653	37.372	39.958	42.371	45.449	48.626
Census Bureau preferred (Campbell, 1996)	32.521	34.441	37.644	41.373	45.278	49.285
Census Bureau alternative (Campbell, 1996)	32.423	33.511	34.968	36.838	39.034	41.480

NOTES: DOF, UC Los Angeles (UCLA), and Census Bureau projections are for July 1st of each year. The UC Berkeley projections are as of April 1st. The USC projections are for January 1st of each year, with April 1st 2000 as the base year. CCSCE is the Center for the Continuing Study of the California Economy.

Our alternative projections bracket the DOF projections, with the low series showing a total population in 2025 that is about 2.1 million people fewer than the DOF projections and the high series showing a total that is about 2.2 million people more (Figure 2.5).

Despite these relatively slow growth rates, absolute increases to the state's population are projected to remain strong. The DOF projections

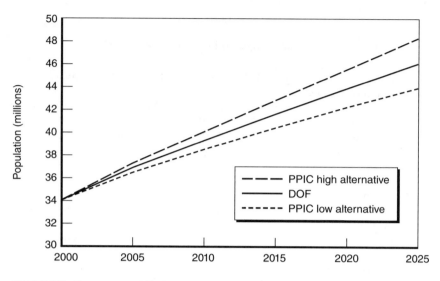

SOURCES: Department of Finance (2004a) and PPIC projections.

Figure 2.5—DOF and PPIC Alternative Population Projections for California, 2000–2025

place the state's growth at 4.7 million between 2005 and 2015 and at 4.5 million between 2015 and 2025. This absolute growth is substantially smaller than that of the 1980s, when the state added more than six million new residents, but larger than the absolute gains of the 1990s, which came to about four million. Indeed, projected growth will be greater in absolute terms than in any other decade except the 1980s and the 1950s. The PPIC low series suggests that between 2005 and 2025, the state will gain about seven million people, whereas the high series places the gain at just under 11 million.

The major forecasters agree that future *growth rates* will be lower than past ones. Indeed, the DOF projections suggest that in the 20-year period from 2005 to 2025, California will experience the slowest rate of change for any two decades in the state's recorded history (Figure 2.6). Even the PPIC high alternative series suggests that future growth rates will be lower than in the 1990s.

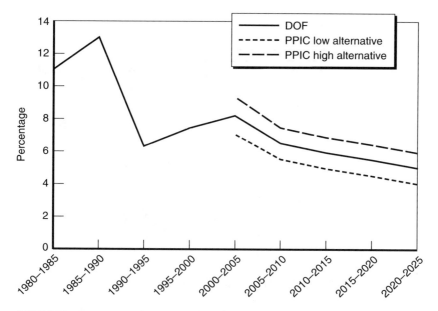

SOURCES: Department of Finance (2004a) and PPIC projections.

Figure 2.6—Five-Year Population Growth Rates for California, 1980–2025

Population by Race and Ethnicity

Two other aspects of the state's demographic future also seem certain. The first is that Latino and Asian population growth will continue to be strong; the second is that the population of non-Hispanic whites will either increase very slowly or actually decline. DOF projections suggest that Latinos will become the largest racial or ethnic group in California by 2011 and will constitute a majority by 2040. Already, Latinos are the largest racial or ethnic group among Californians under age 30 (Figure 2.7). Furthermore, almost half of all births in California are to Latina mothers.

Changes in racial and ethnic categories and identification could alter these projections. No more than two consecutive censuses have used the same racial and ethnic categories. For example, the 2000 census was the

31

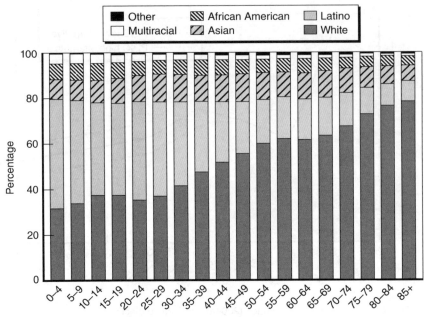

SOURCE: Author's tabulations of 2000 census data.

Figure 2.7—Racial and Ethnic Composition in California by Age, 2000

first to allow respondents to choose more than one race. In that year, less than 2 percent of Californians identified as non-Hispanic of two or more races, and less than half of the children of parents of different races were identified as multiracial (Tafoya, Johnson, and Hill, 2004). Yet multiracial populations could increase substantially over time with increases in intermarriage and changing perceptions.

Nativity

After decades of strong increases, the growth of the foreign-born population is likely to be much less dramatic. By 2025, 30 percent of the state's residents will be foreign-born (Pitkin and Myers, 2004). Although this figure represents an increase in the proportion of foreign-born Californians compared to today, it also indicates a substantial slowdown in that group's rate of growth (Figure 2.8). Although California remains the leading destination for immigrants to the United States, its dominance is not as great as in the past (Hill and Hayes, 2003;

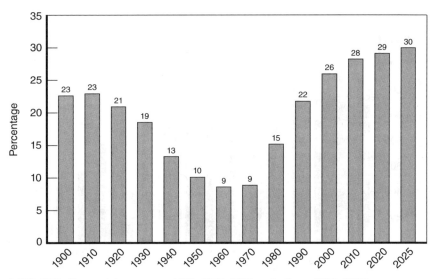

SOURCES: Decennial censuses, 1900–2000; USC projections, 2010–2025.

Figure 2.8—Percentage of Californians Who Are Foreign-Born, 1900–2025

Myers, Pitkin, and Park, 2004). This decline could be due to several factors. The severity of the early 1990s recession in California made finding a job more difficult in California than in other states. The high cost of living, especially housing, may also have deterred some immigrants from choosing California as a destination. Finally, as immigrant social networks expand geographically, information about jobs and housing in other parts of the country become more readily available to new immigrants.

A primary feature of the state's population will be a large increase in the number of second-generation Californians or those with at least one foreign-born parent. In 2003, the vast majority of California's second generation was made up of children (Figure 2.9). With a median age of 15 (compared to age 33 for all Californians), this cohort is poised to finish its schooling and enter the workforce in large numbers. This second generation and its educational and economic success will help determine California's future.

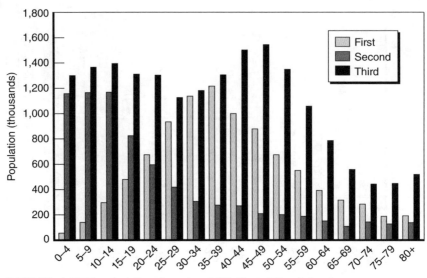

SOURCE: Author's calculations based on 2003 Current Population Survey.

Figure 2.9—California's Population by Generation and Age

Age Structure

The continued aging of California's population is also a safe bet. Older adults have relatively low migration rates and fairly predictable mortality rates; because they are also well counted in the census, projections of their population tend to be accurate. Life expectancies will continue to increase, and baby boomers will begin to reach retirement age in 2011. By 2030, the number of seniors in California will double (Table 2.2), and one in every six Californians will be over age 65. USC's

Table 2.2

California's Projected Population Ages 65 and Over

Year	DOF	USC	UC Berkeley
2000	3,627,000	3,595,000	3,596,000
2010	4,467,000	4,185,000	4,319,000
2020	6,212,000	5,791,000	6,134,000
2025	7,299,000	6,824,000	7,302,000
2030	8,302,000	7,844,000	8,448,000

projections are almost a half million lower than DOF's by 2030, but some of this difference is due to the date of the projection (January 1, 2030, for USC versus July 1, for DOF).

At the other age extreme, the child population of California is expected to change very little over the next 10 years (Table 2.3). As the relatively small baby bust generation has reached childbearing ages, the number of births in California has declined. Declines in fertility rates have also played a role, especially for Latinas; second-generation Latinas have much smaller family sizes than their first-generation parents (Hill and Johnson, 2002). As a result, the number of children ages 5 to 17 is projected to increase only 2 percent from 2000 to 2010, a dramatic slowdown from the 21 percent increase in the number of public school children over the previous 10 years (California Department of Finance, 2003b). The DOF forecast shows a 10 percent increase in the number of school children between 2010 and 2020, whereas the UC Berkeley projections show only 5 percent growth. These differences increase in forecasts of later years and arise primarily because UC Berkeley projections assume lower fertility rates than their DOF counterparts. Both projections assume an increase in the number of women of childbearing age, especially those ages 20 to 34. This increase is largely attributable to the children of the baby boom echo entering the prime childbearing ages, replacing the much smaller baby bust cohort. Nonetheless, even the higher DOF projections assume that population growth rates will be lower for children ages 5 to 17 than for the overall population between 2010 and 2020.

Table 2.3

California's Projected Population Ages 5 to 17

Year	DOF	USC	UC Berkeley
2000	6,781,000	6,763,000	6,767,000
2010	6,932,000	6,879,000	6,869,000
2020	7,608,000	7,338,000	7,210,000
2025	7,979,000	7,681,000	
2030	8,295,000	7,948,000	7,492,000

Changes in the school-age population will not be felt evenly across the state. DOF projections for 2005 and 2025 show declines in the number of 5 to 17 year olds in 15 counties, including Los Angeles, Ventura, Santa Barbara, San Luis Obispo, San Mateo, and Marin Counties. At the same time, many inland counties will experience large gains in that age group. Sacramento, Placer, San Joaquin, Merced, Madera, and Tulare Counties will all experience increases in the school-age population of 40 percent or more between 2005 and 2025.

Note that there is substantial uncertainty regarding the number of school-age children in the future, largely because future fertility rates are less predictable. The PPIC low and high variations of the DOF projections show that relatively small changes in future fertility rates could lead to substantial changes in the number of children ages 5 to 17. If fertility rates in 2025 are only 10 percent higher than those assumed in the DOF projections, the number of school-age children would be 500,000 greater than those shown in Table 2.3; similarly, if fertility rates are only 10 percent lower, the number of school-age children in 2025 would be 500,000 less. The USC projections are slightly higher than the DOF projections, whereas the UC Berkeley median projections are substantially lower.

An easy way to summarize the age structure of a population is to examine the dependency ratio—the number of people of nonworking age (younger than age 18 and over age 65) for every 100 people of working age. It provides a rough indicator of a population's ability to support nonworking members. As shown in Figure 2.10, California's dependency ratio is projected to increase substantially after 2010, as large cohorts of baby boomers begin to enter retirement ages. Because of the certain aging of the baby boomers, there is little variation in projections of overall old-age dependency ratios. However, increasing labor force participation at older ages (beyond age 65) could occur in the future, especially if retirement ages increase. (This has already occurred with Social Security benefits.) In this case, old-age dependency ratios would be lower if they included only older seniors—for example, those over age 70.

To the state government, however, the most important component of the dependency ratio pertains to children, largely because the state is

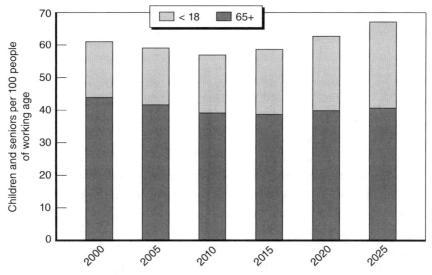

SOURCE: Author's tabulations of Department of Finance projections.

Figure 2.10—Projected Dependency Ratio in California, 2000–2025

the primary provider of school services to children. After a substantial rise in the child dependency ratio during the 1990s, the DOF series projects a decline to 2010, with very little change thereafter (see Figure 2.10). This may be a welcome short-term trend for a state trying to catch up with large increases in public school attendance.

Another group of great importance to the state is young adults between ages 18 and 24. The number of young adults largely determines the demand for higher education. The state is currently experiencing a large increase in this population. The increase is attributable to the aging into young adulthood of children of the baby boomers and the children of the large number of immigrants that came to California in the 1980s. DOF and USC projections suggest that this segment of the state's population will continue to grow rapidly to 2010 and then slow or even decline from 2010 to 2020 before resuming strong growth from 2020 to 2025 (Table 2.4). The decline occurs as the relatively small cohort of children of the baby bust enters young adult ages.

Table 2.4

California's Projected Population Ages 18 to 24

	2000	2005	2010	2015	2020	2025
DOF	3,403,000	3,774,000	4,198,000	4,148,000	3,994,000	4,261,000
USC	3,366,000	3,672,000	4,023,000	4,026,000	4,026,000	4,174,000

Regional Projections

Regional patterns of growth seem fairly set. Inland areas of the state have experienced faster growth rates than coastal areas for over 30 years, and thus their share of the state's population has grown (Figure 2.11). DOF forecasts that between 2005 and 2025, populations will increase 45 percent in inland counties and 17 percent in coastal ones. Absolute increases will also be greater in inland counties (4.8 million) than in their coastal counterparts (4.4 million). In particular, the Inland Empire, the San Joaquin Valley, and the Sacramento Metropolitan Area are projected

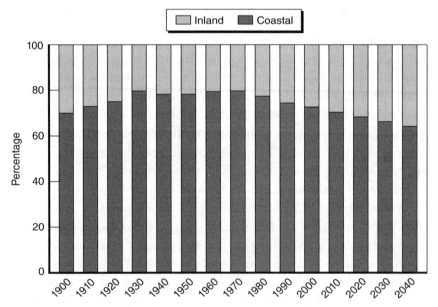

SOURCE: Author's tabulations of Department of Finance projections.

Figure 2.11—California's Population Distribution: Inland Versus Coastal, 1900–2040

to continue to experience the fastest growth rates in the state (Figure 2.12). Each of these areas is projected to grow by half their current population from 2005 to 2025. Especially striking historically has been the Inland Empire. One of the fastest-growing metropolitan areas in the United States for decades, it now has a larger population than metropolitan Cleveland, San Diego, St. Louis, or Denver, and projections suggest that its population could increase from 3.8 million in 2005 to 5.5 million by 2020. (As recently as 1980, the Inland Empire was home to just 1.6 million people.) Riverside County is projected to grow more rapidly than San Bernardino County, as Riverside increasingly becomes home to commuters to San Diego, Orange, and Los Angeles Counties. DOF projects that by 2010, Riverside County will surpass San Bernardino County to become California's fourth most populous county.

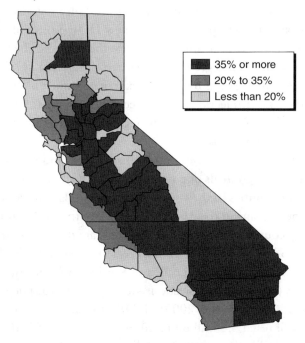

Figure 2.12—Projected Percentage Change in Population Growth in California, 2005–2025

Northern California has the makings of its own Inland Empire as population growth spills out of the Bay Area into the northern San Joaquin Valley. Over the past few years, growth rates in the northern San Joaquin Valley have rivaled those of the Inland Empire. DOF projections suggest that the northern San Joaquin Valley will be the fastest-growing region in the state between 2005 and 2025, with San Joaquin County projected to be the fastest-growing county in the state and Merced County projected to be the third fastest-growing county in the state (Table 2.5).

The DOF projects that by 2040, despite impressive growth rates in inland areas, about 60 percent of the state's residents will still live in coastal rather than inland counties. San Diego and the Bay Area are projected to have growth rates almost as high as in the rest of the state, whereas Los Angeles County will have very low growth rates.

There is some variation in current projections for regions in the state. Compared to their precursors, the new DOF projections show much less growth in the far northern part of the state and the Central Coast and moderately less growth in Southern California. Only the Sacramento Metro region is forecast to experience much higher levels of growth in the latest projections, compared to the previous DOF projections. These shifts reflect recent regional patterns of change as well as input from local officials.

Projections become less certain for smaller areas and populations. Many of the state's councils of governments (COGs) develop population projections for counties in their regions. These COGs are more likely to use local general plans in their forecasts. Because the DOF projections include every county in the state, we can compare the COG projections with those produced by DOF. In most regions, there is fairly close agreement. In San Diego, the DOF and San Diego Association of Governments (SANDAG) projections are very close (San Diego Association of Governments, 2003). DOF projects that the region's population will reach 3.6 million in 2020, compared to SANDAG's forecast of 3.5 million (up from 2.8 million in the 2000 census). In both cases, these projections represent substantial downward revisions from earlier projections. DOF's forecasts for the Bay Area are slightly higher than those produced by the Association of Bay Area

Table 2.5

Population Projections for California Regions and Counties

County	DOF New Projections for 2005	DOF New Projections for 2025	% Change	DOF Old Projections for 2025	% Difference (New vs. Old)
North Coast and Mountains					
Alpine	1,300	1,400	8	1,800	−22
Amador	37,800	43,400	15	41,000	6
Calaveras	45,300	65,300	44	67,000	−3
Del Norte	28,600	31,700	11	44,100	−28
Humboldt	130,900	141,400	8	143,400	−1
Inyo	18,500	18,400	−1	21,500	−14
Lake	64,400	84,700	32	101,700	−17
Lassen	36,300	38,500	6	52,400	−27
Mariposa	18,200	21,600	18	24,700	−13
Mendocino	90,800	103,500	14	126,000	−18
Modoc	9,700	9,100	−6	12,900	−29
Mono	13,900	16,900	21	15,000	13
Nevada	99,600	132,800	33	143,900	−8
Plumas	21,200	20,700	−2	23,400	−12
Sierra	3,600	3,800	7	3,600	6
Siskiyou	45,300	45,800	1	55,600	−18
Trinity	13,500	13,300	−2	15,900	−16
Tuolumne	58,000	67,200	16	81,700	−18
Total	737,000	859,600	17	975,300	−12
Upper Sacramento Valley					
Butte	217,100	270,500	25	335,100	−19
Colusa	21,000	27,900	33	47,400	−41
Glenn	28,300	33,200	17	54,800	−39
Shasta	181,400	244,200	35	254,400	−4
Sutter	88,300	119,000	35	125,000	−5
Tehama	59,800	71,300	19	91,000	−22
Yuba	66,500	91,700	38	90,500	1
Total	662,300	857,800	30	998,200	−14
Sacramento Metro					
El Dorado	174,100	236,500	36	275,900	−14
Placer	303,600	501,300	65	424,000	18
Sacramento	1,394,600	2,120,400	52	1,767,600	20
Yolo	194,400	295,900	52	242,500	22
Total	2,066,600	3,154,000	53	2,710,000	16
San Joaquin Valley					
Fresno	882,700	1,205,400	37	1,210,100	0
Kern	746,600	1,032,300	38	1,196,000	−14
Kings	143,700	204,200	42	204,800	0

Table 2.5 (continued)

County	DOF New Projections for 2005	DOF New Projections for 2025	% Change	DOF Old Projections for 2025	% Difference (New vs. Old)
Madera	138,800	201,500	45	252,000	−20
Merced	244,700	399,100	63	351,500	14
San Joaquin	659,600	1,108,600	68	971,100	14
Stanislaus	508,600	699,600	38	776,600	−10
Tulare	408,300	596,300	46	629,300	−5
Total	3,733,000	5,446,900	46	5,591,400	−3
Bay Area					
Alameda	1,538,100	1,955,800	27	1,867,800	5
Contra Costa	1,034,800	1,436,000	39	1,149,000	25
Marin	251,300	250,600	0	275,800	−9
Napa	134,400	178,300	33	166,000	7
San Francisco	795,300	810,600	2	739,500	10
San Mateo	723,400	802,000	11	882,000	−9
Santa Clara	1,757,300	2,083,600	19	2,299,500	−9
Solano	427,500	616,500	44	589,300	5
Sonoma	486,100	662,600	36	649,700	2
Total	7,148,300	8,796,000	23	8,618,500	2
Central Coast					
Monterey	428,900	531,000	24	634,600	−16
San Benito	58,500	79,200	36	89,900	−12
San Luis Obispo	262,600	319,200	22	426,800	−25
Santa Barbara	419,600	466,500	11	604,000	−23
Santa Cruz	262,300	291,400	11	398,500	−27
Total	1,431,900	1,687,400	18	2,153,800	−22
South Coast					
Los Angeles	10,145,600	11,081,300	9	12,164,600	−9
Orange	3,074,700	3,607,500	17	3,593,000	0
Ventura	817,300	956,200	17	1,054,600	−9
Total	14,037,600	15,645,000	11	16,812,200	−7
Inland Empire					
Riverside	1,871,600	2,923,800	56	3,151,200	−7
San Bernardino	1,942,100	2,613,100	35	3,076,300	−15
Total	3,813,700	5,536,900	45	6,227,500	−11
San Diego					
Imperial	160,500	234,500	46	344,600	−32
San Diego	3,063,300	3,822,800	25	4,194,500	−9
Total	3,223,800	4,057,300	26	4,539,100	−11
State total	36,854,200	46,040,800	25	48,626,100	−5

SOURCE: Author's tabulations of Department of Finance projections.

Governments (ABAG) (2003). DOF projections suggest that the region's population will increase 29 percent between 2000 and 2025, compared to growth of 25 percent forecast by ABAG. ABAG's 2003 series projects 8.5 million people in the Bay Area by 2025, compared to 8.8 million in the DOF series.

Projections for the Southern California Association of Governments (SCAG) region are slightly *lower* in the DOF forecasts (34 percent increase) than in the SCAG projections (39 percent increase) (Southern California Association of Governments, 2003b). The lower growth rates forecast by DOF are due to differences in Los Angeles County, with SCAG showing substantially more growth (Table 2.6). Regional projections for Southern California produced by USC are between the SCAG and DOF projections (22,599,000 for 2030). Although these absolute differences are notable, they are in the context of a region forecast to be home to over 22 million people.

The greatest relative differences are in the Sacramento region. Projections to 2025 are substantially higher in the DOF projections than in the Sacramento Area Council of Governments (SACOG) projections (Table 2.7). Almost all of this difference arises in projections for Sacramento County, with the DOF forecasting growth rates that are almost twice as great as those forecast by SACOG. DOF forecasts suggest that Sacramento County will add almost 900,000 new residents

Table 2.6

Population Projections for Southern California (thousands)

County	2000 Census	2030 SCAG	2030 DOF
Imperial	142	270	255
Los Angeles	9,518	12,316	11,237
Orange	2,846	3,553	3,665
Riverside	1,545	3,045	3,180
San Bernardino	1,709	2,713	2,762
Ventura	753	993	1,026
Regional total	16,513	22,890	22,125

SOURCE: Southern California Association of Governments (2003a) projections.

Table 2.7

Population Projections for the Sacramento Area (thousands)

County	2000 Census	SACOG 2025	DOF 2025
El Dorado	156	194	236
Placer	248	415	501
Sacramento	1,223	1,695	2,120
Sutter	79	135	119
Yolo	169	266	296
Yuba	60	108	92
SACOG regional total	1,935	2,814	3,365

SOURCE: Sacramento Area Council of Governments (2001) projections.

between 2000 and 2025, whereas SACOG's projections suggest growth of fewer than 400,000 new residents. Differences for El Dorado and Placer Counties could be due solely to geographical considerations. SACOG does not include the eastern portion of those counties (the Lake Tahoe basin), whereas DOF projections are for entire counties.

Educational Attainment

Future economic outcomes—and therefore infrastructure and social service demands—depend heavily on the labor force skills of California's adults. Accordingly, we use the population projections to forecast educational attainment levels in the state. Educational attainment distributions are projected by age, race and ethnicity, nativity, and gender and then applied to the DOF population projections to arrive at overall educational attainment projections.[5]

We develop two sets of educational projections for California's population. The first set assumes no change in educational attainment distributions from 2000 levels; thus, 45 to 49 year old white females in 2020 are projected to have the same percentage of college graduates as 25 to 29 year old white females in 2000. For younger cohorts, we take the educational attainment levels observed in 2000 for similarly aged people.

---

[5]Details of our approach can be found in Johnson (2005).

For example, 20 to 24 year old white females in 2020 are projected to have the same percentage of college graduates as 20 to 24 year old white females in 2000. We call these the static cohort projections.

In the second set, termed the dynamic cohort projections, we assume that past increases in educational attainment for a cohort—again defined by age, race and ethnicity, and gender—will continue into the future. Specifically, increases between 1990 and 2000 are assumed to continue to 2010 and then again to 2020. Thus, 45 to 49 year old white females in 2010 are projected to have the same percentage of college graduates as 35 to 39 year old white females in 2000 plus any increase in the percentage of college graduates between 45 to 49 year old white females in 2000 and 35 to 39 year old white females in 1990.

In both sets of projections, for Latinos we develop projections of educational attainment and population by nativity (U.S.-born versus foreign-born). Because educational attainment is much higher among U.S.-born Latinos than foreign-born Latinos, we adjust educational attainment distributions of Latinos for increasing shares of U.S.-born among each adult age cohort.

One of the most striking results of these projections is that older Californians in 2020 will be among the best-educated Californians. This projection derives from the current age profile of educational attainment. As shown in Figure 2.13, Californians with the highest rate of college graduation in 2000 were those ages 50 to 54. This is partly due to differences in the demographic composition of the state's population by age. In particular, Latinos are concentrated at younger ages and tend to have low levels of educational attainment. However, it is also due to historical events that led that cohort to complete college at higher rates than subsequent cohorts. Men ages 50 to 54 in 2000 were of prime draft age for the Vietnam War several decades earlier. For some of those men, attending college allowed them to avoid military service in Vietnam. The phenomenon is not restricted to California. Among U.S.-born white males nationwide, for example, those ages 50 to 54 are the most likely to have graduated from college.

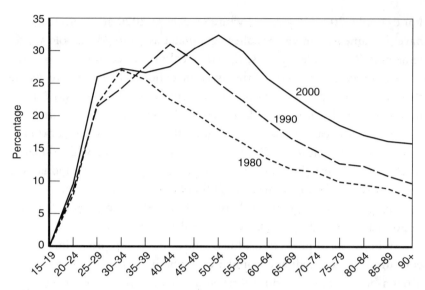

SOURCE: Author's calculations based on decennial censuses.

**Figure 2.13—Percentage of College Graduates in California by Age,
1980–2000**

Because younger cohorts in 2000 (25 to 44 year olds) tend to be less educated than older cohorts (45 to 59 year olds), the static cohort projections suggest that California could face the prospect of a working-age population that is less educated in the future than today. In this scenario, the percentage of college graduates among adults ages 25 to 64 would be lower in 2020, and the percentage of adults not completing high school would be higher in 2020 than in 2000 under the static cohort assumptions (Figure 2.14).

However, if educational attainment continues to improve for each racial/ethnic and nativity cohort in the future as it has in the past, then California's population in 2020 will be better educated than today's population. The dynamic cohort projections show substantial increases in the percentage of adults ages 25 to 64 who are college graduates, although the projected increase is smaller than the historic increase. The percentage of adults not completing high school is also projected to decline, although one in five Californians would still fall into this category. One reason educational attainment levels improved in the past

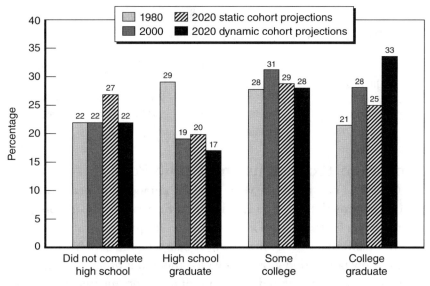

SOURCE: Author's projections.

Figure 2.14—Educational Attainment of California Residents Ages 25 to 64, 1980, 2000, and 2020

is that California attracted relatively well-educated adults from other states and sent to those states less-educated former Californians. Thus, the dynamic cohort projections implicitly assume that California's future levels of educational attainment will rise because it exports less-educated adults and imports better-educated adults from other states.

Overall, California's public and private universities do not produce all of the college graduates demanded by the state's economy. Historically, the state has experienced net domestic migration of college graduates and, more recently, it has attracted large numbers of foreign-born college graduates. (Although most immigrants have low levels of education, a sizable share are college graduates.) As a consequence, most college graduates in California are not native Californians (Table 2.8). Thus, the state's ability to meet the demands of its economy for high-skill labor depends not only on the state's own production of college graduates but also the continued desirability of California to college graduates from other states and from the rest of the world.

Table 2.8

Place of Birth of College Graduates in California, 1960–2000

	1960	1970	1980	1990	2000
California	26%	27%	31%	32%	33%
Rest of United States	65%	64%	54%	47%	39%
Foreign-born	9%	9%	15%	21%	28%

SOURCE: Author's tabulations of decennial census data.

Population Projections and Public Policy

California may be on the verge of a new demographic era. Strong population growth rates, almost a defining characteristic of California, can no longer be assumed. The key question for prognosticators is whether California will become the next demographic New York—a place of slow population growth in which thousands of international migrants arrive each year and thousands of domestic migrants leave—or whether California will return to the population growth patterns that have characterized so much of the state's history, attracting migrants both internationally and domestically. The answer to that question will determine both the pace and magnitude of future population increases in California. If California follows the path of New York, population growth in the state will continue to slow and fall far below national levels. If California returns to its pre-1990s past, the state will experience rapid and formidable levels of population growth. The most likely scenario is that California's future, at least over the next two decades, lies somewhere between the California of the past and the New York of today. The state will continue to experience substantial population growth through international migration and natural increase but will no longer experience large gains from flows of domestic migrants.

In the meantime, California faces many policy challenges as a result of its population growth and change. Absolute increases will be significant if not unprecedented, and they will challenge the state's ability to provide infrastructure, social services, and environmental protection. Perhaps the most important challenge is ensuring that intergenerational educational progress is strong. Almost half of California's current population consists of immigrants and their children, and although many immigrants arrive with high levels of education, many more do not. California's future depends on a well-educated, highly skilled workforce. Although California may continue to attract domestic and international migrants that fit this description, much of the state's workforce will be made up of second-generation Californians. Preparing them for life in California's evolving economy is therefore an urgent priority.

3. California's Economic Future and Infrastructure Challenges

David Neumark[1]

This chapter considers California's economy over the next two decades, emphasizing those features that are likely to influence infrastructure and workforce needs. It draws on existing economic forecasts, combines them with other data sources and predictions, and reviews their implications for some of the challenges the state is likely to face. Specifically, it considers the following:

- The level of economic activity, especially employment;
- The geographic location of that activity;
- Its industrial composition; and
- The skill composition of the workforce.

The first two features influence the magnitude of the infrastructure challenge and where it is likely to be felt. Because industries make different demands on energy, water, and transportation, the industrial composition of economic activity will also affect infrastructure needs. Finally, the skills required to support this economic activity will drive the demand for education—like infrastructure, an investment with a significant public component that has important implications for California's economic growth.

The effects of economic changes on projected infrastructure needs considered in this chapter are less significant than California's sheer population growth. Nevertheless, these economic changes have significant implications for the nature of infrastructure challenges and where they are likely to surface. Moreover, the state's workforce challenges are more closely tied to economic changes than to population

---

[1]For a more detailed technical presentation of this analysis, see the occasional paper *California's Economic Future and Infrastructure Challenges* (Neumark, 2005), available at www.ca2025.org.

growth as such. As a consequence, and because of the strong relationship between workers' skills and their economic well-being, these workforce challenges receive a disproportionate share of attention in this chapter.

It is important to clarify at the outset what this chapter does not do. First, it is not an exercise in economic forecasting as such. Rather, it summarizes and synthesizes existing forecasts to sketch California's economic future. Second, this chapter does not explore specific infrastructure needs associated with different industries and different regions. Instead, it identifies general economic trends and how they might influence infrastructure needs, broadly defined, over the next two decades. Other chapters in this volume address specific infrastructure needs in more detail.

Economic Forecasting

The most venerable method of economic forecasting comes from econometric models, which combine economic theory and statistical methods to model industrial sectors, the government, the labor market, and so on. In addition to the model of the economy, forecasting based on econometric models also requires predictions of the future course of many exogenous variables—for example, population—and typically reflects a good deal of judgment as well. Many institutions—including the Federal Reserve Board and its banks, private banks, and forecasting companies—use these models to produce both national and state-level forecasts.

Forecasts based on econometric models have two strengths. To a trained eye, they are transparent: That is, they have a strong "mechanical" component and are easy to both understand and critique. Also, good econometric models impose the consistency required by economic theory. In particular, they require identities that hold (e.g., all income is either saved or spent) and markets that are in equilibrium (demand equals supply). However, most econometric models are not well suited to our purpose because they focus on the short or medium term—the usual time horizon for financial investors or the Federal Reserve Board. Moreover, over a long time horizon their parameters—which reflect underlying behavior, the state of technology, government policy, and so on—may change in ways that the model will not capture. Also, many exogeneous variables must be forecast in an ad hoc fashion.

For these reasons, professional forecasters are skeptical of long-term projections based on econometric models.

Many government agencies and researchers engage more explicitly in longer-term projections, often for purposes of transportation or manpower planning. Although these projections match the time horizons with which this chapter is concerned, they generally share two weaknesses. First, they tend to assume that present growth rates will continue mechanically into the future. Second, such projections are often done in isolation from what is or what might be happening in other sectors of the economy. Another factor to keep in mind when considering long-term forecasts is the interaction between infrastructure and economic growth and development. Because infrastructure shapes the conditions for such growth and development, there is potentially important feedback from infrastructure to the economy. For example, an economy that depends on a well-functioning transportation network could be threatened by failure to develop the necessary transportation resources. Likewise, if California's economy depends heavily on highly skilled workers, a severe shortage of such workers would threaten the state's economic future.[2]

In short, economic forecasting—even in the short run but especially in the long run—is far from an exact science. Whether based on econometric models or long-term extrapolation, such forecasts do not allow for sweeping changes—in technology, politics, foreign economic development, and so on—that may have profound economic effects. For example, declines in military spending and the dot-com boom demonstrate how government spending and technological innovation

---

[2]In fact, the relationship between economic growth and infrastructure investment is less clear than one might think. Aschauer (1989a) finds that some publicly provided infrastructure investments increase the productivity of private capital, rather than mainly crowding out private investments. His related study (Aschauer, 1989b) finds that investments in "core" infrastructure—streets and highways, airports, electrical and gas facilities, mass transit, water systems, and sewers—have the greatest effect on economic productivity, in contrast to public investments in hospitals, other buildings, conservation and development structures, or the military. However, Kelejian and Robinson (1997) summarize subsequent work that raises serious questions about the marginal productivity of public capital, showing that such estimates are highly sensitive to the econometric specification and that estimates indicating no productive effect are common.

can dramatically influence the composition and location of economic activity within California. Moreover, no single method or approach is uniquely suited to generating long-term economic forecasts for California. In what follows, we therefore consider a variety of existing forecasts and supplement them with expert judgments about possible changes, shocks, or threats to the California economy.

Economic Forecasts for California

There are three main sources of statewide economic forecasts— UCLA Anderson, California's Employment Development Department (EDD), and CCSCE.[3] Each of California's COGs also provides forecasts for its own region (the Bay Area, Sacramento, San Diego, and Los Angeles/Southern California). In addition, the California Department of Transportation (DOT) generates county forecasts that can be aggregated to form a statewide forecast.

The population forecasts that underlie the economic forecasts to the year 2010 project population growth of between 16 and 17 percent (Figure 3.1). Not surprisingly, the range of the forecasts to 2020 is wider—30 to 34 percent. Note that the population forecasts embedded in each economic forecast lie toward the high end of the range of population forecasts. This pattern reflects the economic forecasts using earlier DOF forecasts, which called for higher population growth (California Department of Finance, 2004b). The range of the forecasts for employment growth is considerably wider than that for population growth—13 to 23 percent for the period from 2000 to 2010.[4] There are fewer forecasts available for 2020. The DOT and CCSCE forecasts predict 32 to 34 percent employment growth, whereas the UCLA Anderson forecast predicts 41 percent employment growth from 2000 to

---

[3]For a description of each source's scope and methods, see Neumark (2005).

[4]The levels are not strictly comparable across all forecasts because they are derived from either payrolls (that is, wage and salary workers) or all employment. The growth rates, however, are more comparable. The forecasts done at a later date project lower employment growth (the exception is the EDD forecast), presumably reflecting the economic slowdown at the beginning of the decade.

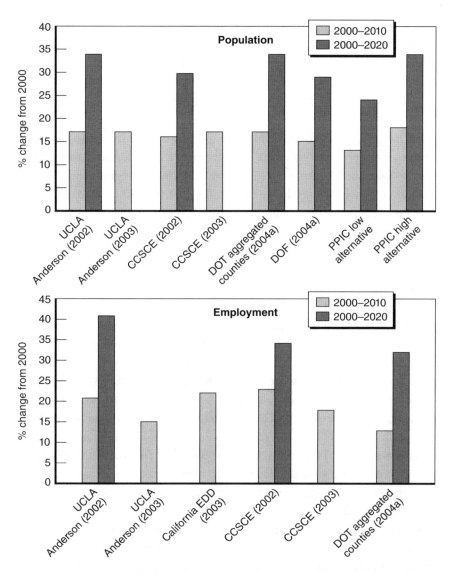

Figure 3.1—California's Population and Employment Forecasts, 2000–2020

2020. Note, however, that the later forecasts from UCLA Anderson and CCSCE revise their projected employment growth downward.[5]

At the regional level, there is considerable variation between COG and DOT employment growth predictions (Figure 3.2). DOT projects the lowest figures for the Bay Area and the highest for the San Diego region, but COG forecasts project the highest employment growth in the Sacramento region and much lower employment growth in San Diego. Employment growth is projected to be near the overall state rate for the North Coast and Mountains, the Upper Sacramento region, and the San Joaquin Valley but lower for the Central Coast. When comparing these forecasts, it is important to note that the COG projections also serve as the basis of regional plans and sometimes project the desired effects of current policies. For example, the 2003 ABAG projections are based on "smart growth" principles that ABAG adopted in 2001. ABAG assumes that policies based on these principles—which would lead to increased housing density in cities and inner suburbs as well as greater reliance on public transportation—will be implemented, at least partially, by 2030 (Association of Bay Area Governments, 2003). In this sense, the projections are somewhat prescriptive as well as predictive. Also noteworthy is the fact that forecasting methods varied significantly across the COGs.

Employment forecasts by industry share two major features (Figure 3.3). First is the projected decline in manufacturing employment, whose share of jobs is predicted to drop 15 to 24 percent by 2010 and 29 to 36 percent by 2020. (Note, however, that projected *levels* of employment in manufacturing are virtually flat over the next two decades.) Second, the forecasts point to sharp increases in services employment—by 7 to 11 percent by 2010 and 15 to 17 percent by 2020. The forecasts also indicate declining shares in mining and construction as well as in transportation, communications, and public utilities. The projected changes for trade, for finance, insurance, real estate, and for government are relatively small. It is important to note, however, that these forecasts

---

[5]Again, the employment forecasts are based on older DOF population forecasts that called for slightly faster population growth; were they based on the current population forecasts, they would presumably be a shade lower.

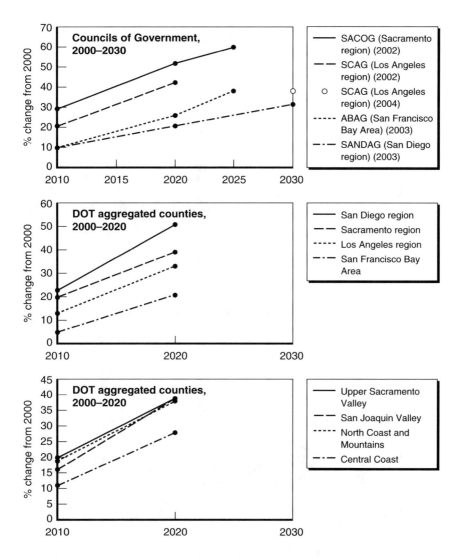

NOTES: The 2004 SCAG forecast contains no detail on the interim years. Employment definitions are as follows: ABAG and SCAG—total employment; SACOG,
SANDAG, and DOT—nonfarm employment. The SANDAG forecast is limited to
civilian jobs.

Figure 3.2—California's Regional Employment Forecasts, 2000–2030

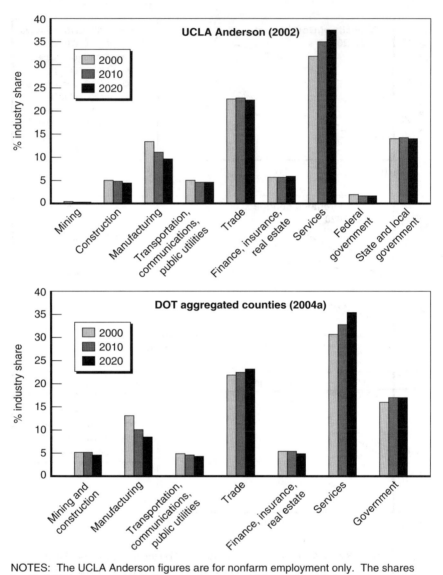

NOTES: The UCLA Anderson figures are for nonfarm employment only. The shares for the DOT forecasts include farm employment, which constituted about 2 percent of employment in 2000.

Figure 3.3—Projected Changes in Shares of Employment in California by Industry, 2010 and 2020

are at the one-digit industry level (using Standard Industrial Classification (SIC) codes) and thereby mask substantial variation within sectors.

Threats to the Forecasts

Finally, we consider expert assessments of developments that could affect the economic future of the state and therefore its infrastructure and workforce needs.[6] Because these assessments are not quantified, we have not incorporated them into our subsequent discussion regarding infrastructure trends and needs. We include them here, however, to serve as a useful backdrop to that discussion. These assessments—on international economic relations, technological change, political decisions, and infrastructure investment and utilization—are summarized in Table 3.1.

Two of the four threats related to international economic relations stem from sharp changes in trade patterns. In general, more trade implies changing demands for output of different industries in California, as well as changes in infrastructure demands, in addition to overall macroeconomic effects. The development of a cheap, alternative fuel would reshape economic and political relations between countries but would most likely benefit a state like California, which is a large consumer of energy and has strong economic ties with Asian countries that would gain from decreased reliance on petroleum. A dramatic change in economic growth in Mexico would also be particularly important to California, which has a large Mexican population prone to cyclical migration, and is an important trading partner.

Sharp technological changes, including the growth and commercialization of the biotechnology and nanotechnology industries, could also alter the course of the state's economy as the rise of the computer industry in Silicon Valley did a generation ago. These changes would affect two key industries—health care and agriculture—most

---

[6]The brief discussion in this section is based on longer reflections on threats to long-term economic forecasts for California provided by four experts: Stephen Levy, Howard Shatz, Christopher Thornberg, and Junfu Zhang. See Neumark (2005) for the full text of their reflections.

Table 3.1

Four Experts' Views on Threats to the Forecasts for California

Unanticipated Development	Likely Major Effects for California
International Economic Relations	
End of globalization	Reductions in demand facing high-tech industries. Slowing of port traffic.
Development of cheap, alternative fuel	Potential economic and political difficulties in oil-exporting countries, including Mexico and Venezuela, which could increase migration to United States. Economic gains for Asian producers, leading to more trade with Asia but also more competition from lower-priced manufactured goods.
Dramatic Mexican economic success	Slowdown or halt to illegal immigration. Possibility even of reverse migration of immigrants from United States back to Mexico. Increasing trade between Mexico and United States.
Elimination of industrial and agricultural tariffs	Opening up of new markets for California exporters, especially in agriculture, but also increased competition from imports. Possible large transitional costs for industries harmed by increased trade. Likely increase in wages and employment prospects for more-educated workers, and declines in opportunities for less-educated workers.
Technological Change	
Deepening of Internet technology	Increases in work online from home or other locations, reducing burden on transportation. Increased efficiency of use of educational infrastructure. Incorporation of "information highway system" into definition of physical infrastructure.
Advancement of biotechnology	Health increases and reductions in mortality. Increased agricultural production.
Commercialization of nanotechnology	Shifts in industrial composition of economy and skill composition of workforce.

Table 3.1 (continued)

Unanticipated Development	Likely Major Effects for California
Political Decisions	
Infrastructure investment directed to manufacturing industries	Disadvantage emerging nonmanufacturing sectors.
Changes in immigration policy	Alteration of population growth scenarios and projected skill composition of the workforce.
Excessive focus on infrastructure-population relationship	Insufficient attention to repair and maintenance of existing infrastructure and improving infrastructure technology.
Infrastructure Investment and Utilization	
Economic growth depends in part on infrastructure investment	Possibly lower economic growth, although evidence linking growth to infrastructure is subject to debate, and infrastructure may be more important as a determinant of quality of life than of economic growth.

NOTE: See Neumark (2005) for detailed discussions of threats to the forecasts.

profoundly. Advances in biotechnology could also lead to declines in mortality, thereby altering the state's demographic profile.

Political decisionmaking, particularly in the area of infrastructure, will almost certainly affect the state's economic future. Some chief concerns include insufficient attention to repair and maintenance, replicating the existing infrastructure stock as opposed to seeking out technological improvements, and paying excessive attention to the infrastructure needs of the manufacturing industry as opposed to those of other industries that may be more important to the state's economic future. In addition, sharp changes in federal immigration policy could affect the state's population trends and the educational levels of the workforce.

Although the precise interactions between infrastructure investment and economic growth are unclear, insufficient investment could very well drop economic growth below what is projected. On the other hand, the ability of government and the private sector to adapt to infrastructure constraints should not be underestimated. This ability, combined with the weak evidence linking infrastructure to economic growth, suggests that at least moderate deviations of infrastructure investment from the trends that might be projected based on economic growth will not seriously threaten that growth. In the end, infrastructure investment may have more to do with maintaining the quality of life as economic growth occurs than with economic growth per se; this does not minimize the importance of infrastructure investment, but it may influence how we think about the "need" for more investment.

Employment Versus Population Growth

Our forecasts also permit us to address imbalances between regional employment growth and regional population projections, which are summarized in Figures 3.4 to 3.6. These imbalances have important implications for transportation and housing infrastructure. For example, if a region is projected to have considerably higher employment growth than population growth, commutes into and out of the region will likely increase, thereby taxing that area's transportation infrastructure.[7] Note, however, that the population projections do not take into account sharp changes in housing availability. A region facing employment growth that outstrips its population growth may be able to partially alleviate this problem by increasing housing availability.

The forecasts exhibit a fair amount of discrepancy on these employment-population imbalances. For example, looking to 2020, the SANDAG forecast implies that employment growth will fall short of population growth by 4 percentage points, whereas the DOT forecast indicates that employment growth will outstrip population growth by 14 percentage points (Figure 3.5). It is difficult to characterize what drives these and other discrepancies. In some cases, the DOT forecast calls for considerably more employment growth than the COG forecast; in others, the opposite is true. These discrepancies notwithstanding, the other DOT figures indicate that employment growth in the SACOG region and the San Joaquin Valley is expected to lag population growth,

---

[7]This assumes that telecommuting or working at home does not increase substantially. In May 2001, 19.8 million persons, or 15 percent of the workforce, worked at home at least once a week (U.S. Bureau of Labor Statistics, 2002). See also U.S. Department of Transportation (2004).

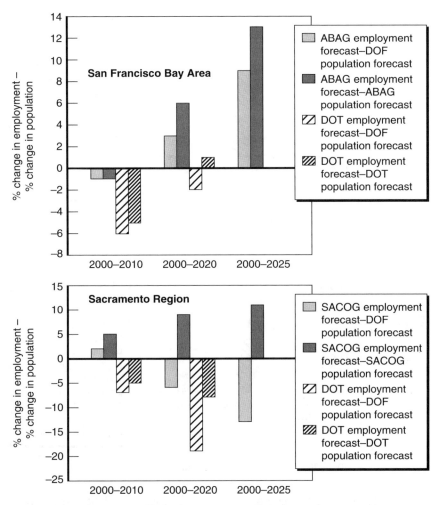

NOTES: The employment figures for COGs are based on COG projections or aggregated county-level DOT forecasts, as indicated. The employment figures for other county aggregations are based on aggregated county-level DOT forecasts. The DOF population forecasts are the disaggregated figures corresponding to the aggregate DOF forecasts. The COG/DOT forecasts are from their economic forecasts.

Figure 3.4—Percentage Change in Employment Minus Percentage Change in Population, Differences in Forecasted Percentage Changes, San Francisco Bay Area and Sacramento Region

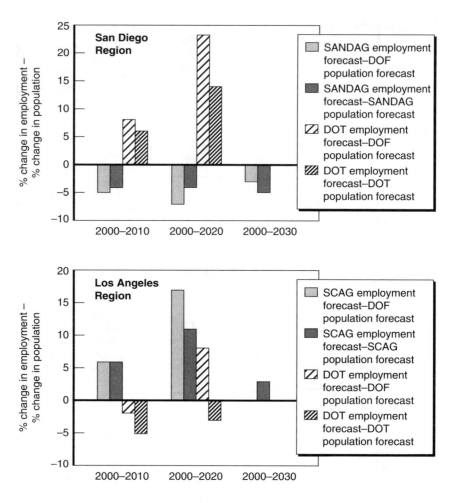

NOTES: See the notes for Figure 3.4. The employment figures for COGs are based on COG projections or aggregated county-level DOT forecasts, as indicated. The employment figures for other county aggregations are based on aggregated county-level DOT forecasts. The DOF population forecasts are the disaggregated figures corresponding to the aggregate DOF forecasts. The COG/DOT forecasts are from their economic forecasts.

Figure 3.5—Percentage Change in Employment Minus Percentage Change in Population, Differences in Forecasted Percentage Changes, San Diego Region and Los Angeles Region

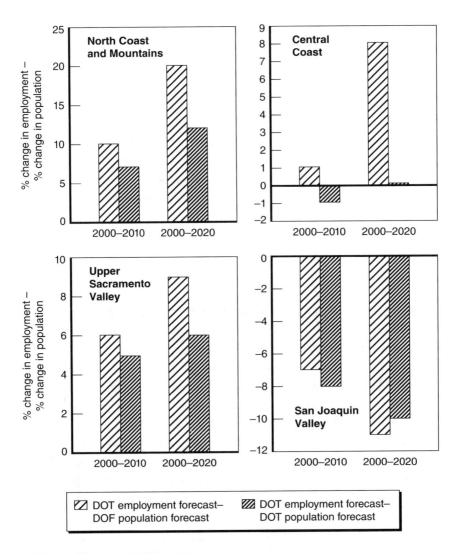

NOTE: See the notes for Figure 3.4.

Figure 3.6—Percentage Change in Employment Minus Percentage Change in
Population, Differences in Forecasted Percentage Changes,
DOT County Aggregations

whereas in the North Coast and Mountains and the Upper Sacramento Valley, employment is expected to grow considerably faster than population. For the ABAG and SCAG regions as well as the Central Coast, the numbers seem to indicate relatively more balance between employment and population growth. All else the same, regions for which employment growth is projected to outstrip population growth are likely to face stronger infrastructure challenges involved with the transportation of distant commuters to work—challenges that can be addressed directly via transportation and perhaps indirectly via increased housing availability. Regions expecting relatively more population growth will face similar (but not necessarily identical) challenges associated with accommodating commuters. Given the discrepancies in the forecasts, however, we are not inclined to draw stronger conclusions about employment-population imbalances by region.

Industrial Composition and Infrastructure Use

The industrial composition of the state's economy has direct implications for infrastructure because specific industries make different demands on transportation, water, energy, and other infrastructure systems. To see how California's changing industrial structure will affect infrastructure needs, we developed an input-output table that highlights infrastructure demands by industry (Table 3.2). We focus on input requirements of each one-digit (SIC) industry—for which we have employment forecasts—for the output of industries in the one-digit industry "transportation, communications, and utilities," and the output of government enterprises.[8] We also focus on inputs from government

---

[8]The two-digit industries that make up transportation, communications, and utilities include railroads and related services and passenger ground transportation; motor freight transportation and warehousing; water transportation; air transportation; pipelines, freight forwarders, and related services; communications; electric services; gas production and distribution; and water and sanitary services. Inputs from these industries do not necessarily constitute infrastructure per se, but they are often strongly associated with infrastructure demands. As an example, the purchase of inputs from the two-digit industry "motor freight transportation and warehousing" will not capture all of the costs associated with highway use (wear and tear, congestion, and so on). Nonetheless, output from this industry will contribute to demands on the transportation infrastructure.

Table 3.2

Input Requirements from Transportation, Communications, and Utilities and Government Enterprises for Output from Other One-Digit Industries

| | Fastest-Declining Employment Shares | | | | | Fastest-Growing Employment Shares | |
	Mining	Construction	Manufacturing	Trade	Finance, Insurance, and Real Estate	Services	Government
	(1)	(2)	(3)	(4)	(5)	(6)	(7)
Railroads and related services; passenger ground transportation	.010	.005	.009	.003	.002	.003	.010
Motor freight transportation and warehousing	.019	.038	.043	.011	.009	.013	.031
Water transportation	.006	.002	.003	.001	.000	.001	.014
Air transportation	.007	.006	.010	.007	.004	.007	.014
Pipelines, freight forwarders, and related services	.003	.003	.005	.003	.001	.003	.005
Communications, except radio and TV	.012	.015	.015	.028	.019	.022	.014
Radio and TV broadcasting	.002	.002	.006	.010	.003	.005	.000
Electric services (utilities)	.023	.009	.019	.013	.005	.011	.031
Gas production and distribution (utilities)	.053	.006	.014	.004	.002	.004	.036
Water and sanitary services	.002	.001	.002	.001	.001	.001	.004
Federal government enterprises	.004	.005	.005	.009	.013	.009	.411
State and local government enterprises	.015	.005	.009	.006	.004	.006	.618

NOTES: Input requirements are calculated from a 1999 national input-output industry requirements table for two-digit industries. Industry input-output coefficients are aggregated weighting by share of two-digit industry in one-digit industry output, based on the industry use table for two-digit industries. (See www.bea.gov.)

enterprises, which may also help to pick up infrastructure demands. The input-output accounts include both federal enterprises (e.g., the postal service and military exchanges) and state enterprises, such as local transit, utilities, water and sanitation services, and parking (U.S. Department of Commerce, 1998).[9]

This analysis requires several important qualifications. First, the industry-level forecasts described above pertain to employment rather than output. If productivity growth differs significantly across industries, a particular industry's employment share may fall even when its relative demands on infrastructure are rising. Second, some industries (for example, tourism) pose infrastructure demands that will not be reflected in the input-output table. Third, the table is likely to underestimate the infrastructure needs that derive from California's role as a gateway for trade originating in or destined for other states.[10] Finally, the fixed input requirements of input-output analysis may not hold over the longer run. Businesses and other agents may adapt to infrastructure shortages or price changes, in which case industry input requirements could change.

The table shows that the declining industries (again, in relative terms) are the most intensive users of infrastructure, whereas the rapidly growing services industry is one of the least intensive users. These input-output calculations suggest that California's emergent industries may make lighter demands on the state's infrastructure than was true in the past. We reemphasize, however, that infrastructure challenges will rise considerably as the population expands; the reductions to which we refer should be interpreted as reductions relative to what would be implied by population growth and the economic structure of the past. Moreover, given many of the limitations discussed above, many factors not captured by this calculation may drive demand for transportation, water, and energy systems. Even so, the input-output analysis helps clarify some of the changes that will accompany the state's shifting industrial composition.

---

[9]For more details on the methods for producing the input-output table, see Neumark (2005).

[10]See Haveman and Hummels (2004).

Industrial Composition and Skill Needs

California's changing economy will make new demands on human capital as well as infrastructure. One dimension of human capital that is strongly influenced by public policy is education. Will California workers be able to provide the skills demanded by industry over the next two decades? This is a complicated question, and we address it in a series of steps. First, we discuss the implications of the state's changing industrial composition, particularly as it implies changes in educational levels for the workforce. Second, we examine educational levels of workers in different industries and changes in those educational levels over time. Third, we look at the implications of changes in the industrial mix of employment at the regional level. Finally, we discuss how the educational attainment of workers in California is likely to adjust to changing requirements on the part of industry. In particular, we consider the extent to which we might expect in-migration of workers with the educational qualifications that are likely to be needed over the next couple of decades.

To predict skill needs by industry, we consider two alternatives. First, we take the educational levels of workers in each industry from the 2002 Current Population Survey (CPS) and assume that the distribution within each industry will remain constant; we refer to this as the static scenario. In this case, the educational requirements of the workforce change only because the industrial mix of employment changes. However, we know that educational levels for the workforce as a whole have been rising, perhaps reflecting the greater skill needs posed by technological changes within industries. Consequently, we also consider a dynamic scenario in which educational trends within industries are projected to continue to follow the same path that they followed from 1992 to 2002.[11] In this case, the educational requirements of the workforce are projected to change as the result of continuing trends in education as well as the shifting composition of employment.

---

[11]Note that we use 1992–2002 rather than 1990–2000 because the classification of education in the Current Population Survey changed in 1992. See, for example, Jaeger (1997).

Using the UCLA Anderson industry employment forecasts for the static exercise, we see that the share of workers with a high school diploma or less is predicted to decline, whereas the share with a bachelor's degree or higher is expected to increase (Figure 3.7). The EDD forecasts show quite similar results. In the dynamic exercise (Figure 3.8), these changes are more pronounced, with sharp projected

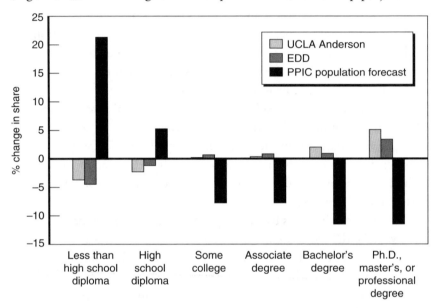

NOTES: Figures for 2000 are based on the educational distribution of each industry in monthly CPS files for 1992 and 2002. In the static exercise (Figure 3.2), these are based on the 2002 educational distribution, and in the dynamic exercise (Figure 3.8), the 2000 distribution is linearly interpolated from the 1992 and 2002 distributions. Figures for 2020 are based on forecasts of employment by industry, coupled with the educational distribution
of workers in each industry in 2002. In the dynamic exercise, there is an additional adjustment for the trend in the educational level of workers in each industry from 1992 to 2002, which is applied to the subsequent years. If a trend projected a negative number of workers with a given educational level in an industry, that number was set to zero, and the additional workers implicitly added to that category were removed from the other educational categories in that industry in proportion to their representation. PPIC population forecasts are from Johnson (2005). The population

Figure 3.7—Percentage Change in Shares of Nonfarm Employment and of Population by Educational Levels in California, Static Exercise, 2000–2020

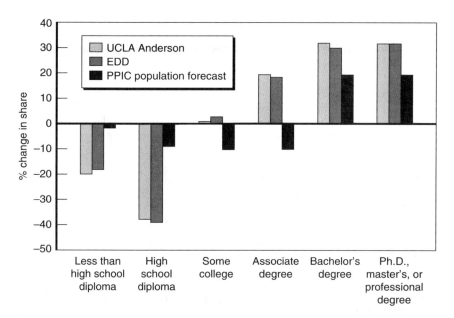

NOTE: See the notes for Figure 3.7.

**Figure 3.8—Percentage Change in Shares of Nonfarm Employment
and of Population by Educational Levels in California,
Dynamic Exercise, 2000–2020**

increases in the shares of workers with associate degrees or higher and
sharp projected declines in the shares of workers with a high school
diploma or less. Assuming that past trends in education within
industries persist, the projections in Figure 3.8 are probably closer to
how demands are likely to change.

These results may be viewed as surprising, given the popular
perception that our economy is moving in the direction of low-wage,
low-skill service jobs. Table 3.3 provides some information on education
levels by industry, which should help to dispel this perception. The top
panel shows the distribution of workers in each industry across
educational categories. This panel demonstrates that mining,
construction, manufacturing, and trade use relatively less-educated
workers, whereas services tend to use more-educated workers. For
example, 27.2 percent of construction workers and 21 percent of

Table 3.3

Educational Levels Across Industries and Trends Within Industries in California

	Less Than High School Diploma	High School Diploma	Some College	Associate Degree	Bachelor's Degree	Ph.D., Master's, or Professional Degree
	(1)	(2)	(3)	(4)	(5)	(6)
2002 share						
Mining	17.7	24.1	13.8	20.8	18.8	4.9
Construction	27.2	36.3	20.2	7.2	7.3	1.8
Manufacturing	21.0	24.8	18.2	8.4	19.8	7.7
Transportation and utilities	9.9	29.0	26.6	11.4	17.8	5.8
Trade	21.1	29.0	25.9	7.3	14.3	2.5
Finance, insurance, and real estate	5.1	19.6	28.3	10.4	28.1	8.5
Services	11.2	17.5	20.6	9.7	25.0	15.9
Public administration	4.0	13.3	28.8	16.3	24.1	13.6
1992–2002 % change in share						
Mining	3.0	–46.0	–41.3	556.5	304.9	–29.3
Construction	11.3	–3.3	–10.6	15.5	0.4	–6.8
Manufacturing	–17.9	–10.8	–1.4	34.2	23.5	33.6
Transportation and utilities	–16.4	–3.3	–6.2	1.7	15.2	53.6
Trade	–1.9	–10.0	0.5	12.7	23.8	–1.9
Finance, insurance, and real estate	–2.7	–21.5	4.0	14.5	6.5	19.1
Services	–16.0	–18.4	–0.2	10.9	19.4	7.6
Public administration	32.7	–38.8	6.3	2.8	9.2	31.5

SOURCE: Figures are from monthly CPS files for 1992 and 2002.

manufacturing workers have less than a high school diploma, compared with 11.2 percent of service workers. Likewise, the services industry has the second highest share (25 percent) with a bachelor's degree; the highest share is in finance, insurance, and real estate. Moreover, service jobs are not becoming less skilled. The bottom panel shows the trends in education within industry. Here we see that in most industries educational levels are rising, but the services industry exhibits relatively robust growth in the share with college degrees.[12]

To shed more light on services, Table 3.4 gives information on education levels for the four subcategories of services that were introduced with the North America Industry Classification System (NAICS)—business and repair services, personal services, entertainment and recreation services, and professional and related services. The top panel of the table reveals that only the personal services industry is characterized by low educational levels, and the bottom panel reveals that the share with a four-year college degree has declined (slightly) in this industry. However, as the first column of the bottom panel shows, this is the only services industry that is in decline; the other services industries—all of which use much more-educated workers—are growing. Thus, the services industry, which is the fastest growing, makes use of relatively more-educated workers, and the trend is toward increased education in this industry. This pattern explains why the projected changes in the industrial composition of employment imply rising educational levels.[13]

In general, changes in skill needs are similar across regions, with declines in manufacturing, mining, and construction, and increases in services (Figures 3.9 and 3.10). There are some exceptions, but we should be cautious in reading too much into any single projection at the industry-by-region level.[14] Similarly, the implied changes in educational levels across regions echo the statewide analysis, with projected declines in workers with a high school diploma or less, and projected increases in workers with an associate degree or higher (Table 3.5).

---

[12]Some of the percentage changes for mining are very large, reflecting changes relative to a very small base.

[13]However, wages in the services industry—for otherwise comparable workers—are lower than in manufacturing and construction (see, for example, Blackburn and Neumark, 1992). The issue of whether the state can or should try to encourage employment in higher-wage industries or take other steps to increase wage levels within industries is beyond the scope of this study.

[14]In particular, the results for the North Coast and Mountains sometimes differ dramatically, but these are based on very small numbers, and this region has a very different industrial structure. For more detail on these projections, see Neumark (2005).

Table 3.4

Educational Levels and Changes in California by Service Subsector

| | Share of Services Employment | Share in Each Educational Category | | | | | |
		Less Than High School Diploma	High School Diploma	Some College	Associate Degree	Bachelor's Degree	Ph.D., Master's, or Professional Degree
	(1)	(2)	(3)	(4)	(5)	(6)	(7)
2002 share							
Business and repair services	22.1	17.5	21.8	20.7	8.4	23.8	7.9
Personal services, incl. private household	9.6	30.0	26.0	20.2	11.1	10.3	2.4
Entertainment and recreation services	8.7	11.0	20.8	25.0	6.4	29.3	7.5
Professional and related services	59.6	6.0	14.1	20.0	10.5	27.1	22.2
1992–2002 change in share							
Business and repair services	.8	–.1	–7.9	–1.3	0	6.6	2.8
Personal services, including private household	–2.7	–3.7	–2.5	1.4	4.2	–.7	1.3
Entertainment and recreation services	1.5	–5.8	2.5	–3.1	–.3	5.1	1.6
Professional and related services	.4	–1.2	–3.4	.8	2.2	7.7	.3

SOURCE: Figures are from monthly CPS files for 1992 and 2002.

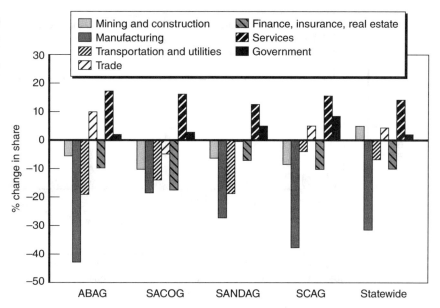

NOTE: All calculations are based on DOT employment forecasts.

Figure 3.9—Percentage Change in Nonfarm Employment Share
by Industry, COG Regions and Statewide, 2000–2020

Educational Attainment and Changing Educational Requirements

The evidence considered so far strongly suggests that California's economy will require large increases in educational levels of its workforce. In that sense, perhaps the most serious challenge posed by California's economic future—aside from the scaling up of all infrastructure required by a growing population—is the need for a more-educated workforce.

A more-educated workforce may, in fact, be forthcoming. Between 1990 and 2000, the following percentage changes in the share of the workforce at each educational level occurred:

- Less than high school diploma, –9.6 percent;
- High school diploma, –16.4 percent;
- Some college, 0.2 percent;
- Associate degree, 12.4 percent;

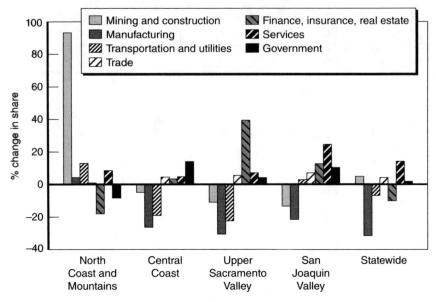

NOTE: All calculations are based on DOT employment forecasts.

Figure 3.10—Percentage Change in Nonfarm Employment Share by Industry, DOT Aggregated Counties and Statewide, 2000–2020

- Bachelor's degree, 18.6 percent; and
- Ph.D., master's, or professional degree, 22.5 percent.

These trends should continue, but the changing demographic mix of the state's population will work in the other direction. That is, the state's population growth is concentrated among groups that now have low levels of education (Figure 3.7). For this reason, the demand for educated workers will likely outstrip the supply generated by California's population. Addressing this shortfall with proactive policies will be an important but difficult challenge. Decisions to obtain postsecondary education are voluntary and respond to the costs, quality, and perceived returns to education. Over time, however, the rising demand for more-educated workers will likely lead to rising educational levels in the workforce. Certainly in California (and elsewhere) educational attainment levels rose for most groups as the economic returns to

Table 3.5

Percentage Change in Share in Each Educational Category Resulting from Changes in the Industrial Composition of Employment, Nonfarm Workers in California, Statewide and by COG Regions and Other County Aggregations, 2000–2020

	Statewide	ABAG	SACOG	SANDAG	SCAG	North Coast and Mountains	Central Coast	Upper Sacramento Valley	San Joaquin Valley
	(1)	(2)	(3)	(4)	(5)	(6)	(7)	(8)	(9)
Static: fixed education within industry									
Less than high school diploma	-4.4	-3.3	-3.7	-3.9	-4.7	2.4	-7.8	-6.9	-15.4
High school diploma	-1.1	-1.8	-2.3	-2.0	-2.1	3.7	-1.8	-1.4	-1.6
Some college	0.7	0.8	-0.3	0.3	1.1	-1.0	1.8	1.6	3.5
Associate degree	0.9	0.4	0.9	1.0	1.4	-2.1	3.1	1.6	5.7
Bachelor's degree	1.0	1.1	1.7	1.6	1.4	-1.8	2.3	2.5	6.7
Ph.D., master's, or professional degree	3.5	4.4	5.1	4.5	4.8	-2.3	4.2	3.3	11.1
Dynamic: trend education within industry									
Less than high school diploma	-18.2	-19.6	-14.7	-18.3	-20.7	-4.4	-21.4	-19.1	-28.7
High school diploma	-39.0	-36.6	-42.6	-38.8	-37.1	-45.2	-37.9	-39.1	-37.0
Some college	2.7	1.3	2.1	1.4	2.0	2.6	7.6	5.0	9.2
Associate degree	18.3	20.0	16.7	19.6	20.8	10.3	20.8	18.6	24.0
Bachelor's degree	29.9	31.4	29.1	31.0	31.6	22.2	32.7	31.6	38.6
Ph.D., master's, or professional degree	31.6	28.9	34.6	30.5	31.0	33.0	30.1	30.5	40.2

NOTES: All calculations are based on DOT employment forecasts. See the notes to Figure 3.7 for description of calculations. Information on education distributions and trends is at the state level, not the county or COG level.

completing high school and obtaining college education increased in the latter part of the 20th century.[15]

Finally, highly educated workers are likely to continue migrating to California.[16] This migration can fulfill the needs of industry without requiring that the state "produce" as many educated workers as its businesses require. However, current residents will probably prefer that their offspring move into these higher-paying jobs. Moreover, the extent to which in-migration is likely to occur depends in part on how the demand for workers of different educational levels evolves in the rest of the country. The final three tables address this question.

In the dynamic exercise, the educational composition of the workforce at the national level will parallel that of California, with decreases in the representation of less-educated workers and increases in the representation of highly educated workers (Table 3.6, bottom panel). The static exercise points to considerably less dramatic changes nationwide, largely because the 2002 UCLA Anderson forecast predicts considerably slower growth of employment in services nationwide than for California (Table 3.7). However, this particular component of that forecast seems anomalous. The last column of the table reports nationwide Bureau of Labor Statistics (BLS) industry employment projections through 2010 (they do not go out to 2020), which suggest much faster growth of services employment. And finally, the more recent 2003 UCLA Anderson forecast—which goes only through 2010 and uses the NAICS—also predicts faster growth of services employment, as does a slightly later BLS projection based on the NAICS (Table 3.8). Thus, it seems safest to say that changes in the industrial composition of employment will be qualitatively similar in California and the nation as a whole.

These results do not imply that more-educated workers will stop migrating to California. They do suggest, however, that similar demand pressures will exist elsewhere and therefore that the state's economy may

---

[15]For evidence on increases in schooling attainment in California, see Reyes (2001).
[16]See Betts (2000).

Table 3.6

Percentage Change in Share in Each Educational Category Resulting from Changes in the Industrial Composition of Employment, Nonfarm Workers in California and the United States

	California		United States	
	2000–2010	2000–2020	2000–2010	2000–2020
	(1)	(2)	(3)	(4)
Static: fixed education within industry				
Less than high school diploma	−1.9	−3.6	−0.1	−0.4
High school diploma	−1.2	−2.2	−0.2	−0.9
Some college	0.2	0.2	0.1	0.1
Associate degree	0.3	0.4	−0.1	0.1
Bachelor's degree	1.0	2.0	−0.1	0.4
Ph.D., master's, or professional degree	2.8	5.1	0.0	1.6
Dynamic: trend education within industry				
Less than high school diploma	−10.0	−19.9	−14.3	−28.6
High school diploma	−19.6	−37.8	−14.3	−29.1
Some college	0.6	0.8	−0.1	−0.5
Associate degree	10.3	19.5	21.1	42.1
Bachelor's degree	16.0	31.9	17.1	34.9
Ph.D., master's, or professional degree	16.4	31.6	11.9	25.7

NOTE: The first two columns repeat the numbers from the UCLA Anderson forecast (2002). The last two columns present the same calculation, but for the UCLA Anderson national forecast, and national data on educational levels and trends.

have to rely, in large part, on boosting educational levels among the state's current residents. The results also suggest that if current residents do not increase their educational attainment, they may increasingly find themselves facing employment difficulties and a lack of higher-paying jobs in the economy of the future. This outcome will affect their quality of life and most likely increase burdens on the state's social and income transfer programs.

Table 3.7

Forecasted Percentage Change in Share in California Employment by Industry, SIC

	UCLA Anderson, California (2002)			UCLA Anderson, United States (2002)			BLS, United States
	1990–2000	2000–2010	2000–2020	1990–2000	2000–2010	2000–2020	2000–2010
	(1)	(2)	(3)	(4)	(5)	(6)	(7)
Mining	−47.8	−9.8	−25.9	−36.4	−15.0	−23.1	−33.3
Construction	11.6	−4.9	−15.1	7.9	8.2	2.9	−2.2
Manufacturing	−18.7	−18.1	−28.6	−19.6	−9.1	−14.5	−11.4
Transportation and utilities	4.9	−8.6	−8.9	1.1	5.0	−3.8	2.0
Trade	−5.0	0.3	−1.2	−2.4	0.9	2.0	−3.5
Finance, insurance, and real estate	−12.5	0.5	3.9	−6.2	3.5	3.6	−6.1
Services	19.1	9.7	17.3	20.3	0.6	4.7	13.2
Federal	−34.9	−12.5	−17.3	−25.2	−13.6	−15.8	−18.8
State and local government	3.0	1.4	−0.3	−2.2	2.0	2.5	−4.2

SOURCE: BLS projections are from Berman (2001).

Conclusion

Aside from the overall scale of the economy, which is tied largely to population, the critical factors regarding the state's infrastructure and human capital needs can be traced to shifts in the industrial composition of the economy. The various forecasts considered in this chapter point to strong relative declines in manufacturing, transportation, and possibly construction employment. In contrast, service industries are projected to grow strongly. The regional effects of these changes will pose a host of infrastructure challenges, but the regional forecasts are too varied to permit more precise analysis of this question. It also appears that the shift away from goods-producing industries and toward service-producing industries will diminish the relative demand on transportation, utilities, and energy systems. We hasten to add, however,

Table 3.8

Forecasted Percentage Change in Share in California Employment by Industry, Later Forecasts, NAICS

	UCLA Anderson (2003), California 2000–2010	UCLA Anderson (2003), United States 2000–2010	BLS, United States 2002–2012
	(1)	(2)	(3)
Natural resources and mining	−46.7	−23.6	−24.4
Construction	1.9	10.5	−1.2
Manufacturing	−26.8	−23.7	−15.0
Transportation, warehousing, and utilities	−4.4	6.3	1.6
Trade	−1.2	−7.9	−2.9
Financial activities	−11.3	−0.0	−3.6
Information	0.7	−5.8	1.7
Professional and business services	8.4	18.6	11.9
Educational and health services	18.6	12.3	13.1
Leisure and hospitality services	5.4	4.0	1.1
Other services	6.3	−0.9	−0.7
All services	13.7	8.9	8.2
Federal	−8.5	−11.5	−13.8
State and local government	3.7	0.9	−2.6

SOURCE: BLS projections are from Horrigan (2004).

that our analysis does not capture all of the demands placed on the state's physical infrastructure. Furthermore, the reduction in the demand for infrastructure is relative to the state's projected growth in population and economic activity. The absolute demand on the state's infrastructure systems will continue to grow.

Although there is some controversy about the contribution of physical capital to economic growth, there is less controversy about the productive effects of human capital, of which education is a large component.[17] A long line of work documents the role of education in

---

[17]Motivated by the "Solow residual" (Solow, 1957), the early work on this topic included Schultz's seminal work (1960, 1961) based on the human capital approach and

economic growth. Projections of California's economic future indicate that the workforce will have to be considerably more educated than it currently is. There are important but unresolved questions concerning what policymakers can do to increase educational attainment among the workforce, but encouraging California's youths to increase educational attainment is particularly important if they are to enjoy high living standards in the evolving economy. A failure to do so is likely to increase their difficulties and potentially increase the burden on public services if they cannot support themselves or their families. The implication of this research is that investment in human capital can go beyond meeting current labor market needs; it can also build the foundation for stronger economic growth. But Barro (2002) emphasizes that efforts to increase educational attainment must not lose sight of continuing efforts to improve the quality of education. Thus, it seems likely that the principal challenge posed by economic change in California over the next two decades is for increased investment in human capital, on which a modern, technologically advanced, and service-oriented economy increasingly depends.

Denison's (1962) and Griliches's (1960) research on the changing composition of the labor force, and extending to consideration of the complementarity of capital and skill by Griliches (1970).

4. Infrastructure Financing in California

Kim Rueben and Shelley de Alth[1]

As a first step toward understanding California's infrastructure needs over the next two decades, this chapter examines how California's state and local governments pay for projects and services. It also presents current spending levels and priorities and shows how they compare to those in earlier periods and in the rest of the country. Finally, it summarizes recent changes in infrastructure financing generally and in four specific sectors—K–12 education, higher education, water supply and quality, and transportation—and how California's decisions have been affected by the ongoing state budget crisis.

There are three basic ways to pay for infrastructure: pay-as-you-go, leasing and private provision, and borrowing. Under pay-as-you-go financing, the government pays for a project out of current revenues. No borrowing occurs, and no interest is paid. This approach limits spending to cash on hand and therefore renders many large projects infeasible. Currently, California uses pay-as-you-go funding principally from federal transfers, which are distributed on a revenue-sharing basis.

Another way to provide infrastructure is for the government to contract with the private sector. Under this approach, private firms may provide services directly to the general public, such as the provision of waste disposal services; or the government can lease public property to private companies, allow them to pay for improvements, and then receive the improved property at the end of the lease agreement. Airport parking lots, for example, are often financed this way.

---

[1]For a more detailed analysis and data appendix, see the occasional paper *Understanding Infrastructure Financing for California* (de Alth and Rueben, 2005), available at www.ca2025.org.

Much of California's infrastructure financing is based on borrowing. By issuing bonds and paying them off over 20 or 30 years, governments can undertake large projects that could not be paid for out of current revenues. Interest payments on these bonds can double the nominal cost of a project, but the cost in real dollars is lower. For large capital projects, borrowing has the added advantage of matching the long-term costs of such projects to their long-term benefits. In effect, the various generations that will benefit from an infrastructure project contribute to its financing.

Infrastructure borrowing is done with general obligation (GO) or revenue bonds. When the state or local government issues GO bonds, it pledges to use its general revenues to pay back the interest and principal, and this debt is backed by the full faith and credit of the issuing government. Revenue bonds, in contrast, are paid back with a revenue stream generated from the infrastructure project itself—for example, tolls generated from a toll road or water fees for a pipeline project—or with special assessments for specific projects. The interest rate for GO bonds depends on the economic and fiscal health of the issuing government; for revenue bonds, rates reflect the expected profitability of the project. At the state level, GO bonds require a simple majority vote; local GO bonds generally require approval from a supermajority in that jurisdiction, but some vote requirements vary by the type of bond being issued.

GO bonds can be separated into two types: self-liquidating and nonself-liquidating. Self-liquidating bonds are backed by project-generated revenue streams (such as mortgages for veterans' housing) and are generally not included when calculating debt-service ratios. Nonself-liquidating bonds are paid back with general fund revenues (Table 4.1). We have included the Economic Recovery Bond, which was passed in March 2004 and allows the government to borrow up to $15 billion, in the category of nonself-liquidating debt. Even though it will be repaid with dedicated sales tax revenues, the services these revenues would have otherwise provided must now be funded with other revenues.[2] In

---

[2]This categorization of the Economic Recovery Bond is open for interpretation. For instance the State Treasurer's Office classifies the bond as self-liquidating, since it is not repaid from the general fund.

Table 4.1

State Bond Types, Typical Uses, and Outstanding Amounts ($ billions)

Uses	State Pays Debt Service?	Voter Approval Required?	Amount Outstanding 12/97	Amount Outstanding 7/04
General obligation (nonself-liquidating)				
Education facilities, seismic retrofit, parks, water projects, Economic Recovery Bond	Y	Y	14.9	43.9
General obligation (self-liquidating)				
Veterans' housing, 1959 California water debt	N	Y	3.8	2.2
Revenue bonds				
State Water Project additions, college dorms, nonpublic projects	N	N	22.2	10.9
Lease-payback revenue bonds				
Prisons, college facilities, state office buildings	Y	N	6.4	7.3

SOURCE: Legislative Analyst's Office (1998a) and California State Treasurer (2004a).

addition, the Economic Recovery Bond will be included in estimating California's future debt load, and the state is responsible for repayment from the general fund if the dedicated sales tax revenues are not adequate.

Revenue bonds are paid for with specific funds and are not backed by the full faith and credit of the state; thus they do not require voter approval. Lease-payback revenue bonds, however, are a subset of revenue bonds that mirror a lease-financing agreement. The debt is used to construct a government-owned facility, and the debt repayment is seen as equivalent to what the government would have needed to pay in rental costs for the space if they had leased it from the private sector. The bond costs are paid for by general fund revenue. These bonds do not require voter approval because the courts have ruled that the lease revenue mechanism does not create constitutional debt but is equivalent to a rental obligation. However, the payments are included by rating agencies in the calculation of California's debt ratio.

State general obligation debt is mainly repaid with general fund revenues from existing tax sources. Because this repayment is not explicitly linked to higher taxes, voters are not always aware that new projects will lead to either new taxes or spending cuts in other parts of the budget. As the state becomes more reliant on debt financing, maintaining future spending on operations may be threatened because of the need to pay off the existing debt burden.

Local Infrastructure Financing

Local governments also finance infrastructure through bonds and dedicated revenue streams. However, when local governments issue general obligation bonds they are usually repaid with voter-approved property tax increases. Local revenue bonds—used extensively for water and sewer projects—are repaid with revenues from services, local sales and parcel taxes, developer and user fees, and benefit assessments. This myriad of revenue sources is also used to provide some spending directly on infrastructure projects, most notably local sales tax revenues for transportation projects. Local governments also receive state and federal money for projects in a variety of sectors.

Over the last generation, statewide ballot initiatives have limited local governments' ability to raise tax revenue.[3] Passed in 1978, Proposition 13 capped the property tax rate at 1 percent, limited changes in property value assessments to when property is sold, and required a two-thirds majority for the passage of special taxes. In 1986 voters approved a statutory measure that required voter approval (a simple majority) for passing other general taxes. Some counties have also passed sales taxes for transportation projects. Initially, these sales taxes required approval by a majority of voters and were considered general taxes, but the courts have decided that such taxes are special taxes and therefore now require a two-thirds supermajority for passage or renewal.

User fees and special assessments are also used to provide infrastructure for local governments. These fees may vary with consumption (as with fees for electricity or water) or may be assessed as a

---

[3]For more information on these statewide limitations on local revenues see Rueben and Cerdán (2003).

flat monthly charge. User fees do not require voter approval if they do not exceed the "reasonable cost of providing service." User fees that exceed a reasonable cost require the same level of voter approval as a special assessment, which local governments can levy for such public-benefit-related services as flood control and streetlights. Following the passage of Proposition 218 in 1996, special assessments require a two-thirds majority of voters or a simple majority of property owners for passage. There are ongoing debates and court battles over the differences between user fees, special assessments, special taxes, and general taxes, as well as what is a "reasonable" cost for a service, but it is clear that local governments increasingly face the need for public approval to carry out new or ongoing projects.

The one area in which raising new funds has become easier for local governments in recent years is K–14 education. In November 2000, voters approved Proposition 39, which decreased the supermajority requirement for local school bond measures from two-thirds to 55 percent.[4] Although there is talk of statewide initiatives to lower the passage rate for other types of local GO bond measures, none has been approved so far.

Finally, local governments have also relied on development fees for infrastructure financing. The local government can negotiate these fees while approving new developments, which are asked to bear the burden for new services. However, this approach is more difficult to use if local governments wish to build new infrastructure in existing areas.

Spending Patterns in California

Infrastructure spending in California has varied over time as the result of changes in public attitudes, revenue availability, and population demands.[5] The Pat Brown era (1959–1967) is often seen as a boom

---

[4]This lower majority requirement comes with additional restrictions on the bond funds including an enumeration of projects that will be funded and the presence of a voter oversight committee. In addition, the lower requirement is available only if the bond is proposed during an election where a federal, state, county, or city election is also occurring.

[5]To examine infrastructure spending over time, we use U.S. Census Bureau, Governments Division data available from 1957–2002 in five-year increments. Because of changes in state Controller reporting methodology in 2002, there is missing information in the census numbers on capital expenditures for nontransportation special

period of infrastructure building and was characterized by increased federal spending, bipartisan support for infrastructure, and increased tax revenues. Since that time, the political support for infrastructure provision has changed. Beginning in the late 1960s, per capita state and local capital outlays declined in California, reaching a low point following the passage of Proposition 13 in 1978. Although this decline was more dramatic in California, it was similar to capital outlay expenditure patterns found in the United States as a whole (Figure 4.1).[6]

The drop in infrastructure spending predated Proposition 13 and reflected temporary declines in both federal capital funds and school capital spending because of a decline in size of the school-age population.

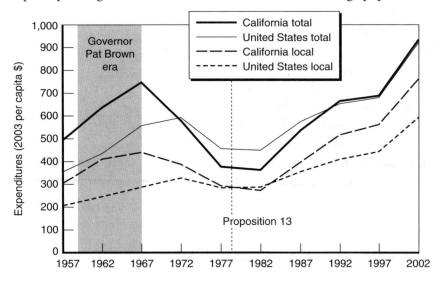

SOURCES: *U.S. Census Bureau* (1957–2002a); California State Controller (2001–2002).

Figure 4.1—Per Capita State and Local Capital Outlay Expenditures, 1957–2002

districts. We have therefore augmented the census numbers with information from the Controller's office about changes in net assets for special districts (California State Controller, 2004). For more information, see the data appendix in de Alth and Rueben (2005).

[6]Unless otherwise noted, all dollar amounts are given in 2003 dollars.

Per capita capital expenditures began increasing again in 1982, with dramatic increases in the last few years. In 2002, California spent $931 per person on capital, compared to $917 in the country as a whole. This is over one-third more than the amount spent in 1997 and one-quarter more on a real per capita basis than was spent in 1967—the former high point in California infrastructure spending. California has also always spent more of its capital funds locally than the rest of the country. In 2002, local governments carried out 83 percent of capital expenditures in California, compared to 65 percent in the country as a whole. There has been a shift in where this money is coming from, with California's state government funding an increasing share of local projects.

Although California's overall per capita spending levels now approximate those in the rest of the country, how the state spends that money has diverged from the national pattern (Figure 4.2). In 1997, California spent significantly more than the United States as a whole on resources and community development ($95 per capita versus $56) and

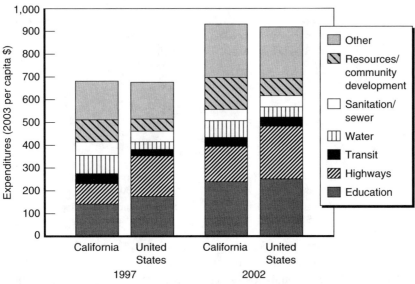

SOURCES: U.S. Census Bureau (1997, 2002a); California State Controller (2001–2002).

Figure 4.2—California Versus United States State and Local Capital Outlay, 1997 and 2002

water ($79 versus $34)[7] and less on highways and roads ($92 versus $176) and educational facilities ($140 versus $175). By 2002, California was still spending less on highways and roads ($156 versus $233) and more on water and resources (including levee, irrigation, and drainage special districts). However, California had almost caught up with the nation as a whole for spending on educational facilities ($239 versus $250).

The spending priorities reflected in California's state budget have also changed over time. In 1965–1966, transportation infrastructure took the largest share of the state's capital expenditures, and spending on resources (mainly water) was the next largest slice. K–12 capital constituted only 9 percent of state spending but now makes up 69 percent of capital outlay (Figure 4.3), a result of the shifts in state and local responsibilities occurring after Proposition 13.

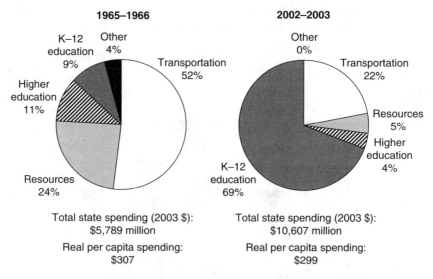

1965–1966

K–12 education 9%
Other 4%
Higher education 11%
Transportation 52%
Resources 24%

Total state spending (2003 $): $5,789 million
Real per capita spending: $307

2002–2003

Other 0%
Transportation 22%
Resources 5%
Higher education 4%
K–12 education 69%

Total state spending (2003 $): $10,607 million
Real per capita spending: $299

SOURCES: California Department of Finance (1967–1968, 2004–2005).

Figure 4.3—State Capital Outlay Expenditures, 1965–1966 and 2002–2003

---

[7]Although California has historically spent more on water projects than the nation as a whole, its water project spending is on par with that of other arid Western states.

Likewise, the state's capital funding sources have shifted significantly since the early 1960s. Most notably, the state has moved away from pay-as-you-go financing, with a corresponding increase in reliance on bonds (Table 4.2). The amount of direct payments from the general fund for infrastructure payments has plummeted from the level found in the early 1960s, with general fund revenues now mainly being used to pay back debt.[8] Special funds are usually limited to specific programs, with the State Highway Account being the largest. Federal funds make up a significant portion of the state's pay-as-you-go infrastructure funds ($1.5 billion in 2002–2003, about 45 percent of capital outlay revenue excluding K–12 local assistance) and provide money to local governments to pay for highways, mass transit, flood control, and veterans' homes.[9]

Since 1972 California voters have approved $82.6 billion (nominal $) in GO bonds for various purposes (Figure 4.4). About 45 percent of

Table 4.2

State Revenue Sources for Infrastructure Financing

	1960–61	1965–66	2002–03
General fund	13.5%	1.8%	0.9%
Special funds	44.2%	27.9%	7.5%
Bond funds	15.8%	42.2%	77.5%
Federal funds	26.6%	28.0%	14.1%
Total real amount (2003 $ millions)	4,104	5,789	10,607
Amount per capita ($)	259	307	299

SOURCES: California Department of Finance (1962–63, 1967–68, and 2004–05).

NOTES: Includes K–12 local assistance for facilities. Percentages may not sum to 100 because of rounding.

---

[8]It is important to note that the shift in how California funds infrastructure makes comparisons in how much general fund revenues are spent on infrastructure projects somewhat misleading. In the ad campaigns favoring Proposition 53 (on the October 2003 ballot), proponents highlighted this decline in general fund spending without recognizing the larger role of special funds and shift to bonds to pay for new investment.

[9]California Budget Project (1999); Legislative Analyst's Office (2004a); California Department of Finance (2004–05).

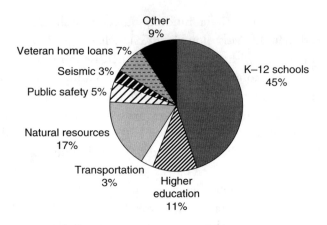

Other 9%

Veteran home loans 7%

Seismic 3%

Public safety 5%

Natural resources 17%

Transportation 3%

Higher education 11%

K–12 schools 45%

SOURCE: California Department of Finance (2004–05) updated by authors.
NOTE: The figure does not include the Economic Recovery Bond.

Figure 4.4—Distribution of State General Obligation Bonds for Infrastructure, 1972–2004

this amount has been used to finance K–12 school construction. The next largest categories are natural resources ($15 billion) and higher education ($10 billion).

The increase in reliance on bond funding has implications for the state's debt-service ratio—the portion of annual general fund revenues that are devoted to principal and interest payments on debt. This ratio was at 3 percent in 2002–2003, lower than usual because of the recent refinancing of outstanding debt in response to the state budget shortfalls. In March 2004, Californians passed an additional $27.3 billion of general obligation bonds; half of this will finance school infrastructure and the other half will help solve the state's current budget crisis. In November 2004, voters approved an additional $3 billion initiative to fund stem cell research and $750 million for children's hospitals. The result will be increasing debt-service ratios, rising above 7 percent in 2007–2008 and remaining at that level until after 2010 (Figure 4.5). A reasonable debt service ratio is 6 percent or less (Legislative Analyst's Office, 2004a). This suggests that California's capacity for new bonds is limited in the near term, since more money must be earmarked to repay debt in the next few years.

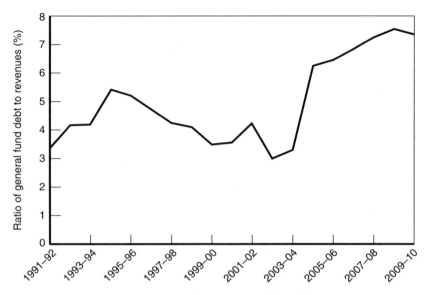

SOURCE: Legislative Analyst's Office (2004b).
NOTE: Includes general obligation bonds passed in 2004, including payments on
the Economic Recovery Bond.

Figure 4.5—California's Debt-Service Ratio, 1991–1992 to 2009–2010

K–12 Education

To flesh out our picture of infrastructure spending, we turn now to
specific sectors, beginning with K–12 education. Per student outlays on
school facilities have been anything but steady over the last 30 years.
Even before the passage of Proposition 13, school capital financing was
falling (Figure 4.6). Per pupil capital spending began to increase in the
mid-1990s, well before the lower supermajority requirement for local
school bond measures was passed. Between 1999 and 2002, local
governments increased per pupil capital spending by over $140. This
additional level of spending reflects the growing support for schools
generally and school facilities specifically.

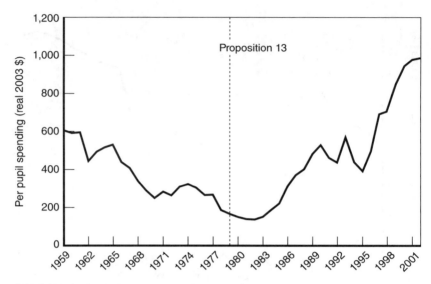

SOURCE: California Department of Education (various years).

Figure 4.6—California per Pupil School Infrastructure Spending, 1959–2002

By 1986, K–12 capital finance relied more or less equally on state bond money, local bonds, and developer and other local fees.[10] This pattern continued into the 1990s, with local districts paying for just over two-thirds of capital outlay costs for K–12 education through a combination of local general obligation bonds (32%), developer fees (11%), and other sources (27%), and with state GO bonds covering the remaining third (Brunner and Rueben, 2001).

During the recent past, voters have been willing to pass large state GO bonds to fund K–12 education (Table 4.3).[11] Before recent reforms, however, this funding system suffered from some serious weaknesses, with school districts uncertain when funding would be

---

[10]Following the passage of Proposition 13 in 1978, it was unclear how school districts would locally finance new facilities. Several reforms occurring in the mid-1980s reestablished local funding sources. For more information see Brunner and Rueben (2001).

[11]Some state bond measures combined financing for K–12 and higher education. In this section, however, we list the funds solely for K–12 districts. We will discuss higher education financing in the next section.

Table 4.3

State K–12 Education General Obligation Bonds, 1974–2004
($ millions)

Years	No. Proposed	No. Passed	Amount Proposed	Amount Passed	Real Amount Proposed (2003 $)	Real Amount Passed (2003 $)
1974–80	3	1	700	150	1,601	419
1981–85	2	2	950	950	1,423	1,423
1986–90	5	5	4,000	4,000	5,253	5,253
1991–95	3	2	3,800	2,800	4,524	3,400
1996–00	2	2	8,725	8,725	9,176	9,176
2001–04	2	2	21,400	21,400	21,573	21,573
Total	17	14	39,575	38,025	43,550	41,244

available and how much to expect. Although the State Allocation Board's decisionmaking process has changed frequently, it historically allocated bond money on a first-come, first-served basis bond by bond. Moreover, it required matching funds from localities.[12] Until 2000, school districts needed to reapply each time a bond was passed. This money was usually depleted entirely before new bonds were authorized, creating a "hill and valley" revenue stream, which impaired districts' capacity to plan and raise local supplemental funds.

Moreover, the finance system led to considerable inequities, with many California children schooled in inadequate facilities. In 2001, one in three children attended schools that were overcrowded or in need of modernization, with estimated costs to correct these problems at $30 billion (Legislative Analyst's Office, 2001). Following litigation surrounding the distribution of Proposition 1A funds (passed in 1998), the state revamped its formula for distributing bond funds, specifically allocating a portion of new bonds for school districts with critically overcrowded schools and maintaining a list of projects to be funded from

---

[12]Hardship funds were allowed for school districts that could show an inability to raise local funds. For more information on the details surrounding specific limits on school facility finances see Brunner and Rueben (2001).

one bond pool to the next. The new formula also limited the state match to a certain amount per pupil for each type of district.

After these changes were put into place, voters passed Proposition 47 in 2002 and Proposition 55 in 2004, which authorized $21.4 billion in new state bond funds for K–12 facilities. These bonds included money to fund existing approved projects off the Proposition 1A waitlist ($4.8 billion), projects in critically overcrowded schools ($4.1 billion), modernization projects in existing schools ($3.7 billion), and new construction to accommodate projected growth in enrollments ($8.8 billion). Although there is a per pupil cap on state contributions, most money is still distributed on a matching basis, so school districts with higher property values are able to raise more local funds, thereby possibly becoming eligible for more state money.[13] However, hardship provisions assist districts that are unable to raise their local match.

Concerns about the ability to raise local revenues have been lessened in the last few years. Since the passage of Proposition 39, which lowered the vote requirement for the passage of school bonds in local elections from two-thirds to 55 percent, school districts passed more than 250 bond measures for more than $20 billion. Slightly less than half of these measures would not have passed without the lower supermajority requirement (Table 4.4).

Table 4.4

Local K–12 School Facility Bonds Since Proposition 39
($ billions)

	Number	Amount
Passed	256	20.3
Not passed	50	1.7
Proposed	306	22.1
Passed with less than 2/3	119	9.9

NOTE: Includes the November 2004 election.

---

[13]There is a limit on the level to which school districts can raise property tax rates, so districts with lower property values may be constrained in how much state funding they will be able to receive.

In the aftermath of Proposition 39, the state may wish to examine its role in financing school facilities. The Legislative Analyst's Office has suggested allocating education capital funds on an ongoing per pupil basis and moving away from a reliance on bond revenues, which would address equity concerns and provide a predictable facility revenue stream (Legislative Analyst's Office, 2001). Alternatively, state revenues could be allocated based on a local match that takes into account the fact that the same tax rate raises different amounts of revenues across different districts (because of differences in assessed property values across districts). The state could equalize this system by using state money to top off the revenues raised by a given local property tax increase to equalize levels across the state. This would give lower-wealth districts a higher state match rate for new construction programs.

Although the increased level of state and local bond funding seems promising for schools, we are allocating much of the next decade's school infrastructure funds today. In particular, if there are future unexpected demographic shifts, some growing districts may find that they are unable to provide adequate facilities once the current funds have been spent. The increased surge in funds has also had at least one unintended consequence: The costs of building schools have increased dramatically, with the demand for construction exceeding the supply of school construction firms. Therefore, higher costs may produce fewer classrooms than originally anticipated. This pattern might have been avoided if money had been allocated on a more regular basis.

Higher Education

A mix of federal, state, and local district sources finances the University of California (UC), California State University (CSU), and California Community College (CCC) capital outlays. In 1999–2000, capital spending represented only 8 percent of total higher education spending. State funds for capital and operating expenditures totaled about $11 billion in 1999–2000 and came from education bonds, earmarked special funds, and the state general fund. Student fees and private funds now augment state funds, adding $1 billion for capital and $8 billion in operating expenditures in 1999–2000. As with overall capital spending, capital outlays for higher education declined rapidly during the 1970s, especially after the passage of Proposition 13, but increased during the late 1980s and 1990s. Census of Governments data for higher education capital outlay show a real per student spending peak of $1,652 in 1967 and a trough of $592 in 1982. By 2002, California was spending $767 per full-time student.

Before Proposition 13, local community college districts funded their own building programs through local bonds and property taxes with some matching funds from the state. Roughly 10 to 15 percent of UC and CSU capital funding came from federal sources through the 1963 Higher Education Facilities Act. Tideland oil revenues from state-owned land also financed UC, CSU, and CCC capital outlay. These revenues were deposited in the Capital Outlay Fund for Public Higher Education (COFPHE) and totaled $964 million (in nominal dollars) between 1965 and 1986—about 19 percent of all higher education capital outlay spending in that period (California Postsecondary Education Commission, 2003a).

Following the passage of Proposition 13, community colleges lost the ability to propose new local bond measures, and federal funds for UC and CSU dried up in the 1980s. Also in 1985, oil prices dropped dramatically, decreasing revenue available from the Tideland Oil Fund. The state then shifted to using bond measures to fund higher education infrastructure projects. In 1986, the legislature proposed and voters passed Proposition 56, a bond measure for higher education raising $400 million. This was the first time state bond funds were used to fund facilities for UC or CSU. State bond measures are now used regularly to fund higher education capital outlay (Table 4.5). Until 1996, measures for higher education and K–12 capital outlay were proposed separately, but because of stronger voter support for K–12 bonds, propositions are now joint K–university bond acts.

Before 2000, higher education bond funds had been split into thirds for UC, CSU, and CCC. Proposition 47 (2002) and Proposition 55 (2004), which made nearly $4 billion available for higher education projects, increased the community college share to 40 percent, with UC and CSU receiving 30 percent each.

UC has been fairly successful in securing private money for capital building, raising $4.6 billion through private and other nonstate funds

Table 4.5

State Higher Education General Obligation Bonds, 1972–2004 ($ millions)

Date	Proposition No.	Amount Proposed	Real Amount Proposed (2003 $)	Proposition Passed?
November 1972[a]	1	160	572	Y
June 1976[a]	4	150	359	N
November 1986	56	400	568	Y
November 1988	78	600	794	Y
June 1990	121	450	562	Y
November 1990	143	450	562	N
June 1992	153	900	1,093	Y
June 1994	1C	900	1,012	N
March 1996[b]	203	975	1,043	Y
November 1998[b]	1A	2,500	2,616	Y
November 2002[b]	47	1,650	1,675	Y
March 2004[b]	55	2,300	2,300	Y
Total		11,435	13,156	11,223

[a]These bond measures are for community colleges only.

[b]These bond measures also include K–12 money.

Table 4.6

State Capital Outlay Revenue for Higher Education, 1996–1997 Through 2000–2001 ($ millions)

	State General and COFPHE Funds	GO Bonds	Revenue Bonds and Special Funds	Other Nonstate Funds	Total
UC	10.0	981.9	195.9	4,621.8	5,809.6
CSU	35.6	945.9	11.7	258.3	1,251.4
CCC		1,004.5	1.5	(a)	1,006.0
Total	45.6	2,932.4	209.0	4,880.1	8,067.0

SOURCE: California Postsecondary Education Commission (2003a).

NOTE: Community college numbers do not include local district revenues, which are discussed below.

from 1996–1997 through 2000–2001 (Table 4.6). Additionally UC can finance new research facilities through bonds backed by future research revenue, a recently recommended step (Legislative Analyst's Office, 2004c). The CSU system has been less successful in private fund raising, raising only $258 million from nonstate funds over this same period.

Although community colleges have not raised substantial amounts of private money, the passage of Proposition 39 has helped them raise over $9 billion in local district bonds since 2001 (Table 4.7). Nearly three-quarters of these measures would not have passed if the two-thirds supermajority had been required.

Table 4.7

Local Community College Facility Bonds Since
Proposition 39 ($ billions)

	Number	Amount
Passed	46	9.1
Not passed	5	1.0
Proposed	51	10.0
Passed with less than 2/3	33	6.6

NOTE: Includes the November 2004 election.

Water Supply and Quality

California water resources are used for agricultural, residential, industrial, environmental, recreational, and other purposes. To accommodate these various uses, California has a vast infrastructure system for water supply, conveyance, and quality control. In 1999–2000, capital spending for water supply and water quality totaled $4.7 billion, and operating expenses totaled $9.6 billion. About one-third of this spending is used for sewer systems and wastewater treatment centers.

City water agencies and nearly 1,300 local water districts and other entities spend most of this money either to provide water directly or to meet water standards for municipal wastewater discharge. User fees are the largest source of both city and special district funds. In 1997–1998, cities brought in $4.1 billion in water and sewer service charges, or 80 percent of city water and sewer functional revenues (California State

Controller, 1997–98). Water special districts brought in $4.3 billion in fees, nearly 60 percent of water district total revenues in this year (Legislative Analyst's Office, 2002a). As Ellen Hanak and Elisa Barbour show in Chapter 5, average yearly water fees in 2003 were $363, and only 3 percent of communities faced fees greater than 1.5 percent of median household income.

Although local water utilities are primarily responsible for delivering water to end users, several state and federal projects established significant conveyance and storage infrastructure during the mid-20th century to supply these local utilities. These include the federal Central Valley Project (CVP), the State Water Project (SWP), and the federal Colorado River Project. These projects have authority to levy fees and charges for capital costs. The U.S. Bureau of Reclamation (USBR) constructed the CVP beginning in 1937 and still controls the facilities. The project was financed through federal appropriations and repayments from water users, including agriculture, municipal and industrial users, and power customers. Total construction costs totaled $3.3 billion in nominal dollars as of 1999 (Dowall and Whittington, 2003). The Colorado River Project, also administered by USBR, allocates water from the Colorado River among the Western states, with California historically receiving a significant share.

The California Department of Water Resources (DWR) runs the SWP, which furnishes a substantial portion of the water supplies for urban Southern California as well as agricultural users in the southern San Joaquin Valley. Construction on these conveyance and storage facilities began in the 1960s, when voters approved a $1.75 billion general obligation bond ($8.2 billion in 2003 dollars) to finance initial construction. Water supply contractors became responsible for repayment of this GO bond and passed on these costs to users in the form of fees. Subsequently, revenue bonds have been used to finance additional SWP facilities in Southern California and along the Central Coast and are also paid off with user fees.

California voters have been asked to approve 15 statewide water-related GO bonds over the last 30 years, and have done so for all but one of these, for a total of $9.9 billion (Table 4.8). The vast majority of

Table 4.8

State Water General Obligation Bonds, 1972–2004
($ millions)

Date	Proposition No.	Purpose	Amount Proposed	Real Amount Proposed (2003 $)	Proposition Passed?
June 1974	2	Clean water	250	698	Y
June 1976	3	Drinking water	175	419	Y
June 1978	2	Clean water and conservation	375	753	Y
November 1984	25	Clean water	325	473	Y
November 1984	28	Drinking water	75	109	Y
June 1986	44	Water quality and conservation	150	213	Y
November 1986	55	Drinking water	100	142	Y
November 1988	81	Drinking water	75	99	Y
November 1988	82	Conservation	60	79	Y
November 1988	83	Clean water and reclamation	65	86	Y
November 1990	148	Water supply	380	475	N
November 1996	204	Water supply	995	1,064	Y
March 2000	13	Drinking water, clean water, watershed, and flood control	1,970	2,008	Y
March 2002	40	Clean water	300	305	Y
November 2002	50	Water supply, clean water, drinking water, and wetlands	3,440	3,492	Y
Total			8,735	10,415	9,941

these bonds have focused on water-quality-related issues, for both urban supply ("drinking water") and wastewater (usually called "clean water") programs. The most recent bonds have also focused on ecosystem restoration and grants to local water districts to increase water use efficiency and augment local supplies.

A large portion of the most recent bonds—$1.5 billion—has been allocated to the CALFED program, a multiagency state and federal effort to restore the Bay-Delta fisheries, ensure water and environmental quality, and secure the water supply. Representatives include urban, environmental, agricultural, and other interests. CALFED does not directly control or manage water supply but attempts to coordinate activities of various water actors in the state, including the CVP, SWP, and local agencies. CALFED's long-term financial plan follows a "beneficiary pays" principle, with project benefits and costs as closely correlated as possible to avoid or minimize subsidies. However, to date, the state bond funds have been the primary revenue source, with relatively little money forthcoming from either federal sources or local users. CALFED partners have recently completed a 10-year finance plan that allocates costs among federal, state, and local authorities. In October 2004, federal legislation authorized $395 million from 2005 to 2010 to support the federal share of CALFED expenditures.

The recent state bonds also provide substantial resources to help local agencies improve water quality, a shift from the policy in the 1990s, during which relatively limited state funding was available. In the first decade following the passage of the federal Clean Water Act of 1972, federal grants provided about 75 percent of the capital costs for upgrading wastewater systems to meet the new water quality standards. This program was then substantially downsized and converted into a Clean Water State Revolving Fund, with 20 percent state matching funds, to provide low-interest loans to wastewater utilities. In 1996, the Safe Drinking Water State Revolving Fund was established to assist water utilities. California spent $134.6 million in federal funds for water quality in 1999–2000. Currently Congress is considering bills that would provide additional federal money for local water treatment plant infrastructure, motivated by September 11 security issues and concerns raised by local governments and environmental groups regarding the growing costs of clean water programs.

The State Water Resources Control Board (SWRCB) administers clean water programs, covering wastewater and storm water runoff. The recent passage of Propositions 13, 40, and 50 have greatly increased the state's ability to provide local assistance for clean water projects. In 2003–2004, estimated expenditures from these bond funds total $559 million, or three-quarters of the estimated $750 million in local assistance from the SWRCB.

The Department of Health Service's (DHS) Office of Drinking Water administers the state's safe drinking water programs. Here, too, bond funds are dramatically increasing spending. In 1999–2000— before the bonds—it lent $21.3 million to local entities for drinking water projects (half of which was from federal sources) and made a small number of capital grants. The DHS drinking water budget appropriation in 2003–2004 includes $115 million in local assistance from the recently passed Proposition 50, representing one-third of that year's DHS local assistance budget.

Whereas user fees are a straightforward local funding source for water and wastewater systems, there are questions about the funding of a relatively new area of water quality regulation—storm water. It is uncertain whether increases in local charges to pay for storm water management require two-thirds voter or property-owner approval for the increase or implementation of property-related fees or assessments. If so, without federal or state subsidies, local governments will be responsible for meeting standards but may face difficulties raising revenue.

Another question involves funding for the restoration of fish and wildlife habitats. Recent state bonds and efforts such as the CALFED Environmental Water Account, which buys and stores water to mitigate competing environmental and water user needs, show the public's and state's willingness to fund water for the environment. To meet the continued funding requirements of the CALFED program and new ecological challenges, however, funding mechanisms will have to keep pace.

Transportation

How people and goods travel through California will help determine the state's quality of life and continued prosperity. Transportation infrastructure financing has undergone dramatic shifts since the large-scale freeway projects of the 1950s and 1960s. Although the overall level of spending on highways and roads is now comparable to that of the earlier period, less of this money is now spent on construction and more is spent on operations. In 1967 and 2002, the combined capital and operating expenses for highways and roads totaled $315 and $332 per capita, respectively. In 1967, $231 went to capital, versus only $156 more recently. Mass transit has, meanwhile, emerged as a key sector. In 1972, California spent $20 per capita on transit construction; in 2002, it spent twice that.

In 1999–2000, capital outlay spending on highways and roads was evenly divided between state and local projects, with each spending slightly less than $1.9 billion. Much of the local spending is allocated by cities and counties but is coordinated through regional transportation planning agencies, which receive revenue from the federal and state governments.

For transit, state and local capital outlay spending in 1999–2000 was $2.6 billion—about 65 percent of the amount devoted to operating expenditures. Virtually all of the transit capital money is spent locally, although much of it comes from federal and state sources. Capital spending on mass transit was unusually high that year largely because of federal grants and local funds for the Bay Area Rapid Transit (BART) and the Los Angeles County Metro Transportation Authority to complete extension projects. In 2001–2002, total transit capital expenditures fell to $1.5 billion, a more representative level of recent transit infrastructure financing.

Traditional sources of revenue for transportation have been user fees such as federal and state fuel taxes, sales taxes on fuel, vehicle registration fees, motor vehicle weight fees, drivers' license fees, and tolls. These revenues are deposited into special funds administered by the state and earmarked for transportation, including the Federal Highway Trust Fund, State Highway Account, and the Public Transportation Account. About one-third of the state gas and diesel tax is distributed to local governments for streets and roads; the remainder is deposited into the State Highway Account. California's federal gas and diesel tax contributions are deposited into the Federal Highway Trust Fund and redistributed. Additionally, 4.75 percentage points of the 6 percent state sales tax on diesel fuel has historically been allocated to the Public Transportation Account for transit operating expenses and improvements (Legislative Analyst's Office, 2002b). Table 4.9 shows the most recent revenue sources for state capital outlay transportation spending. Note that this does not include state or federal money passed

Table 4.9

State Transportation Revenue for Capital Outlay, 2002–2003
($ millions)

	Revenue	%
Highway		
Bond funds	32.3	1.4
Seismic Retrofit Bond Act of 1996	32.3	
Special funds	725.8	32.0
State Highway Account	486.3	
Toll Bridge Seismic Retrofit Account	190.9	
Traffic Congestion Relief Fund	48.6	
Federal Trust Fund	1,480.7	65.2
Transit		
Special funds	31.7	1.4
State Highway Account	23.7	
Public Transportation Account	0.3	
Traffic Congestion Relief Fund	7.7	
Total	2,270.5	100.0

SOURCE: California Department of Finance (2004–05).

through to local governments for capital, including most transit capital funding.

State and federal gasoline and diesel taxes are still important—funding about half of transportation spending and raising more than $3 billion each in California annually. However, fuel tax increases have been sporadic and politically difficult to pass, making it hard to maintain revenues in real terms (Table 4.10). Additionally, this revenue source has become less reliable over time. Even with dramatic increases in vehicle travel, fuel consumption (and therefore real tax revenue) has declined because of increasing vehicle fuel efficiency.

The federal highway program used to be the largest source of federal aid to the states, and the federal share of state and local capital spending on highways reached 46 percent in 1960. But since the mid-1960s, federal money has shifted away from highway development and toward transit, local roads, and operations and maintenance. Federal authority has also devolved to regional transportation agencies and local control.

Table 4.10

State and Federal Gas Tax Rates (cents per gallon)

Year	California	Federal	Total	Total Real Rate (2003 $)
1950	4.5	1.5	6	45.8
1951		2	6.5	46.0
1953	6		8	55.1
1956		3	9	60.9
1959		4	10	63.2
1963	7		11	66.1
1983	9	9	18	33.3
1987		9.1	18.1	29.3
1990	14	14.1	28.1	39.6
1991	15		29.1	39.3
1992	16		30.1	39.5
1993	17	18.4	35.4	45.1
1994	18		36.4	45.2
2003	18	18.4	36.4	36.4

SOURCE: California Department of Transportation (n.d.).

The current mix of transportation financing still represents a primarily pay-as-you-go system. But as gasoline tax revenue and federal funds have eroded, the state has turned to ballot initiatives to fund transportation capital projects (Table 4.11). In 1990 and 1996, voters approved GO bonds for rail transit ($3 billion) and seismic upgrades of bridges and highways ($2 billion). Californians also approved Proposition 42 in 2002, which earmarked 80 percent of the 6 percent state sales tax on gas to be spent on transportation projects, including highway improvement and repairs, mass transit, and local road and street repairs. (That revenue had previously been allocated to the general fund.) Proposition 42 is estimated to raise about $1.2 billion per year in revenues for transportation. However, the funds can be allocated back to the general fund by a two-thirds majority vote of the legislature, and this occurred at least partially in each of the subsequent budget years to help address the state's budget crisis.

Table 4.11

State Ballot Measures for Transportation Capital Outlay Funds, 1990–2004 ($ millions)

Date	Proposition No.	Amount Proposed	Real Amount Proposed (2003 $)	Proposition Passed?	Purpose
June 1990	108	1,000	1,250	Y	Rail transit
June 1990	116a	1,990	2,487	Y	Rail transit
June 1990	122	300	375	Y	Seismic
November 1992	156	1,000	1,214	N	Rail transit
June 1994	1A	2,000	2,249	N	Seismic
November 1994	181	1,000	1,124	N	Rail transit
March 1996	192	2,000	2,139	Y	Seismic
November 2002	42b	6% sales tax		Y	Infrastructure

a$29.9 million of Proposition 116 was allocated to the Alameda Corridor project, which facilitated shipping container rail transportation.

bProposition 42 allocated most of the existing 6 percent sales tax on gasoline for transportation projects.

Although voters have passed bond measures and initiatives to earmark funds for transportation, it is unclear in practice how this will translate into transportation capital funding in the near term. Future Proposition 42 funds are not guaranteed, repayment of loans from the general fund are uncertain, seismic retrofit costs have turned out to be higher than expected, federal fund levels are unknown, and a conversion to ethanol fuel will lower federal apportionments unless legislative action is taken.

The decline in state gas tax revenues and federal funds has prompted some local governments to seek new funding sources through the primary option at their disposal—a state-sanctioned optional sales tax.[14] Historically, local governments funded street and road construction predominantly through local general fund revenues (largely from property taxes) and their share of the gasoline tax pass-through from the state. In 1971, state voters also passed a quarter-cent general sales tax on

------

[14]Counties that have passed additional sales taxes for transportation usually pass a half-cent rate for roads, and in the counties served by BART and in Los Angeles, another half-cent tax has been passed for mass transit projects.

all sales to fund local transit, which is deposited into each county's Local Transportation Fund; this tax raised about $1 billion for transit operating and capital funds in 1999–2000 (Table 4.12). Since 1978, 20 counties approved local supplemental sales taxes of between 1/4 and 1 percent dedicated for highway, street, road, and transit projects.

The optional county sales taxes are now the largest local revenue source for transportation, constituting one-third of local revenues; in 2003, they nearly equaled state gasoline excise tax revenues. Because much of state revenue is distributed with a match requirement, the ability to raise local sales taxes affects the distribution of state transportation funds as well.

Getting voter approval for introducing or renewing this funding source has become more difficult since 1995, when the voter threshold shifted from a simple majority to a two-thirds supermajority. Bay Area and Southern California coastal counties have been most successful in passing these supplemental sales taxes (Figure 4.7). Nineteen counties currently have county sales taxes for transportation, an additional 15 counties have tried and failed to pass a tax at least once, and San Benito County passed a sales tax in 1988 that expired in 1998. Marin and Sonoma Counties recently passed transportation sales taxes in November

Table 4.12

Local Transportation Revenue, 1999–2000
($ billions)

Source	Revenue	%
Optional local sales tax (1/4 to 1 cent sales tax)	2.6	34.7
Local Transportation Fund (1/4 cent sales tax)	1.0	13.3
Transit fares, property taxes, and local operating assistance	1.4	18.7
Other local funds	2.5	33.3
Total	7.5	

SOURCE: Legislative Analyst's Office (2000a).

NOTE: Other local funds include local general funds, bond proceeds, fines and forfeitures, and road taxes.

SOURCE: Surface Transportation Policy Project (2002) updated by authors.

Figure 4.7—California Counties That Ever Passed a Local Transportation Sales Tax

2004 after failing to pass taxes in multiple earlier elections, and it has taken other counties several attempts to pass or renew these taxes.

Recent state budget shortfalls also affect local transportation funding. Some local government transit districts are facing a loss of funds as part of the governor's negotiated deal with local governments. Under this deal, local governments forgo $1.3 billion in local property taxes in each of the next two years in exchange for support of a ballot measure to safeguard local funds in future years.

It is clear that local governments are playing a larger role in transportation funding through the local sales taxes. The primary concern raised by this is the new supermajority requirement and the ability of counties to maintain these taxes. There are also geographical equity issues because these local taxes are largely concentrated in coastal communities. Additionally, increasing reliance on sales tax revenue further divorces transport use from transportation financing. Allocating the costs of transport to users of the system encourages more efficient behavior and can reduce such negative effects as congestion. Forward-thinking strategies on transportation financing that consider the incentives on system use will be crucial to consider as California prepares for its transportation future.

Conclusion

California currently spends about as much as the rest of the country on infrastructure projects but less on transportation infrastructure and more on water and resources than other states. Our current level of spending surpasses that of the 1960s, but the priorities have shifted.

Over the last decade, support for K–12 facilities has increased dramatically. Going forward, there are still important questions to be addressed. Should school districts be more responsible for facilities financing in the aftermath of Proposition 39? Should the state become less reliant on bond financing for school facilities and shift to an annual per pupil allocation of funding? Should revenues be distributed to reflect differences in district wealth? Should state distributions be based more on future predicted growth or current enrollments? In higher education, where facilities represent a relatively small percentage of total higher education spending, questions of overall access are likely to be more pressing than infrastructure needs.

California continues to spend more than the national average of its infrastructure dollars on water supply and quality, although spending levels are in line with other Western states. Water users bear most of these costs, but rates are relatively low as a percentage of household income, and most water districts and municipalities have been able to meet their revenue needs. Going forward, the main water financing issues center around water quality and ecosystem restoration. Local governments are largely responsible for ensuring water quality, but because the costs of controlling storm-water runoff are not linked directly to benefits received by specific households, local governments could face a two-thirds vote requirement to pass new fees. Thus, local authorities may be faced with clean-up costs without a clear way of paying for them. For ecosystem improvements, the question is whether voters will continue to support state bonds, since contributions by the federal government and water users have been relatively limited.

Transportation infrastructure seems to be the main area where California has fallen behind in investment. Today, many more of our highway dollars are used for maintenance rather than new construction. Transportation revenues are also increasingly allocated to mass transit programs that may or may not be cost-effective. Furthermore, traditional sources of revenue are declining in real terms. Federal and state fuel taxes, which currently raise 36.4 cents per gallon of gasoline, have not increased since 1994, and although Californians are driving more, increased fuel efficiency and higher project costs have further eroded the real value of the fuel tax revenue.

Increasingly, highway, road, and transit infrastructure is financed with other taxes, most notably dedicated county sales taxes. Renewal of these sales taxes might now face opposition as vote requirements have changed to require a two-thirds majority for passage or renewal. General sales taxes do not tie road use to the cost of providing roads, nor do they promote the efficient use of transportation infrastructure as much as a user-based gas tax or toll does.

Transportation questions go beyond the arithmetic of funding sources. How much of transportation costs should the actual users of transportation pay? How does building new highways affect growth and congestion? Should transportation revenues go for roads or mass transit? These questions must be answered as California considers its infrastructure future.

Finally, California's increasing reliance on debt financing in recent years to help solve the state's budget crisis also limits the state's options in undertaking new projects. Our current debt load is projected to be about 7 percent for the next five years, higher than the level deemed prudent by credit rating agencies, which can limit our future ability to undertake new projects at the state level. Local governments also are faced with an increasingly restrictive environment for raising new revenues as voter approval is required for a growing list of sources. As new infrastructure projects are examined, these constraints might mean that new options for funding infrastructure will be necessary.

5. Sizing Up the Challenge: California's Infrastructure Needs and Tradeoffs

Ellen Hanak and Elisa Barbour[1]

Since the late 1990s, reports by government agencies and independent groups have sounded a common alarm: Decades of rapid population growth, unmatched by corresponding increases in public investments, are straining the capacity of California's public facilities.[2] In this view, the telltale signs of this problem—overcrowding in schools, record rates of traffic congestion, growing vulnerability to drought, and threatened ecosystems—are likely to reach crisis proportions without actions to fix the way we fund and deliver new infrastructure projects as well as maintain older ones.

These calls for reform have met with some success. In 1999, the state legislature passed AB 1473, which requires that the governor prepare an annual five-year infrastructure plan. The passage of Proposition 39 the following year lowered the voter requirement for local school bonds from two-thirds to 55 percent, paving the way for significant increases in local funds for school facilities and for community colleges. In March 2002, voters also approved Proposition 42, which dedicates revenues from the state sales tax on gasoline to transportation projects. Education bonds passed in November 2002 and March 2004 made a total of $25.35 billion available for K–12 and higher education facilities. Three environmental bonds were passed between 2000 and

---

[1]For a more detailed analysis, see the occasional paper *Sizing Up the Challenge: California's Infrastructure Needs and Tradeoffs* (Hanak and Barbour, 2005), available at www.ca2025.org.

[2]See California Business Roundtable (1998); Legislative Analyst's Office (1998b); California State Treasurer (1999); Center for the Continuing Study of the California Economy (1999); Dowall (2001); Neuman and Whittington (2000); Dowall and Whittington (2003).

2002, making available $5.7 billion for water quality and supply projects and $2.3 billion for the acquisition and improvement of open space and public parks.

Despite these successes, some core funding questions remain. The passage of new local taxes and bond finance for other key sectors, such as transportation, still require a two-thirds supermajority, and the statewide ballot initiatives do not tap new revenue sources to fund infrastructure. (Proposition 42 earmarked the use of existing revenues for transportation, and state bonds are repaid through the general fund.) The gasoline tax, a major source of roadway funding, has not been adjusted for inflation since 1994. In May 2004, water agency opposition scotched a proposal for water user fees to help restore threatened ecosystems. Among major sectors, only higher education has seen fee increases; since the onset of the budget crisis, student fees are up by over 50 percent and rising. Thus, California faces the future without a clear mandate to raise funds at the state level for infrastructure projects. Moreover, local spending (except in education) still faces high voter thresholds. It is therefore appropriate to revisit a central question posed by the numerous reports on infrastructure: Are we spending too little on our public investments to secure a sound economic future and quality of life?

The conventional method for addressing this question, sometimes referred to as "gap analysis," begins by assessing infrastructure "needs," pricing them, and then comparing the total price tag to actual spending. The discrepancy between the price tag and actual spending is then dubbed the "funding gap." Gap analysis usually assumes that unfunded needs should be met with public subsidies and tends to ignore or discount the policy tradeoffs that those subsidies entail. Perhaps the major problem with gap analysis, however, arises from the way it defines and estimates infrastructure needs. It typically follows an engineering approach, gauging needs by matching a targeted per capita level of services to population projections. As a result, it tends to overstate the level of needs in sectors where market mechanisms (especially prices) might shape the demand for those services. For example, estimates of water supply needs will be high if the analysis does not acknowledge that different pricing approaches might lead to conservation. Likewise, the perceived need for new highway lanes will be greater if the analysis declines to consider alternative transportation modes and incentives to encourage carpooling.

Such overestimations of need are often compounded by the nature of infrastructure finance. When agencies compete for public funds, they have various institutional incentives to inflate their requirements. The result is often a wish list that does not distinguish agency desires from a definition informed by the notion of consumer demand. Various techniques for distinguishing needs from desires—often grouped under the heading "demand management"—have grown in importance over the last 10 to 15 years. The appropriateness of these techniques, which rely on price mechanisms and other incentives to ration scarce resources, varies across sectors, depending on their social consequences. Political opposition can also block greater reliance on fees even when they would be appropriate. In this chapter, we will refer to these approaches, along with those that emphasize new technologies and the efficient use of existing assets, as "modern" approaches to infrastructure needs analysis. In our evaluation of needs and tradeoffs, we will also highlight the extent to which infrastructure planning has incorporated these approaches. Instead of asking only whether we are spending enough to secure a sound economic future and quality of life, we will also ask whether we are making the most of our available public resources.

We focus our analysis on the three main areas in which California spends its public investment dollars: education, water supply and quality, and transportation. Together, these sectors represent over 85 percent of proposed state-level spending in the most recent five-year infrastructure plan, and over 60 percent of all state and local capital spending in recent years. After a general description of each sector, we turn to needs assessments and funding mechanisms and, where appropriate, alternative approaches to meeting infrastructure needs. We then look at the potential for "smart growth" approaches to help California reconcile the pressures of growth and environmental protection as it channels its investment dollars.

K–12 Education

California's massive public school system encompasses more than six million students, 9,000 schools, and 1,000 school districts. Its sheer size makes the system a key infrastructure concern, but it is also unique in at least one other respect: The state constitution guarantees residents equitable access to primary and secondary schools. For this reason, demand-management techniques are inappropriate for this sector, and a modern approach to needs assessment must focus on mobilizing resources, using them efficiently, and ensuring their equitable distribution.

The primary driver of school facilities needs is growth of the school-age population. Rapid enrollment growth during the late 1980s and 1990s, during a time of limited investment, created a facilities backlog. As the baby boom echo ages its way through the K–12 system, this pressure should subside. Growth rates for the K–8 cohort are projected to be negative in the short term and to begin climbing again around 2010 (Figure 5.1). Growth rates for high school students are expected to rise until 2005–06, subside and even become negative by the end of the decade, and then begin rising again around 2015. Much of the new growth will occur in inland areas—the Inland Empire, the San Joaquin Valley, and the Sacramento metropolitan region—where existing capacity is likely to be more limited.

Taking into account the facilities backlog and new enrollment growth, planners predict that 35,000 more classrooms will be needed to accommodate nearly one million additional students by 2008 (Table 5.1). Modernization needs will also become more prevalent as aging buildings deteriorate. The Department of Education estimates that 73 percent of classrooms are more than 25 years old.

School Facilities Funding Needs and Gaps

Under the current system for funding K–12 facilities, the state provides 50 percent of new construction costs and 60 percent of modernization costs for school districts requesting assistance. State grants are standardized based on average cost factors for per pupil new

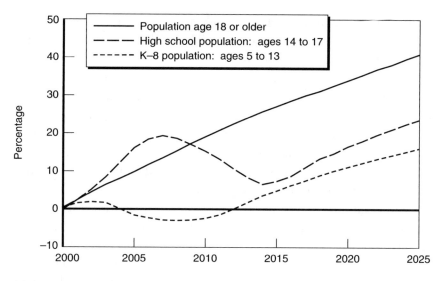

SOURCE: California Department of Finance (2004a).

Figure 5.1—Projected Population Growth in California by Age Group, 2000–2025

Table 5.1

Statewide Classroom Needs for New Construction and Modernization of K–12 Public School Facilities, 2003–2008

Grade Level	New Construction		Modernization	
	Projected Unhoused Students	Classrooms Needed	Students in Classrooms Over 25 Years Old	Classrooms to Be Modernized
K–6	373,446	14,938	500,827	20,033
7–8	160,184	5,933	223,133	8,264
9–12	388,335	14,383	352,394	13,052
Total	921,965	35,254	1,076,354	41,349

SOURCE: California Department of Education (2004).

construction and for modernization of classrooms over 25 years old (or portable classrooms over 20 years old). The local match can be waived or reduced for districts facing hardship.

School facilities funding has benefited enormously from recent statewide and local ballot initiatives. The recent state education bonds made $21.4 billion available for K–12 schools. Following the passage of Proposition 39, local voters have approved $20.3 billion in local school bonds. As Kim Rueben and Shelley de Alth show in Chapter 4, nearly half of these local measures would not have passed without a relaxation of the two-thirds majority vote requirement.

Although the recent surge in bond funding has addressed school facilities needs, a funding gap remains. The Department of Education recently estimated a need for $16.9 billion in school facilities funding over the next five years (Table 5.2). However, the most recent five-year infrastructure plan from DOF—which includes remaining state bond funds—proposed only $10.4 billion, leaving a gap of about $6 billion. Judging by the overall ratio of local to state bond funds over the past four years ($20.3 billion versus $21.4 billion, respectively), it is likely that a comparable effort will be needed at the local level as well.

Table 5.2

State Share of Funding Needs and Proposed Spending for New Construction and Modernization of K–12 Public School Facilities, 2003–04 to 2007–08 ($ billions)

	Department of Education Projected	Department of Finance Proposed
New construction	13.0	4.6
Modernization	3.9	3.4
Hardshipa		2.4
Total	16.9	10.4

SOURCES: California Department of Education (2004); California Department of Finance (2003b).

aThe California Department of Education figures include hardship allocations.

Alternative Approaches to Meeting Needs

This funding gap suggests the need to reduce costs, provide a more stable source of funding, or both. As pressure on school facilities increased during the 1990s, proposals were advanced to reduce costs and make fuller use of existing facilities. These include

- The use of lower-cost technology, especially portable classrooms;
- A shift to multitrack schooling; and
- Management or organizational reforms.

The use of portable classrooms increased considerably with the introduction of class size reduction policies in 1996. In 2000–2001, portable classrooms made up almost one-third of the state's stock of K–12 classrooms. Their advantages include low initial cost, fast installation, and portability from school to school. However, concerns have also been raised about their environmental effects (health, aesthetics, loss of playground space), and their durability and quality have led to concerns about their long-term cost effectiveness (California Air Resources Board and California Department of Health Services, 2003; EdSource, 1998).

Multitrack schooling—which staggers three or more tracks of students with different schedules throughout the calendar year—can also increase a school facility's student capacity. Since the 1980s, the state has offered incentives to promote multitrack programs in schools with space constraints, and by 2002–2003, 22 percent of K–12 students in California were enrolled in these programs (California Department of Education, 2003). The approach has met with a number of criticisms, however. For one, it may complicate or even prevent other educational reforms, such as extension of summer schooling. Additionally, some administrators argue that the multitrack schedules, which include more frequent disruptions than a regular school year, are detrimental for learning and for efforts to improve educational quality in low-performing districts (Little Hoover Commission, 2000a).

The remaining cost-savings proposals are still on the drawing board. One proposal would imply an overhaul of the current incentive structure for local districts. To discourage cost overruns, the state's current 50–50 state-local partnership system allows districts to keep any of the state funds not spent on construction. Some observers argue that a better policy would reward projects that produce long-run savings over the life cycle of buildings in terms of maintenance, operation, and renewal costs, in addition to construction costs. Another proposal argues that economies of scale could be achieved by regionalizing school facilities management. School administrators focus only sporadically on construction projects and are rarely in a position to innovate successfully or develop cost-saving expertise (Little Hoover Commission, 2000a). Similarly, some advocate consideration of joint-use facilities as a way of achieving economies of scope: Such facilities would enable a range of local agencies to provide a diverse set of services to the community (Metropolitan Forum Project, 1999).

Some analysts have called for a more complete overhaul of the finance system for school facilities. The Legislative Analyst, for example, recommends that the state provide facilities funding on an annual per pupil basis—similar to the way it funds school operating budgets—after a transition period in which districts are brought to a comparable starting point (Legislative Analyst's Office, 2001). The proposal also includes an ability-to-pay adjustment to address disparities in local school districts' capacity to raise matching funds. Capital expenditures are not currently subject to the equity requirements established for school finance equalization. However, as Manuel Pastor and Deborah Reed discuss in Chapter 7, the state has agreed to channel additional resource and attention to facilities in low-performing schools as part of a recent legal settlement.

Higher Education

California's system of public higher education is the largest in the nation, with enrollments of over 2.3 million students (California Department of Finance, 2003c). It includes the 10 UC campuses, the 23 CSU campuses, and the 109 CCC campuses. The Master Plan for Higher Education, first adopted in 1960, laid out distinct roles for each segment. It also set ambitious goals for the overall system, promising an accessible, low-cost, high-quality postsecondary education to all who could benefit from one. The Master Plan guided the development of all three segments and produced what many observers regard as the most successful system of public higher education in the world.

Under the Master Plan's generous low-fee premise, facilities planning for higher education uses population growth as the primary driver of enrollment potential. The college-age population is expected to grow more rapidly than the population as a whole until 2012 (Figure 5.2). Growth in the 18 to 24 year old age group is then expected to decline and remain negative until 2021. Indeed, if facilities are expanded over the next decade to fully accommodate the "Tidal Wave II" generation (the name college planners have given to the baby boom echo"), some of California's postsecondary institutions may experience excess capacity between 2015 and 2025.

The expected pressure on facilities over the coming decade is nevertheless substantial. DOF projects a 26 percent increase in enrollment from 2003 to 2012, to a total of 2,859,206 students (Figure 5.3). Some of this growth reflects increased participation rates among 18

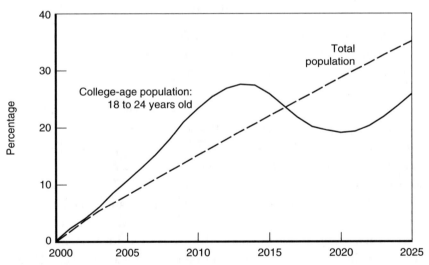

SOURCE: California Department of Finance (2004a).

Figure 5.2—Projected Growth of the College-Age Population in California, 2000–2025

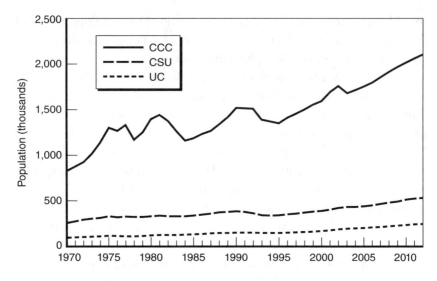

SOURCE: California Department of Finance (2003c).

**Figure 5.3—Public Higher Education Enrollment in California,
1970–2012**

to 24 year olds. In 2000, the California Postsecondary Education
Commission (CPEC) estimated that improved participation rates would
account for over one-quarter of enrollment growth between 1998 and
2010 (California Postsecondary Education Commission, 2000). Further
progress in the late 1990s led CPEC to revise this share upward in its
most recent projections (California Postsecondary Education
Commission, 2004). Increased participation rates imply more college
attendance by economically disadvantaged groups, particularly Latinos,
who are growing as a share of this age cohort.

In 2000, CPEC estimated that the UC system had reached its
capacity limits and that the CCC and CSU systems would reach theirs
within a few years. It also estimated that the state's independent colleges
and universities could add an additional 35,000 students between 1998
and 2010. In 2004, it predicted a capacity shortfall of more than
686,000 students by 2013: in effect, one-third of the total full-time-
equivalent (FTE) enrollment for all three public segments. The CCC

system would experience three-quarters of the capacity shortfall and the CSU system 19 percent.

Higher Education Funding Needs and Gaps

CPEC's 2004 update explicitly assumed that state funding, student fees, and course offerings would return to levels observed during the economic boom years of 1996 to 2001. In the new millennium, California's higher education system has been one of the casualties of the state government's massive budget deficit. Between 2001 and 2004, undergraduate fees for a full academic year in the UC system jumped from $3,859 to $6,230 (61%). CSU fees climbed from $1,876 to $2,860 (52%), and CCC fees rose from $330 to $676 (105%).[3] Student fee hikes and course cancellations led to an enrollment decline in the CCC system of about 90,000 students (about 5%) from fall 2002 to fall 2003. Given a projected growth rate for the same year of 5 percent, the CCC system argued that roughly 10 percent of potential students were "denied access," although the decline was considerably smaller (1.7%) in FTE terms (Legislative Analyst's Office, 2004d).

In 2004, proposed state budget cuts to UC and CSU would have reduced freshman enrollment by 10 percent. More than 7,000 eligible students were to be diverted to community colleges and guaranteed transfers by their junior year. Although funding for most of these diverted students was subsequently restored, this was the first such violation of the access tenets of the state's Master Plan since its passage in 1960. Continued uncertainties over the state's long-term budget situation leave open the possibility of further cuts or fee increases.

The CCC mission may be especially vulnerable to cuts in funding and student fee hikes. The proportion of students completing two-year terminal degrees has risen over time, and many members of the next wave in enrollments will come from families of limited means. Funding cuts have been hardest on the least-prepared students at CCCs, who tend to be first-generation, low-income, and minority (Hayward et al., 2004). In addition, students in more-expensive vocational programs may have

---

[3]California Postsecondary Education Commission (2003b); University of California (2004); California State University (2004).

suffered from cuts along with older working adults who attend evening and weekend classes.

These cutbacks were the product of reduced operating budgets, not a lack of facilities. Although the UC system faces immediate capacity constraints on some campuses, space is available elsewhere to accommodate students. Even as operating budgets were cut, the outlook for higher education capital budgets actually improved substantially during the early 2000s, thanks to the passage of state and local bond measures. The two most recent state education bonds provided nearly $4 billion for higher education facilities. Like primary and secondary schools, community colleges have benefited from the lower majority required on local bonds following the passage of Proposition 39. Since then, local bonds totaling $9.1 billion have been passed for community college facilities. Over two-thirds of the total were passed at the lower voter threshold.

How far these new funds will go in addressing the projected shortfalls in space depends on a number of factors, including assumptions about requirements for research facilities and institutions' ability to mobilize outside funds. It also depends on how one assesses costs for new instructional facilities for higher education. Although the legislature has imposed space and utilization standards, each segment uses its own method of cost estimation.

Table 5.3 presents an overview of four recent capital needs estimates for all facilities: two self-reported estimates by the segments for inclusion in *California's Five Year Infrastructure Plan for 2003* and two estimates using CPEC's 2000 and 2004 10-year enrollment projections. The first CPEC column reports the results of a detailed cost assessment done in conjunction with the 2000 study of projected enrollment and facilities needs to 2010. The second CPEC column reports our rough estimates of the cost implications of the June 2004 enrollment projections to 2013, which point to greater facilities shortfalls in the CCC and the CSU systems and slightly lower future needs in the UC system. The update raises total annual costs from $1.5 billion to $2.1 billion, still 17 percent lower than the segments' own requests for funding, which were based on lower enrollment projections. The discrepancies between

Table 5.3

Needs Estimates (Annualized) and Bond Revenue for California Higher Education ($ millions)

	Self-Reported Needs, 2003–07[a]		CPEC Needs Estimates		Funding Proposed/Available		
Segment	Request to DOF	Request Plus Deferred Needs	1998–2010[b]	2003–2013[c]	DOF Proposed[a]	State Bonds Since 2001 (Total)[d]	Local Bonds Since 2001 (Total)[e]
UC	670	770	618	583	335	1,098	
CSU	556	556	359	550	312	1,186	
CCC	1,329	2,769	526	988	427	1,666	9,100
Total	2,555	4,095	1,503	2,121	1,074	3,950	9,100

SOURCES: [a]California Department of Finance (2003b); [b]California Postsecondary Education Commission (2000); [c]authors' calculations based on California Postsecondary Education Commission (2004); [d]Proposition 47 passed in November 2002, and Proposition 55, passed in March 2004; [e]de Alth and Rueben (2005).

CPEC estimates and the self-reported figures are greatest for the CCC system.

The right-hand columns of the table present two estimates of available funding: the administration's proposed expenditures in the *Infrastructure Plan*, and the cumulative amount of state and local bonds made available since 2001. The Department of Finance proposed to fund only two-fifths of the segments' request and only two-thirds of the CPEC estimates then available. The discrepancies were greatest for UC, possibly reflecting the fact that a large share of UC capital funds is raised from nonstate sources (California Postsecondary Education Commission, 2003a).

Given the continued state budget woes, these funding proposals—which include contributions from the general fund—may be unreliable guides to future funding. It is therefore useful to assess how far the one sure source of public funding—the bond revenues—will go toward alleviating facilities needs. Table 5.4 summarizes the number of years of capital needs that could be met under the different needs scenarios,

Table 5.4

Years of Capital Costs Covered by Public Bonds and Nonpublic Sources in California

	Projected % Share of Nonpublic Funds	Self-Reported Needs		CPEC Needs Estimates	
		Request to DOF	Request Plus Deferred Needs	2000–2010	2003–2013
UC (1)	80	8.2	7.1	8.9	9.4
UC (2)	50	3.3	2.9	3.6	3.8
CSU	21	2.6	2.6	4.1	1.5
CCC	0	8.1	3.9	20.5	10.9

NOTE: For the UC, scenario 1 includes nonpublic funding at late 1990s levels. Scenario 2 assumes a drop in nonpublic funding to 50 percent.

assuming that the same share of capital outlay is contributed from nonstate sources for UC and CSU as during the period from 1996–97 through 2000–01.[4] It also includes a scenario with lower nonstate funding for UC.

The figures highlight the importance of nonstate sources to meet facilities expansion needs in the current era. Overall, CCC's situation has improved dramatically with the passage of local bonds, which outnumber state bonds for this segment by five to one. Depending on future enrollment patterns, which respond to fees and course offerings, funds are available to cover from 11 to 20 years under CPEC cost estimates. Even with the high-enrollment scenario, this would potentially cover statewide facilities expansion throughout 2012, the period of projected enrollment growth. However, some districts may still face challenges because local bonds are not evenly distributed. By CCC's own needs estimates, bond funding will be adequate for four to eight years of capital investment.

With limited expectations of outside funding, the CSU system is in the worst position, with enough funds for just two to four years. Thanks to outside funding, the UC system appears to be in relatively good shape,

---

[4]The share of capital outlay funds contributed from nonstate sources was calculated from data for the period from 1996–97 through 2000–01, from California Postsecondary Education Commission (2003a).

with adequate facilities funds for seven to nine years. This figure is more than halved, however, if outside funding falls from 80 to 50 percent of the total. Moreover, the ability of different campuses and programs to raise external funds varies widely. Older, more established campuses and programs are better able to raise funds from alumni and donors, yet newer programs may face more pressing expansion needs. These mismatches could significantly alter the projection of adequate facilities funding.

Alternative Approaches to Meeting Needs

These innovations in facilities finance notwithstanding, public higher education in California is at a crossroads. As CPEC warned in 2000, "If a second great surge of students is coming—and Commission analysis . . . shows clearly that Tidal Wave II is a reality—then business as usual will clearly be insufficient" (p. 11). In response to that warning, numerous reform proposals have been put forward to reestablish or reinterpret the social contract in the Master Plan.[5] Many proponents argue for the need to restore higher and more predictable levels of state funding from the general fund, which has been susceptible to cuts during periods of budget difficulties and has declined as a share of rising real per student costs. However, modern approaches recognizing the limits and tradeoffs involved in public funding are also increasingly common. As with K–12 education, these include supply-side proposals to improve the system's productivity and cost-effectiveness. In contrast to the K–12 sector, there is also explicit consideration of demand-management techniques. Many of these proposals have found fertile ground in today's revenue-constrained environment.

Well before the recent fee increases, a number of observers had begun to call for greater reliance on user fees. Instituting a long-term policy of higher fees (or tuition) would influence demand for schooling and put a formal end to the Master Plan's commitment to low-cost access. The justification for higher fees is that many students could pay a

---

[5]For summaries of major reports during the late 1990s, see Breneman (1998) and California Postsecondary Education Commission (1999). Also see Joint Legislative Committee to Develop a Master Plan for Education (2002).

greater share of the costs without undue hardship, thus providing a stable source of funding to the system. Higher fees may also relieve some pressure on enrollment demand in the public sector by shifting some students to private institutions and encouraging students to finish their degree programs more quickly. Some observers also advocate varying fees (or prioritizing access) according to the level of education, training, and profession. In spite of the hefty increases in recent years, fees for California schools remain low compared with fees in counterpart schools in other states (Legislative Analyst's Office, 2004d). To avoid limiting access, a program to raise fees must be accompanied by increased financial aid for needy students.

Fee increases alone may not be enough to solve the system's problems. Park and Lempert (1998) found that to maintain historic levels of access into the next decade, California would need to increase fees well beyond levels envisioned in current debates unless the system becomes far more productive in its use of resources. Proposals for greater cost-effectiveness include

- Increasing performance and accountability standards;
- Providing incentives or mandates for more efficient use of space;
- Mobilizing outside funds for research facilities;
- Reallocating students from high-cost to lower-cost institutions;
- Realizing economics of scope through regional linkages; and
- Introducing new technologies.

Performance and accountability standards can serve as incentives for both learners and institutions. For example, state aid might be geared toward demonstrated achievement of performance goals such as rapid time-to-degree. Such incentives could encourage institutions to facilitate more streamlined course loads for students.

In the area of space utilization, one much-discussed option is to extend summer sessions or even institute full year-round operations. According to the Legislative Analyst's Office (1999), year-round operation could increase the number of students accommodated with existing facilities by up to one-third and save several billion dollars. Year-round operation has been phased in slowly at some UC and CSU campuses, and most financial aid programs have not been restructured to accommodate summer programs. The call for summer programs is part of a more general push for improved space and utilization standards (the Legislative Analyst's Office, 2002e). Many administrators also believe that the decades-old space standards should be overhauled, and the CSU Chancellor's Office has introduced incentives for space conservation and sharing (California Postsecondary Education Commission, 2000; Dowall and Whittington, 2003).

Specific issues arise for research facilities. For the same square footage, these facilities are about twice as expensive to construct as classrooms, and they have expanded in the UC system at almost twice the rate of instructional space (including laboratories) over the past decade. Research space in the UC system accounts for about 80 percent of academic space; the comparable figure at peer universities nationally is roughly 50 percent (Legislative Analyst's Office, 2004c). The policy debates, however, center less on these proportions than on the role of the state in funding them. Arguments in favor of state sponsorship stress the role that research facilities play in the quality of graduate instruction and in the contribution to the regional economy. The Legislative Analyst maintains that the UC system can fund these facilities through sponsored research.

Another way to reduce the public outlay for higher education is to emphasize CCC's role as a feeder institution to the UC and CSU systems, given the CCC system's far lower costs per student. However, most UC- and CSU-eligible students are unlikely to shift to the community colleges voluntarily, and efforts to divert such students to the CCC system for 2004–05 were unsuccessful. Other proposals that would help achieve economies of scope include greater intraregional coordination among educational institutions and more joint use of space. Improved linkages to the K–12 system offer the potential for better student preparation for postsecondary education and more streamlined movement of students through the system. Finally, technological solutions such as distance-learning have been advanced.

To be successful, many of the reforms proposed in the name of cost savings may require additional financial contributions from the state or other sources. Year-round enrollment, for example, may be feasible only if the state provides full financial support. Technological upgrading would require expensive up-front investments even as it promises long-run savings. Furthermore, efforts to reduce the state's financial contribution to higher education, by increasing fees or compressing costs, necessarily involve tradeoffs. The economic rationale for public support to higher education is that the benefits to society of an educated workforce are likely to outweigh the benefits for individual students. Attempts to reduce public costs may provoke concerns about loss of quality as well as equity. For instance, diverting some students to CCCs may permit cost savings, but those institutions may also provide a lower-quality education. Raising fees without adequate financial aid will reduce access for those groups least able to afford a higher education.

These choices have consequences not only for individuals but also for the economic health of the state as a whole. In today's more global, competitive, and high-tech-oriented economy, higher education is increasingly the ticket needed to obtain the best jobs. Indeed, as David Neumark points out in Chapter 3, economic projections for California predict the greatest job growth in sectors that are relatively skill-intensive, such as business and professional services, education, and health care. Thus, Californians will need to consider the potential costs of *not* pursuing policies to ensure greater access, quality, and affordability—the major elements enshrined in the Master Plan.

Water Supply and Quality

California's water resources are expected to meet multiple, potentially competing, objectives: safe, reliable, and affordable drinking water supplies for the growing residential population; reliable, low-cost supplies for water-dependent agricultural and industrial businesses; and clean and adequate supplies to ensure the health of the state's waterways, lakes, and beaches as well as the wildlife and recreational activities that depend on them.

Although state and federal agencies play a role in all aspects of water management, the frontline institutions are local utilities and governments. Retail water utilities—a mix of special districts, municipal departments, and private companies—are responsible for meeting drinking water standards. Roughly 400 large retailers serve most

California homes and businesses; over 8,000 additional systems deliver water to smaller communities and public facilities such as parks. Nearly 600 local wastewater utilities—many of which double as water retailers—are responsible for meeting the clean water standards for municipal wastewater discharge, the primary fixed or "point" source of water pollution in California.

Over the past decade, municipal and county governments have progressively become responsible for managing a key form of diffused or "nonpoint" source pollution—storm-water runoff. Finally, hundreds of agricultural water districts manage the water resources for California's farmers. Because they deliver "raw" (untreated) water, they are not subject to drinking water standards, but they are increasingly being targeted to manage agricultural runoff, the other main nonpoint pollution source. Because agriculture uses about four times more water than all municipal and industrial uses combined, these districts are also key players in the discussions about statewide supply policies. Since the mid-1990s, a multiagency, federal-state partnership known as CALFED has brokered agreements among water users and environmentalists for ecosystem restoration and water supply reliability improvements in the hub of the state's water system, the San Francisco–San Joaquin Bay Delta.

California's water sector is in the midst of a paradigm shift in the way public investments are planned and paid for. Municipal water services have a strong tradition of direct user-fee finance. Many agricultural users have benefited from federally subsidized projects to develop water supplies. Since the 1980s, there is a growing recognition, backed by court rulings and legislation, that both sectors were taking too much water out of the system. To support fish and wildlife habitat, some water has been reallocated to instream uses. The modern approach to water planning emphasizes the importance of demand management as a guiding principle for future water investments. In theory, water users have adopted this approach, by agreeing to a "beneficiary pays" principle, whereby users pay for those investments that benefit them directly, and tax dollars pay for public benefits, such as ecosystem restoration. In practice, implementing this policy is proving contentious, because public funds are in short supply.

Supply-Related Needs

California's water supply concerns arise because urban demand is growing, traditional supply sources are shrinking, and the environment is perceived to have unmet needs. In a conventional approach to water supply planning, this pattern could imply the need for vast new quantities of water. At current levels of per capita use, and with a projected population increase of 14 million inhabitants, municipal use would expand by 3.6 million acre-feet between 2000 and 2030. Between now and 2015, California will also have to reduce its use of Colorado River supplies by about 0.8 million acre-feet. Finally, the most recent California Water Plan Update, still in draft at the time of this writing, has set two environmental goals that would also require new water: increasing instream flows to support aquatic wildlife and eliminating the overdrafting of groundwater basins. To meet all these demands, while leaving agricultural uses at their current levels, California would need an additional 5.9 to 7.4 million acre-feet by 2030, an increase of 7 to 9 percent over 2000 levels (Table 5.5).

However, this extreme scenario overstates new supply needs by a considerable amount. California's residential water users can still make

Table 5.5

Current and Projected Water Use in California
(millions of acre-feet)

| | | Net Change to 2030 | |
	2000	Extreme Scenario	Moderate Scenario
Municipal	8.9	3.6	3.1
Agriculture	34.3	0.0	−3.2
Environment	39.4	0.5–1.0	0.5–1.0
Total use	82.6		
Colorado River surplus	0.8	0.8	0.8
Groundwater overdraft	1.0–2.0	1.0–2.0	1.0–2.0
Total "new" water needed		5.9–7.4	2.2–3.7

SOURCE: California Department of Water Resources (2004); extreme and moderate scenarios calculated by authors using information from this source (Hanak and Barbour, 2005).

large savings through conservation. By one recent estimate, average per capita use will fall by nearly 5 percent if utilities simply continue to implement conservation programs to which they have already agreed. Economic factors are also likely to reduce agricultural water use. Every year, some farmers sell land for new housing developments, and others use water more efficiently as they shift to higher-value crops. Taken together, these patterns could cut in half the amount of new supplies needed—a figure reflected in the moderate scenario of Table 5.5. Water no longer used by agriculture provides the opportunity for transfers to urban and environmental users, reinforcing a trend in water marketing that got underway in the early 1990s (Hanak, 2003). Unused agricultural water can also contribute to reducing groundwater overdraft.

Numerous supply options are available to fill the remaining gap, including traditional sources, such as surface storage, along with conservation measures and nontraditional sources, such as storage in underground aquifers, desalination, and recycling. Figure 5.4 shows the most recent estimates of supplies available from these sources from the California Water Plan Update.

Simply summing these strategies overstates the potential, because some—for instance surface and groundwater storage—could compete for the same supplies. Globally, however, they indicate scope for expansion well above the range of expected growth in urban and environmental demand. The optimal mix of supply solutions depends on costs and reliability and will vary by locality and region. Some sources, such as conservation, groundwater banking, and water transfers, can make water available at a very low cost—$100 to $200 per acre-foot or less per year. Others, such as desalination, recycling, and surface storage, require considerable up-front investments as well as high operating costs, bringing annual costs above $600 per acre-foot and in some cases over $1,000.

There are no comprehensive estimates of how much California's water sector would need to invest each year to expand supplies to meet urban and environmental demands. To provide a very rough gauge, we can cost out the increases in net water demand implied under the moderate scenario presented above, which range from 75,000 to 135,000 acre-feet per year. Assuming average development costs in the range of

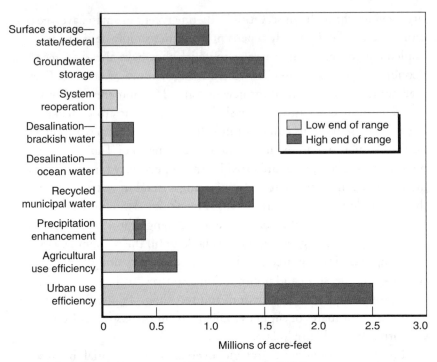

Figure 5.4—Potential New Water Supply Sources in California, 2000–2030

$3,000 to $5,000 per acre-foot, this implies annual investment needs for new water on the order of $220 to $615 million statewide.[6]

Quality-Related Needs

Many observers stress that managing water quality is at least as great a challenge as securing new supplies. New public health evidence on drinking water contaminants is raising the bar for water utilities, and new environmental regulations on polluted runoff are reshaping the way we will need to manage a wide range of activities. Some public works and environmental advocates have also argued that insufficient

---

[6]Average investment costs are based on data presented in California Department of Water Resources (2004).

investment by drinking water and wastewater utilities is leading to an impending water quality crisis.[7]

Estimates of the investment costs to maintain and expand California's local water delivery systems and treatment facilities are presented in Table 5.6. On balance, they suggest that capital expenditure requirements for water quality far exceed the costs of developing new supplies. For drinking water, the range is from $1 billion to $2.8 billion per year, and for wastewater from $1 billion to $1.8 billion. The relatively modest figure for managing storm-water and other nonpoint source pollution, with capital costs of $60 million per year, could reflect an undersampling of agencies responsible for these activities, although there are also debates about costs. These estimates exclude costs for runoff management by farmers and by the California Department of Transportation (Caltrans), which are also uncertain (California Department of Finance, 2003d). They also exclude the costs of ecosystem restoration, another water quality concern, which the

Table 5.6

Annual Drinking Water and Clean Watershed Investment Needs in California (millions of 2000 $)

| | EPA Needs Surveys | | EPA Gap Analysis | | CBO Estimates | |
	California Total	California Share (%)	Low	High	Low	High
Drinking water	874	12.6	969	2,806	1,459	2,529
Clean water						
Sewage	663	8.2	1,355	1,842	1,064	1,711
Storm water	18	6.3				
Nonpoint source	40	5.8				

SOURCES: U.S. Environmental Protection Agency (2001, 2002, 2003); Congressional Budget Office (2002).

NOTE: CBO estimates include financing costs.

---

[7]For national studies, see American Water Works Association Water Industry Technical Action Fund (2001); Water Environment Research Foundation (2000); Water Infrastructure Network (2000); and Natural Resources Defense Council (2004). For commentary on the California situation, see California Rebuild America Coalition (2003).

California Department of Water Resources (2004) has priced at $150 to $300 million per year statewide. Some ecosystem funds are destined for protection of the seismically vulnerable Delta levees, whose failure could jeopardize drinking water supplies for Southern California and irrigation supplies in the San Joaquin Valley for months, if not years. A levee break in June 2004 has renewed debates on the best strategies for tackling this problem, with costs potentially much higher than those envisaged in current funding plans.[8]

Is There a Funding Gap?

The high costs of these investments, particularly for water quality, have led to calls for increased public subsidies. Advocates hearken back to the 1970s, when the federal government provided massive subsidies to upgrade wastewater treatment. However, our analysis suggests that California's municipal water and wastewater utilities are largely on track to meet regulatory demands and accommodate growth with the current funding system, which again relies mainly on user fees. In real terms, water-related capital spending, including both supply augmentation and drinking water facilities, increased from $2.6 billion to $3.3 billion between 1997 and 2000.[9] This lies at the high end of the range of projected annual needs for these activities of $1.2 billion to $3.4 billion. Wastewater spending has been relatively stable at around $1.7 billion per year, well in line with annual capital needs.

This healthy state of affairs is due in no small part to utilities' straightforward system for raising revenues. Generally, they need only a simple majority vote from their governing board to raise fees. Moreover, current user fees are low as a share of household income, suggesting scope for fee increases without causing across-the-board hardship (Table 5.7). In a recent statewide survey of utilities, only 3

---

[8]CALFED's 10-year finance plan targets funding for levees at $446 million (CALFED, 2004). Some analysts argue that propping up the levee system is an unsustainable strategy, and they call for reconsideration of the decades-old plan to sidestep the Delta with a peripheral canal (Leavenworth, 2004a).

[9]Data are in 2000 dollars (de Alth and Rueben, 2005). More recent data for water and sewer are less reliable because of a change in reporting methods for capital investment by special districts.

Table 5.7

Water Charges as a Share of Median Household Income in California, 2003

	No. of Communities in Sample	Average Yearly Water Fees ($)	Water Fees as % of Median Household Income	Fees > 1% of Median Income	Fees > 1.5% of Median Income
Bay Area	109	444	0.6	5	0
Southern Coast	176	385	0.7	13	1
Central Coast	38	457	0.9	29	11
Inland Empire	60	322	0.7	17	8
San Joaquin Valley	55	207	0.5	5	0
Sacramento Metro Area	34	248	0.5	3	0
Rest of State	64	344	1.0	41	8
California	536	363	0.7	15	3

SOURCES: Authors' calculations, using water fees from Black and Veatch (2003). Median household income is from the 2000 census, adjusted for inflation with the consumer price index for urban areas (CPI-U).

percent (covering 1% of the sampled population) had charges greater than 1.5 percent of median income, the cutoff for eligibility under targeted drinking water programs. Regions where water rates are high—such as the Central Coast and some North Coast and Mountain communities included in the "rest of state" category—appear more vulnerable than the Central Valley, where water rates are generally quite low. Moreover, modern water pricing techniques—which increase rates for higher levels of use to encourage conservation—have built-in protections for lower-income residents, who tend to consume less water than wealthier households with larger lots.

Mandatory system upgrades, however, could pose real financial difficulties in some low-income communities. The potential is greatest in smaller communities, where unit costs tend to be higher. Some existing programs address these concerns. For drinking water systems, the state revolving fund, co-financed by federal and state authorities, gives priority grants and low-interest loans to low-income communities. California also has a small communities grant program for wastewater systems, and the U.S. Department of Agriculture targets financial assistance to rural (typically low-income) communities for wastewater and drinking water. As regulatory pressures increase—for instance to meet new standards on arsenic in drinking water—policymakers will need to keep an eye on the adequacy of these programs, which currently account for a small share of total state and federal support in this sector.

Two other areas of the water portfolio are more problematic: providing funds for the environment and managing polluted runoff. The estimated costs of environmental water and ecosystem restoration are considerable—on the order of $500 million annually. Many agricultural users hold the view that the environmental price tag should also include some restoration of supplies returned to instream uses through involuntary cutbacks in the early 1990s. Since 2001, environmental programs (including levee maintenance) have been funded with state bonds, and there is enough money available to cover another two to three years. The presumption behind CALFED's tentative peace accord between water users and environmentalists was that public funds would continue to be available for these activities. With no assured long-term funding, environmentalists are now calling for increased user fees (in effect, an environmental tax) to finance the program. The strongest opposition to such proposals comes from farmers, who maintain that the water supply promises of CALFED have yet to be met.

Given the likelihood that federal contributions will remain limited, Californians probably will be asked to make ballot-box decisions on whether to devote substantial new bond funds to support ecosystem restoration and perhaps to help fund the development of new supplies. Because state bonds are repaid through the general fund, this form of financing amounts to subsidies from the general taxpaying public. Under the alternative of eco-taxes on water, a much higher burden would fall on farmers.

For runoff, regulations are clamping down on the construction industry, local governments, transportation authorities, and farmers. With management techniques still in the process of development, cost estimates vary widely, but it appears likely that a flexible mix of technologies and policies can keep costs down. A plan in San Diego allows cities to work with developers to install systems covering entire drainage areas rather than individual projects, thereby reducing per acre costs from \$50,000 to \$10,000 (Rogers, 2002). In San Bernardino County, local governments and water managers are exploring the possibility of tying storm-water management programs to aquifer recharge. By reducing impervious surfaces (e.g., curbs, pavement) and directing the flow of runoff, they hope to increase local supplies while reducing the discharge of pollutants to local rivers and lakes. Even in areas where recharge benefits are not available, the introduction of more drought and pest-tolerant native plants can simultaneously conserve water and reduce pesticide-laden runoff. Integrated watershed management approaches are also seen as a way to combat source contamination of drinking water, reducing the need for treatment.

Nevertheless, there are clearly challenges to paying for runoff programs, prompting some to consider this as yet another "unfunded mandate." Private construction activities are the only ones with a direct mechanism for recouping costs—that is, through higher sales prices. Under the current legal system, storm-water fees may be considered taxes, requiring a two-thirds popular vote. In this sense, the unfunded mandate critique rings true: Municipalities and transportation agencies are given responsibility for implementing regulations but lack the authority to generate the necessary funds.

Transportation

California's transportation system, the most extensive in the nation, is made up of more than 50,000 state highway miles, 8,000 miles of railroad, 250 general aviation and 28 commercial airports, and over 200 public transit systems. As the leading global gateway for Pacific Rim trade, California's ports handle more than one-third of the value of all U.S. and foreign trade, totaling \$200 billion (California Department of Finance, 2003b; California Department of Transportation, 2003a; Haveman and Hummels, 2004).

Transportation planning is a hybrid of federal, state, regional, and local responsibilities. During the 1990s, federal and state policies augmented the regional role. Today, regional transportation planning agencies (RTPAs) program 75 percent of funds from state and federal sources designated for transportation capital improvements in California. The remaining 25 percent is allocated for projects of interregional significance chosen by Caltrans. Regional agencies in urban areas with a population of 50,000 or more are required by federal law to produce 20-year regional transportation investment plans and update them every three years. The plans must address air quality standards, mobility, access, congestion relief, equity, energy efficiency, and safety, among other objectives.

This planning takes place against a backdrop of rising vehicle use. Between 1967 and 1997, vehicle miles traveled on state freeways grew almost three times faster than population, and car use is projected to continue outpacing population growth in the future (Figure 5.5). Contributing factors include a rise in the number of two-earner households and a continuing shift of jobs and residents to less densely developed suburban and "edge city" locations. Goods-related traffic has also contributed to the increase in road use, especially in Southern

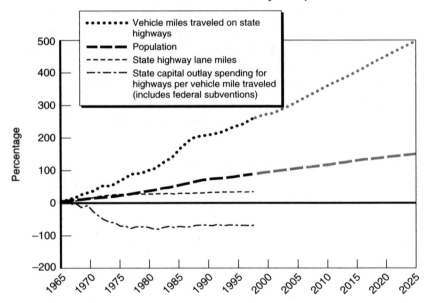

SOURCE: Author's calculations, using various federal and state statistics (Hanak and Barbour, 2005).

Figure 5.5—Growth in Key Highway-Related Indicators in California, 1965–2025

California. California roads and highways carry more truck traffic than any other state in the nation—more than a billion tons of freight annually (California Department of Transportation, 2003a; The Road Information Program, 2004). In 2002, trucks accounted for 29 percent of total vehicle miles traveled in the state (California Department of Transportation, 2003b).

Despite increasing vehicle use, highway construction has been curtailed as a result of rising costs and declines in its major source of dedicated revenue. In inflation-adjusted terms, capital expenditure for each new U.S. road mile was more than three times higher during the 1990s than during the early 1960s.[10] Rights-of-way, labor and materials, high design standards, and growing community and environmental concerns accounted for much of the cost increase (Taylor, 1992). Meanwhile, the state and federal excise taxes on gasoline did not rise with inflation, and increases in fuel efficiency put downward pressure on those revenues. In real terms, California fuel tax revenue per vehicle mile traveled today is worth approximately 36 percent of what drivers paid in 1970. Capital outlays on highways declined during the high inflation years (Figure 5.5); and, from 1980 to 2000, California increased its highway lane miles by only 6 percent.

The steady rise in vehicle miles traveled, coupled with limited capacity expansion, means that Californians have been using their roadways more intensively over the past few decades. Traffic delays, especially at peak periods, are a natural outcome of this process. Traffic congestion has become a feature of life in California's metropolitan areas, and judging by public opinion polls, a source of daily consternation. Census data indicate that between 1990 and 2000, average travel time to work increased by two to five minutes for residents of California's major metropolitan areas, or 7 to 19 percent (Table 5.8).

Another view of trends and relative magnitudes across metropolitan areas is provided by the Texas Transportation Institute's (TTI) estimates of annual hours of congestion-related delay (Figure 5.6). For coastal regions, the sharpest increases in congestion occurred during the 1980s. Congestion continued to rise in San Diego and in fast-growing inland

---

[10]For details, see Hanak and Barbour (2005).

Table 5.8

Travel Time to Work for California Residents, 1990 and 2000 (minutes)

County of Residence	1990	2000	Increase	% Change
Los Angeles	26.5	29.4	2.9	11
Orange	25.5	27.2	1.7	7
San Bernardino	27.4	31.0	3.6	13
Riverside	28.2	31.2	3.0	11
San Diego	22.2	25.3	3.1	14
San Francisco	26.9	30.7	3.8	14
Santa Clara	23.3	26.1	2.8	12
Alameda	25.8	30.8	5.0	19
Contra Costa	29.3	34.4	5.1	17
Sacramento	21.7	25.4	3.7	17

SOURCE: Authors' calculations, using U.S. Census, 1990 and 2000 STF3

NOTE: Workers are all workers age 16 or older who did not work at home.

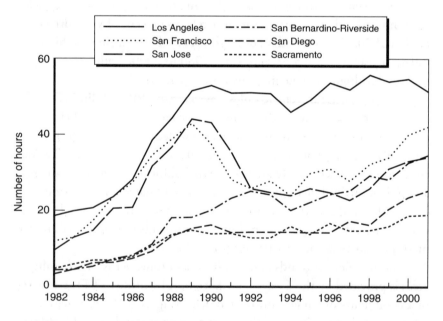

SOURCE: Texas Transportation Institute (2003).

Figure 5.6—Annual Hours of Delay per Person on Highways and Major Arterials in California Metropolitan Areas, 1982–2001

areas during the 1990s. In 2001, the average annual delay per capita ranged from 19 hours in Sacramento to 52 hours in Los Angeles.

These time delays and the associated extra fuel costs have been used to generate very large estimates of the costs of congestion to California's economy. For 2001, TTI set the cost at $20.4 billion for the state's seven largest urban areas, or about 40 percent more than all public spending on transportation in California. Such figures suggest that Californians might be willing to pay substantial sums to alleviate congestion—in the Los Angeles area, for example, just over $1,000 per year for every man, woman, and child. However, other studies suggest that commuters' valuations of time vary considerably (Calfee and Winston, 1998; Small, Winston, and Yan, 2002).

Moreover, broad measures of congestion are not necessarily the best indicators of transportation system needs. Building enough capacity to eliminate congestion during peak travel periods would create considerable excess capacity for the rest of the day. Given the high costs of road construction, this would be an inefficient use of scarce public resources. Modern approaches to congestion focus on strategic investments to tackle bottlenecks and demand-management techniques. These include encouraging drivers to carpool, to spread out their travel across the day, and to use transit alternatives during peak periods.

Mass transit investments in California increased as the construction of new highway lanes diminished. Per capita expenditures on California transit projects more than doubled between 1972 and 1997 as four major cities—San Diego, Los Angeles, San Jose, and Sacramento— opened new rail systems during the 1980s and 1990s. In recent years, transit has accounted for 20 to 40 percent of the combined capital outlay for transit, highways, and roads. Transit serves multiple goals, including mobility and access for low-income, disabled, and elderly residents without cars. However, an important motivation for shifting investment toward transit was to provide an alternative to road use to alleviate congestion during peak periods.

Progress toward attainment of this goal has been less than stellar. Between 1990 and 2000, transit use for trips to work in five major metropolitan areas barely increased, moving from 5.5 to 5.6 percent (Table 5.9). The recent numbers are somewhat better for densely

Table 5.9

Means of Transportation to Work in Major California Metropolitan Areas

Mode of Travel to Work	Los Angeles	San Francisco	San Diego	Sacramento	Average
% drove alone					
In 2000	72.4	68.1	73.9	75.3	71.5
% point change 1990–2000	0.1	-0.2	3.0	0.1	0.3
% carpooled					
In 2000	15.2	12.9	13.0	13.5	14.2
% point change 1990–2000	–0.3	–0.1	–0.7	–0.1	–0.3
% used bus/streetcar					
In 2000	4.3	5.7	3.1	2.4	4.4
% point change 1990–2000	–0.2	–0.5	–0.1	0.3	–0.3
% used subway/rail					
In 2000	0.3	3.5	0.2	0.3	1.2
% point change 1990–2000	0.3	0.6	0.2	0.0	0.4
% worked at home					
In 2000	3.6	4.1	4.4	4.0	3.8
% point change 1990–2000	0.8	0.6	–0.6	0.9	0.6
% used other means					
In 2000	4.2	5.7	5.4	4.5	4.8
% point change 1990–2000	–0.7	–0.4	–1.8	–1.2	–0.8

SOURCE: Authors' calculations using data from the U.S. Census.

NOTE: The data are for metropolitan statistical areas, which comprise counties and include undeveloped areas within them.

traveled corridors—38 percent of trips along the San Francisco Bay Bridge corridor, 30 percent to downtown Los Angeles, 18 percent to downtown San Diego.[11] But it is difficult to dismiss the critique that overall, these investments are not living up to expectations, with costs—including high operating subsidies—that far outweigh the benefits. Often, we have been making the wrong transit investments, favoring

[11]Data are from California Transit Association and California Association for Coordinated Transportation (1999). See also Fielding (1995).

suburban light-rail systems that may never pencil out over more flexible bus systems and selective rail investments in densely populated areas (Wachs, 1997, 2003a; Garrett and Taylor, 1999).

Federal and state funding allocations have contributed to this spending bias by favoring new transit capital investment over operating subsidies, rail over bus service, and track or vehicle mileage or population over ridership. As a consequence, suburban systems tend to receive much deeper subsidies per transit rider than central city systems (Taylor, 1991; Wachs, 1997; Garrett and Taylor, 1999). The governance system for ratifying regional transportation plans also plays a role. The one-government, one-vote system used by most metropolitan area COGs—entities that generally coincide with regional transportation planning authorities—works against identifying priorities that are truly regional.

In addition to coping with capacity issues, officials have stressed the need for more maintenance and rehabilitation of existing transportation facilities. Although maintenance and rehabilitation have consumed increasing shares of spending, a significant backlog remains; deferred maintenance for state highways alone is estimated at $587 million (Legislative Analyst's Office, 2004e). California's roadway system has been characterized as the second roughest in the nation, about one-fifth of the pavement on state highways is considered in need of rehabilitation or major reconstruction, and more than half the state's bridges require rehabilitation or replacement (California Department of Transportation, 2003a). Once again, however, these measures cannot always be taken at face value. Road and bridge conditions are often checked visually, and it is not obvious that the entire roadway system should be maintained to the same high standard. Given the competing objectives for public funds, many believe that planners should use new technology to assess conditions and prioritize expenditures based on usage.

Looking ahead, the volume of goods moving by all modes within the state is expected to double by 2020. Many of the state's major airports will soon reach capacity (California Department of Transportation, 2003a). In the greater Los Angeles area, air passenger travel is expected to double before 2030, with suburban airports forced to accommodate much of the increasing demand (Southern California Association of Governments, 2004). A study recently completed for Caltrans projected future road and transit travel demand to 2025 as a function of various demographic and land-use variables, assuming that transportation infrastructure is provided at similar levels as today (Crane et al., 2002). Car use will continue to be the predominant mode of travel, and traffic congestion will worsen as a result of population growth in urban centers, the Central Valley, peripheral edge cities, and the highway corridors linking these areas. Time spent traveling is projected to rise by 48 percent. Transit trips will rise at a substantially faster rate than car trips but will remain a small share (less than 10%) of overall trips in most areas.

Transportation Funding Needs and Gaps

The complexity of the transportation system makes it particularly difficult to assess whether we are spending enough in this sector. In the early 1990s, transportation agencies were required to move away from a conventional wish list approach to assessing needs, toward revenue-constrained planning. This new system has the advantage of forcing planners to consider tradeoffs among different investment options in meeting such goals as mobility and congestion relief, while meeting air quality requirements. However, the fiscal constraint requirement also hampers their ability to evaluate potential benefits from additional investments.

One recent study by the California Transportation Commission (1999) surveyed state, regional, and local transportation agencies for their *unfunded* 10-year needs for system rehabilitation, operations, and high-priority expansion projects. The combined total was between $107 billion and $117 billion, of which three-quarters was for system expansion and one-quarter was for rehabilitation or retrofit of existing assets. Taking 1999 and 2000 capital expenditures as an estimate of the *funded* needs, this suggests total capital spending needs on the order of $16 billion to $17 billion per year. To meet this total, capital spending on transportation would have to be more than double the amount actually expended in these years, a time of budget surpluses.

Because this exercise did not weigh the costs and benefits, however, it is not a reliable guide to what we should be spending. Caltrans and the regional agencies have been working to develop system performance measures to permit cost-benefit comparisons across different modes and projects, but progress has been slow, as the endeavor is both technically and politically demanding. Several regional agencies have begun to model scenarios with different revenue alternatives. Such scenarios can then be presented to the public to see whether it will support the tax or fee increases to fund the more costly alternatives.

Since the late 1990s, both the public and the state legislature have lent support to transportation funding but with mixed results. In 2000, the legislature passed the Transportation Congestion Relief Program, a six-year program to direct $7.6 billion in state general funds for specific congestion relief projects around the state. In 2002, voters passed Proposition 42, which permanently dedicated state sales tax revenue on gasoline toward transportation improvements.[12] However, as Kim Rueben and Shelley de Alth show in Chapter 4, these actions were rapidly undone by the state's growing budget crisis. California is also likely to experience a contraction of federal funds by more than $600 million per year when it converts to ethanol-blended fuel, which is taxed at a lower rate than fuel with no ethanol content (Transportation California, n.d.).

Historically, California has relied heavily on user fees to raise transportation revenue—specifically, the state and federal gasoline taxes, which now stand at 18.4 cents and 18 cents per gallon, respectively. Neither is indexed to inflation, and the state tax has not been raised since 1994. As the real revenue from this funding source declined, California allowed counties to propose half-cent sales tax increases for transportation projects, subject to voter approval. Such measures have passed in 20 counties, and by the late 1990s, this source accounted for one-third of local funding for transportation (Legislative Analyst's Office, 2000a; Goldman, Corbett, and Wachs, 2001).

County sales taxes are a problematic source of funds from several standpoints: They reduce flexibility by committing transportation authorities to spending on a specified set of projects; they favor showcase

---

[12]The sales tax on gasoline, introduced in 1972, had been principally destined to the general fund, as is the case for other state sales taxes. This tax should not be confused with the per gallon gasoline tax, considered a user fee, which has always been dedicated to transportation funding.

(but not necessarily cost-effective) projects that appeal to suburban voters; they are geared to meet needs defined at the county not the regional level; and they frequently lock in state and federal matching funds for the same projects. The shift to county sales taxes also raises questions of funding stability. In many counties, these funds risk nonrenewal under the two-thirds voter threshold introduced with Proposition 218. Finally, unlike the gas tax, sales taxes provide no incentives to drivers to modulate car use.

To improve funding stability and user incentives, many policy analysts have recommended a state transportation finance system based on growth-indexed user fees. For example, the LAO recommends that voters be asked to repeal Proposition 42, to increase the gasoline tax to replace the lost funding, and to index that tax to inflation (Legislative Analyst's Office, 2004f; see also Taylor, Weinstein, and Wachs, 2001). A greater reliance on user fees also clears the way for revenue bonds, a form of long-term borrowing secured by a project revenue stream. Revenue bonds, which do not require voter approval, offer the prospect of greater funding stability.

Alternative Approaches to Meeting Transportation Needs

Many of the pathways for maximizing the effectiveness of transportation spending center on modern approaches: demand-management policies such as user fees to encourage more efficient use of existing systems and improve cost recovery, and supply-side innovations to provide services more cost-effectively and enable greater capacity utilization. Some of the greatest potential lies in combinations of both demand- and supply-side approaches.

To date, the primary demand-management technique to mitigate congestion has been the high-occupancy vehicle (HOV) lane, reserved for carpoolers and mass transit vehicles. This technique imposes no out-of-pocket costs on drivers but instead encourages them to group their travel to save time and (sometimes) tolls. State and federal mandates require consideration of HOV expansion in all highway expansion planning. As a result, the majority of new capacity added to the state highway system over the last 15 years has been for HOV lanes. By 2000, 925 lane miles of California state highways had been designated as HOV lanes (2% of state highway lane miles). About 70 percent were in Southern California. In 2000, the state's HOV lanes carried nearly 60 percent more people per hour during peak congestion periods than mixed-use lanes. HOV lanes were especially efficient when complementary efforts to promote bus service and carpooling had been implemented (Legislative Analyst's Office, 2000b). Aided by "casual" carpooling arrangements at East Bay transit stops, the four HOV lanes at the San Francisco Bay Bridge toll plaza carried 63 percent of all people crossing during the morning commute, while 18 mixed-flow lanes carried the remaining 36 percent. Statewide, about two-thirds of total maximum HOV capacity was being used, suggesting that some of these lanes still have room to accommodate users.

Tolls are another alternative both for raising revenue and helping manage transportation demand. With the advent of electronic toll technology, it is now possible to vary tolls by location and time of day, a practice known as "congestion pricing." Five toll roads opened in Southern California in recent years, and at least two have been used in conjunction with HOV access, a hybrid known as a HOT (high-occupancy toll) lane. Long considered politically infeasible, HOT lanes allow drivers to use carpool lanes by paying a toll, which varies according to the congestion in the cost-free lanes. In San Diego, where a stretch of Interstate 15 uses this form of congestion pricing, revenues in 2000 averaged about $5,000 per month and were used to finance transit service on the corridor (Legislative Analyst's Office, 2000b).

A similar HOT lane was designated on Orange County's State Route 91, one of four demonstration projects for toll roads in Southern California financed by the private sector (Taylor, Weinstein, and Wachs, 2001). These "public-private partnerships" have met with mixed success to date. For example, the Orange County Transportation Authority bought back the Route 91 toll lanes after it concluded that the 35-year "no compete" clause prevented the expansion of adjoining public highway space (Shigley, 2003). The Route 91 project has been running successfully since then, with funds earned on tolls going to improvements in other capacity.

Although tolls have raised equity concerns, some research suggests that equity effects may be small and that policies could mitigate the effects for poor households (Taylor, Weinstein, and Wachs, 2001). A Legislative Analyst's Office study (1998c) suggested that welfare recipients and other low-income drivers could be provided a monthly transportation subsidy in the form of toll credits or "lifeline" toll rates, similar to the reduced lifeline telephone and energy rates. Equity implications are also less urgent if toll roads lie close to or alongside nonpaying lanes. In such cases, toll roads are perceived as providing relief even to nonusers by relieving congestion on nearby routes.

Parking charges are another pricing mechanism to discourage solo driving. Approximately 95 percent of automobile commuters in California receive free parking at work (census data cited in Legislative Analyst's Office, 2002c). The availability of free parking is partly a function of local planning codes. Local governments impose minimum off-street parking requirements on new development, generally pegged to peak levels of demand (Shoup, 1997, 1999a). Studies have shown that solo driving and car use generally are reduced substantially when workers must pay to park (Legislative Analyst's Office, 2002c).

In 1992, California passed a parking cash-out law requiring that certain employers offer cash in lieu of parking. Although the program was found to be quite effective in reducing solo driving and increasing transit use, its scope was very limited, applying only to employers who lease, rather than own, parking space (Legislative Analyst's Office,, 2002c). Other options being tested by California cities include in-lieu parking fees for developers (in lieu of the requirement for providing free off-street parking space), employer-paid transit passes, and curb-parking fees with revenue targeted for improvements to the specific neighborhood to help overcome public opposition to higher parking fees (Shoup, 1993, 1997, 1999b).

New transportation strategies to enhance system capacity include advances in information technology to improve transportation management (Wachs, 2002). Smart technologies such as ramp metering, electronic toll collection at bridges, and traffic lights that respond to sensors at key locations are already reducing congestion and providing air quality benefits as vehicles spend less time idling and in low gear. Sensors also have potential to improve the precision of road and bridge quality assessments for maintenance scheduling. Some analysts argue that more could be done to support the adoption of smart technologies (Deakin, 2002). One constraint is that regional spending plans are tied down many years in advance by the programs agreed to in county sales tax ballot measures, leaving little opportunity to respond to new ideas.

Transit planners are also looking for less costly alternatives to light rail. Bus rapid transit (BRT), which involves operating buses on exclusive bus highways or HOV lanes, is gaining new adherents. Average capital costs per mile for BRT projects have been less than half the cost for light rail, although operating costs have been variable (U.S. General Accounting Office, 2001). California urban areas implementing BRT include San Diego, San Jose, and Los Angeles. To be effective, however, BRT requires a level of density that currently exceeds those in many metropolitan areas. In less densely populated areas, an expansion of regular bus capacity and access to HOV lanes would be a better option.

Planners are also seeking innovations to mitigate the effects of goods-related traffic. Many of these innovations seek to exploit the fact that the industry itself has much to gain financially by enhanced mobility. The flagship effort to date is the Alameda Corridor, a public-private partnership that has reduced rail and road congestion between the Long Beach ports and Los Angeles through grade separation (Haveman and Hummels, 2004). The corridor is funded primarily by revenue bonds that will be repaid with charges to the railroad and port shippers. Plans are also under consideration for the construction of dedicated truck toll lanes in the Los Angeles region.

Integrated Strategies and Smart Growth

California's rapid growth has exposed a fundamental tension between environmental protection and economic development. Transportation systems pollute our air and water. Expanding water supplies can harm aquatic wildlife. Construction of all types contributes to water and air pollution and can endanger critical natural habitats. Since the early 1990s, planners and environmental and community activists have increasingly sought to craft solutions to these problems through integrated approaches. Rather than taking land-use decisions as given, these "smart growth" approaches aim to shape these decisions. By influencing how and where we build, proponents see the potential not only to improve environmental outcomes but also to generate other social benefits, including more affordable housing, healthier lifestyles (more walking and biking), greater community development, and more cost-effective use of transportation facilities.

California's four major metropolitan areas—the Bay Area, San Diego, Los Angeles, and Sacramento regions—have officially embraced this philosophy in their most recent regional transportation plans, which target more compact, transit-oriented development. A primary aim of these strategies is to increase housing affordability, with more housing and a greater mix of housing types than would occur with the single-family tract developments envisioned in the "business as usual" scenarios. Legislation passed in 2002 (AB 857) also calls for the state to embrace this smart growth approach by investing strategically to support infill development, efficient development at the urban fringe, and the preservation of open space.

The explicit adoption of smart growth goals by regional councils of government, through processes involving substantial citizen input, is significant. It suggests that elected officials are buying into the idea that concerted planning is the best way to ensure that growth is accompanied by wider social benefits. Moving from planning to execution of these goals will be challenging, however. Many of the benefits of linking public investment to private land-use decisions will accrue at the regional scale through more housing opportunities, more open space, better air quality, better source water protection, and potentially also improvements in social equity. Some of the costs, meanwhile, are concentrated at the local level with those who have to implement or accept changes in land use.

To make these strategies truly "win-win," fiscal and legal reforms may be needed to increase the incentives for denser development. To succeed, however, smart growth strategies also depend on the willingness of California's residents to accept more compact living. As Mark Baldassare and Jon Cohen report in Chapter 8, when surveyed, most residents say that growth will make the state a less desirable place to live. Both housing affordability and air quality are routinely listed as primary concerns. However, Californians appear more split on the type of tradeoff they want to make in terms of housing and location, with about half preferring single-family homes, even if it means long commutes, and the other half preferring denser living and easier access to work (Baldassare, 2002a). This suggests that there is already a potential market for compact, transit-oriented development. If compact development programs succeed in making housing more affordable, they may win over more converts.

Conclusion

This chapter set out to shed light on two central questions for public investment in California. First, are we spending enough to secure a sound economic future and quality of life? Second, are we making the most of the public resources available? Our review of three major sectors—education, water, and transportation—provides ample evidence that there is no single answer to the first question, if only because there is no objective measure of "needs." Whenever it is appropriate for those who use public services to contribute to their cost, the demand for those services—and hence the level of investment needed—depends in part on how much users are willing to pay. Recognizing the scope for cost-saving innovations and developing suitable user incentives are pathways to spending public resources judiciously. This is the essence of what we have termed a "modern approach" to infrastructure planning. California's public investment planners have been moving in this direction over the past 10 to 15 years, experimenting with different ways to provide and pay for infrastructure. The challenges include striking the right balance between efficiency and equity goals and setting up appropriate funding mechanisms.

In K–12 education, voter support for state and local bonds since 2000 has gone a long way toward redressing a serious backlog of school facilities shortfalls. A key contributing factor was the easing of voter requirements for local school bonds, which now require only a 55 percent majority (down from two-thirds). Recent reforms have also begun to redress inequities across school districts, by focusing more resources on overcrowded schools in low-income neighborhoods. These equity concerns are part of a larger question of how to raise performance levels in California's public schools, which is especially poor in low-income districts (Rose et al., 2003). Higher per student spending levels—now relatively low in California—may be a part of the solution.

In higher education, funding innovations have also helped address the facilities constraints pressing upon the system as the children of the baby boomers reach college age. Thanks to the lower pass rate on local school bonds, the community colleges have generated enough local funds to ensure expansion well into the next decade. If the UC system continues to attract as much outside funding as in the recent past, it too will be in a good position. With limited outside funding, the CSU system is worst placed.

Facilities are not the biggest question mark for this sector, however: California's recent budget woes have the potential to reshape some basic tenets of the Master Plan for Higher Education, established in 1960. In particular, proposals now call for additional increases in student fees (already up more than 50 percent since 2001) and for increasing the role of the lower-cost community colleges as feeder schools for the four-year institutions. Demand management through higher fees offers many potential advantages, as long as it is accompanied by means-tested financial aid. This is, nevertheless, a break with the social contract of the Master Plan, which promised low-cost, universal access to California residents. Californians will need to consider the role they want the higher education system to play in the future, in which jobs requiring college training are expected to be an increasing share of all jobs.

Although many raise the specter of impending water shortages as California grows, more efficient use of existing resources, through conservation and reallocation through water marketing, can considerably diminish this challenge. Moreover, municipal water and wastewater utilities, financed through user fees, are making substantial investments to accommodate growth while meeting regulatory goals for clean and safe water. The big questions in this sector therefore concern paying for environmental programs for which no one wants to take ownership. Without continued bond funding for ecosystem restoration and water for aquatic wildlife, urban and agricultural water users will be asked to pay eco-taxes, a prospect farmers consider particularly onerous. Managing polluted runoff is another unfunded environmental mandate. New watershed approaches offer potential to achieve this goal at low cost; however, local funding sources will also need to be secured through user fees or local taxes. Raising these funds is considerably more difficult than for utility charges, because it requires a two-thirds voter majority.

Transportation agencies face the challenge of providing mobility and access, managing congestion, and attaining air quality goals in a far different environment from the heyday of freeway expansion in the 1950s and 1960s. Real costs of building highway lanes have more than tripled since then, and the value of traditional roadway user fees—gas taxes—has eroded through inflation and higher fuel efficiency. In today's more built-up environment, the greatest potential lies in strategic investments to relieve bottlenecks and to encourage drivers to carpool, modulate their travel schedules, and use transit alternatives.

Over the past decade and a half, roadway investments have focused on these approaches, with the majority of new capacity in HOV lanes. Promising experiments are also under way with the greater use of tolls. Better pricing of road use would also improve ridership on transit systems, many of which go underused. Transportation finance would also greatly benefit from shifting back to user fee support and away from general sales taxes that have progressively replaced the gas tax. Making this move will depend on the public's willingness. The alternative is a future in which we manage demand by default, through longer and longer delays.

In recent years, strategies that aim to achieve multiple goals, by focusing on how and where we build our communities, have increasingly come into the spotlight. Councils of Government in California's four major metropolitan areas have embraced the smart growth philosophy in their most recent regional transportation plans, which target more compact, transit-oriented development. A primary aim of these strategies is to increase housing affordability, with more housing and a greater mix of housing types than would occur with traditional "sprawl" pattern of development (single-family tract developments on the suburban edge). To make these strategies truly "win-win," fiscal and regulatory reforms may be needed to reduce the disincentives to denser development. To succeed, smart growth strategies also depend on the willingness of California's residents to accept more compact living. The public currently appears split on this issue; it is more united in expressing concerns about the effects of growth on housing affordability and air quality.

The message that emerges across all sectors is that Californians have choices about the future we want to build. One part of the choice is deciding what level of public services we want to provide. Another part is deciding how we want to pay for them. The more we link payments to the use of facilities, the better we encourage residents and businesses to use them efficiently. As the examples of water and wastewater show, user fees offer the potential to be robust, stable funding sources. To be sure, it is important to be aware of the equity implications of more reliance on user fees. But there are many ways to provide safety nets to protect those unable to afford basic services, and equity should not be used as a pretext for subsidizing those who can afford to pay for the services they use.

6. California Comes of Age: Governing Institutions, Planning, and Public Investment

Elisa Barbour and Paul G. Lewis[1]

When infrastructure is working, most of us do not think about it. When it becomes crowded or rundown, we think first about fixing or expanding it rather than the decisionmaking process for providing it. However, if the institutional framework for making decisions about long-term public investment no longer reflects or facilitates underlying social and political agreements, it may need to be revisited. These turning points may be experienced as crises, and we are fortunate that they are rare. However, they also provide opportunities to adapt to changing needs.

Has California reached such a turning point? By the late 1990s, a series of policy reports indicated that the state faced critical infrastructure deficiencies.[2] Voters and elected officials subsequently increased spending on new infrastructure and on the rehabilitation and maintenance of existing facilities, but their efforts were soon undercut by a series of political crises, including electricity system breakdowns, an unprecedented budget gap, and the recall of a sitting governor. More long-standing political concerns such as widespread voter discontent with

---

[1]For an extended discussion of the themes raised in this chapter and for more details regarding the three infrastructure sectors, see the occasional paper *California Comes of Age: Governing Institutions, Planning, and Public Investment* (Barbour and Lewis, 2005), available at www.ca2025.org.

[2]See Legislative Analyst's Office (1998b); California Business Roundtable (1998); California State Treasurer (1999); Center for the Continuing Study of the California Economy (1999); Neuman and Whittington (2000); California Commission on Building for the 21st Century (2002); Dowall and Whittington (2003).

government, partisan gridlock in the state legislature, recurrent budget crises, and antagonism between the state and local governments only added to worries about governments' ability to plan, finance, and deliver an adequate level of infrastructure.

In considering these problems, many commentators pointed to an earlier so-called "golden era" in California, when under the leadership of Governors Earl Warren (1943–53), Goodwin Knight (1953–59), and particularly Edmund "Pat" Brown (1959–67), the state built higher education, water supply, and highway systems that became the envy of the nation and even the world. Comparing that era to the current one has led many to conclude that the state's governance system is failing to provide for current and future needs for public investment.

This chapter seeks to answer several questions. How do California's infrastructure concerns relate to its system of governance? What are the origins of current governance challenges for public investment, and what are potential solutions? Can we draw useful parallels to dilemmas faced by state leaders of the past; and if so, what can we learn from their responses? We address these questions by tracing changes in government decisionmaking for surface transportation, water supply, and higher education since World War II. Turning to the future, we conclude the chapter by evaluating emerging opportunities for governance reform.

California's Golden Age

California's largest public projects—including the State Water Project, the Master Plan for Higher Education, and the state highway system—were passed during Pat Brown's tenure about four decades ago. Although much has changed since that time, the political context of that era forms a useful parallel to the current period. Many policy challenges were similar, including strain on existing infrastructure facilities following decades of rapid population growth and lagging investment, pressure to enhance educational opportunities resulting from demographic change and economic restructuring, and planning and governance challenges posed by new patterns of urban development.

As today, lawmakers in the postwar period were concerned about the need to expand infrastructure facilities. During the Great Depression and World War II, many projects such as new roadways had been placed on hold, but the war launched California as a major economic power and the state experienced a postwar economic and population boom. One hundred new cities, mostly suburbs, were incorporated in the state during the 1950s and 1960s. Rapid suburbanization was fueled by economic prosperity and by public policies, including federal homeownership assistance, new road building, and financing and service-delivery innovations—special-purpose districts, in particular—that enabled smaller suburban jurisdictions to escape dependence on central cities (Fishman, 1987; Hise, 1997; Pincetl, 1999).

Although the state's young, fairly homogeneous population was willing to invest in growth and development, governing arrangements inherited from the past were not well-suited for a major expansion of facilities. In earlier decades, central city governments had built many of the large-scale infrastructure projects, but new patterns of urban development rendered this approach inadequate. As suburbanization transformed metropolitan areas into aggregates of multiple, diverse jurisdictions, local governments petitioned the state for help with large projects. Yet, even as funding was increased for many programs, certain broad governance conflicts still forestalled large-scale expansion plans. For example, proposals for expanding water supplies opened up divisions between the northern and southern parts of the state and between agricultural users and city dwellers. Similarly, as higher education was widely advocated to support the state's burgeoning high-tech manufacturing industries, competition for college and university campuses intensified among regions and segments of the educational system.

A concerted state approach finally emerged under the tenure of Governor Pat Brown, who had support from the state's first Democratic-controlled legislature in the 20th century. As the economy entered a recession, pressure to sustain spending for social services had led to large deficits, focusing lawmakers' attention on the need for more efficient, coordinated growth policies. A rise in federal aid for domestic infrastructure also helped propel Brown's expansionist approach to state infrastructure. Most infrastructure "mega-projects" of the 1950s and 1960s in the United States were largely financed with federal money and carried out by state agencies and regional authorities, leaving just a minor role for local governments (Altshuler and Luberoff, 2003). The confluence of population growth, legislative support, and federal financing allowed Governor Brown to broker difficult political deals to create large infrastructure projects.

None of these projects, however, represented a radical departure from those undertaken or proposed by his predecessors. Rather, Brown's effectiveness lay in his ability to translate the prevailing sense of urgency for reform into pressure to force political compromises among warring interest groups, thereby translating pending proposals into long-term commitments. Brown also galvanized support for the new projects by passing the first significant tax increase since the early 1940s and using large bonds for capital construction for the first time.

Brown's legacy suggests that a major priority for leaders at such turning points is to forge consensus and to prod key interest groups to negotiate so that public investments can move forward. The plans ratified under Brown's leadership also led to new institutional arrangements, which have been as influential in shaping development and nearly as long-lasting as many of the physical systems themselves. To illustrate this point, we turn to the three infrastructure sectors.

A Statewide Freeway System

California was the first state to make a substantial, sustained commitment to metropolitan freeway construction after World War II. Under Governor Brown, the pace of building reached full throttle. The state highway system, today worth $300 billion (California Department of Finance, 2003b), is the largest public works project built in the United States by a single organization (Taylor, 1992).

The State Highway Plan, adopted in 1959, was the culmination of policies that consolidated the state government's role in urban road-building. The state had passed a gasoline tax in 1923, but funds were directed to rural road maintenance. As property taxes flattened out during the Great Depression and World War II, local governments petitioned the state for help. Los Angeles, for example, developed the earliest and boldest plan for metropolitan freeways in the nation in 1939, but the project was shelved for lack of funding. In 1947, the State Division of Highways was given major responsibility for designing and building urban freeways, and motor vehicle fees were increased. The federal Interstate Highway Act of 1956 set the freeway-building era in full motion, as Congress committed $28 billion to build a 41,000-mile Interstate Highway System, with funds provided on a nine-to-one matching basis to states (Jones, 1989).

The federal legislation also charged state highway departments, such as California's Division of Highways, with planning and construction of the new system. In 1958, the division prepared a dramatic 20-year, statewide plan to upgrade 12,240 miles of highway to limited access design in a latticework system based on the Los Angeles model. The plan met with near-universal support (Jones, 1989, Taylor, 2000). From 1956 to 1972, more than 1,300 centerline miles (12,700 total miles) of new freeway were added, increasing total state system miles by 28 percent.

However, because federal and state agencies were paying for the new highways, their prerogatives frequently won out over local land-use plans. For example, Los Angeles's highway aspirations helped prod the state, but the freeway system eventually built there differed markedly from the city's original vision. The initial Los Angeles plan, which emphasized regional parkways integrated with transit lines and park and recreation facilities, was jettisoned in favor of uniform federal and state highway design standards (with higher speeds, more grade separation, wider lanes, and longer ramps) imposed without regard for potential joint development with transit or local redevelopment (Jones, 1989; Taylor, 1992; Wachs and Dill, 1999). In their efforts to avoid protracted intergovernmental planning and interfering with metropolitan land uses, state planners primarily accommodated a particular pattern of local land use—auto-dependent suburban development (Taylor, 1992).

A State Water System

Water policy followed the same general pattern as transportation policy. In the postwar era, the state government adopted a more active and dominant role to develop a statewide system. This required a monumental engineering feat in a state in which the majority of residents lived in the south but the majority of water originated in the north. It also required an equally impressive political feat, as Governor Brown secured the support necessary to build the world's largest and most complex hydraulic system.

Local governments were the most ambitious builders of water systems in the early 20th century. Los Angeles and San Francisco built aqueducts to meet existing needs and to propel new growth. Attempts to develop a state water plan during the 1920s and 1930s evolved into a more limited effort—the Central Valley Project, soon transferred to the federal Bureau of Reclamation—to deliver water from the Sacramento River to the San Joaquin Valley. It remains the state's largest single water supplier.

During the postwar boom years, the state government moved to coordinate a system for increasing supplies statewide, responding especially to needs in Southern California, where agriculture was threatened by depletion of groundwater. In 1945, the State Engineer released an audacious plan for the California Water Project (also called the State Water Project or SWP). The Feather River would be dammed and a conveyance constructed to direct water south along a 750-mile route first to the San Francisco Bay Delta, then through an aqueduct to the San Joaquin Valley, and from there to Southern California. The plan contemplated building two of the world's biggest dams, the world's longest aqueduct, and the world's most powerful pumps to convey water over the Tehachapi Mountains (Reisner, 1993). In 1956, the Department of Water Resources was established to implement the plan, consolidating 52 other agencies (Hundley, 2001).

However, formidable political obstacles stymied this ambitious vision. Northerners resisted efforts to send "their" water south. Although San Joaquin Valley farmers strongly supported the proposal, Los Angeles did not. Another obstacle was the project's cost, which was projected to be as high as $3 billion, equivalent to about $14 billion today. Governor Brown made passage of the plan a personal crusade on which he staked his political reputation. "I was absolutely determined that I was going to pass this California Water Project. I wanted this to be a monument to me," Brown later recalled (Reisner, 1993, p. 349). Crossing the state to meet with stakeholders, he offered a series of key concessions, offering bond sales for local projects to northerners and reassuring southerners that water contracts under the plan would not be abrogated while the bonds remained outstanding (Hundley, 2001). Costs of the project were downplayed; a bond issue of $1.75 billion was proposed that would only partially complete it. Nevertheless, the bond was nearly as big as the entire state budget itself and was at the time the largest ever considered by any state. Brown secured legislative passage of the measure in 1959. Although voters in 48 of 58 counties voted against the bond measure, support in the southern counties helped carry the measure (Reisner, 1993).

The scale of the State Water Project and the bond measure to pay for it attest to the scale of Brown's political accomplishment. More even than the highway and higher education systems, the water system concretely unified the state through a statewide development strategy. But the slim margin of victory for the bond measure and its partial payment for the whole plan indicate that the underlying consensus was weak and that more conflicts would likely lie ahead.

A Master Plan for Higher Education

Perhaps more than any other product of the Brown era, California's system of public higher education became a national, even international, model. The state's Master Plan for Higher Education, a compact reached under Brown's leadership, committed California to a social contract as well as a set of governance arrangements. More than 40 years later, it still frames programmatic and facilities requirements for higher education.

In the years after World War II, many states attempted to create more coherent higher education systems. Unlike other large states, California based its system on the relative autonomy and the sharp delineation of its three segments—the California Community Colleges, the California State University system, and the University of California system. The elements of this tripartite system can be traced to Progressive Era policies around the turn of the last century when the University of California was granted an unusual degree of autonomy in the state constitution and the nation's first network of junior colleges also was established (Douglass, 2000). By the 1920s, UC's reluctance to build new campuses prompted a "regional college movement" calling for state support in transforming existing teaching and technical colleges into full-fledged liberal arts colleges that would eventually coalesce as the CSU system.

Enrollment demand soared in the postwar years as veterans took advantage of the GI bill and workers sought training for jobs in manufacturing and technology. Proposals for rapid expansion, especially of state college campuses, brought policymaking turmoil (Smelser and Almond, 1974). UC officials fought attempts by the state colleges to expand into graduate training. Lawmakers introduced bills to establish campuses, viewed as critical for regional development, in their districts. Segmental leaders, especially UC officials, attempted to resolve differences; but negotiations frequently broke down. By indicating that he was willing to exert his full authority to achieve a more orderly path of expansion, Governor Brown helped produce a compromise that formed the basis for the 1960 Master Plan. Segmental leaders viewed the moment as their last chance to control the outcome and retain autonomy from state government. Their compact—reached at the eleventh hour and ratified by the legislature—delineates the segmental missions and governance arrangements. UC retained a virtual monopoly over academic research and the granting of doctoral degrees, and the CSU system gained governing autonomy.

With 10 campuses today, UC is designated the state's primary research and doctorate-granting institution. Under the Master Plan, it must offer admission to any California resident in the top one-eighth of his/her high school graduating class. The CSU system, with 23 campuses today, is a regional system whose primary mission is to educate through the master's degree level, especially to provide technical and teaching degrees. CSU must offer admission to the top one-third of the state's high school graduates. The 109 locally oriented campuses of the CCC system are charged with providing academic, vocational, and remedial instruction at the lower-division levels and must admit any student capable of benefiting from instruction. The Master Plan also links these institutions through matriculation policies. This so-called transfer function makes California's system greater than the sum of its parts (Douglass, 2002, p.85).

The structure was promoted as a cost-saving measure, which helped earn legislative approval. Clear policies for admission, transfers, and funding permitted orderly planning, including for facilities. Yet as Douglass (2002) notes, "The Master Plan did not represent a major shift in the policy development of California's higher education system. Rather, it represented a political compromise at a critical historic moment" (p. 96). That compromise has proved remarkably durable and influential. The stable policy environment enabled California to provide high rates of access and high quality at low cost to taxpayers and students, compared to peer state systems.

Retreat and Transition

The highways, water systems, and college campuses built during the 1950s and 1960s are still with us, but the confidence and consensus that launched them began to wane by the 1970s. The investments of the postwar era helped transform the state in ways that provoked public backlash and led to higher costs for development, ultimately rendering the postwar policymaking approach obsolete. Communities protested against invasive projects such as highways, and government costs increased for mitigating negative local impacts. A broad environmental movement emerged in response to air and water pollution; and federal and state environmental bureaucracies were created to enforce new regulations for clean air and water, endangered species protection, and toxic waste disposal, among others. Requirements for environmental review slowed down development planning and increased its cost. Project costs also rose because of the very prosperity fostered by postwar investments, as land acquisition costs skyrocketed in increasingly built-up metropolitan areas and labor and materials also became more expensive. Anti-tax sentiment emerged among voters in response to rapidly rising property taxes, and voters passed a series of statewide ballot initiatives (starting with the landmark Proposition 13 in 1978) to constrain governments' ability to raise revenue.

As the state and federal governments increasingly were forced to absorb new (or overlooked) social and environmental transactions costs of investment, infrastructure investment declined both in California and nationally. The two California governors during the period—Ronald Reagan (1966–1975) and Pat Brown's son Edmund "Jerry" Brown (1975–1983)—were from different parties but shared the view that growth in public spending should be limited. The lower investment levels of the new "era of limits" are reflected in Figure 6.1, which shows

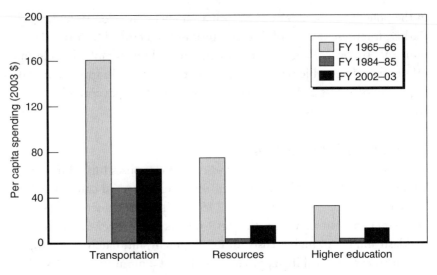

SOURCE: de Alth and Rueben (2005).

**Figure 6.1—Per Capita State Capital Outlay Expenditures by Budget Area,
Fiscal Years 1965–66, 1984–85, and 2002–03**

declines in real per capita capital outlay expenditures in the three state
budget areas pertaining to the sectors discussed in this chapter, from
fiscal year 1965–66 (late in Pat Brown's tenure) to 1984–85, a low point
in state infrastructure spending (Dowall and Whittington, 2003). Even
by fiscal year 2002–03, state capital outlay spending in these areas was
well below postwar levels.[3]

---

[3]Capital outlay expenditure is not only the responsibility of the state government,
of course. de Alth and Rueben (2005) compiled data from the Census of Governments
on state and local capital outlay spending in California in five-year intervals since 1957.
Their data indicate that real per capita spending for higher education facilities in
California dropped from a peak in 1967 of $51 (in 2002 dollars) to 55 percent of that
level by 1982 and has not exceeded 79 percent of the peak level since. Combined state,
federal, and local spending on highways and roads in California also peaked in 1967, at
$227, declined to a low of 28 percent of that level in 1982, and remained below half the
peak level during the 1980s and 1990s before rising sharply to 68 percent of the peak in
2002. Spending on mass transit facilities—tracked only starting in the 1970s—increased
steadily in relation to highways and roads from about one-tenth as much during the
1970s to half as much by 1997. However, even when mass transit, highway, and road
spending are combined, total transportation capital outlay spending did not regain even
half the peak 1967 level for highways alone until 1992. Even the sharp increase in
transportation spending between 1997 and 2002 (44%) raised spending to only 85

In transportation policy, the era of limits was reflected in a shift in direction during the 1970s toward promoting mass transit as an alternative to highways and roads. This reflected concerns about rising air pollution, congestion, and fuel shortages (Jones, 1989). However, the rapid demise of the state's highway building boom also reflected a "cost-revenue squeeze," as costs rose rapidly for construction, urban rights-of-way, and community and environmental mitigation, whereas gasoline tax revenues declined in real terms as mandated vehicle fuel efficiency standards reduced the amount of fuel sold (Jones, 1989; Taylor, 1992). In 1973, the Division of Highways was replaced by Caltrans, a new multimodal transportation agency whose mandate emphasized flexibility, efficient use and maintenance of existing resources, and greater collaboration with local and regional agencies (Taylor, 2000).

Water policy also faced serious constraints. The State Water Project bond passed under Pat Brown could not deliver the full 4.2 million acre-feet that had been promised to cities and rural irrigation districts, and Governor Jerry Brown attempted to complete his father's project. Finishing that project was far more difficult than launching it, however, as costs for the completion stage were projected to be two to five times more than for the initial stage. Moreover, Brown's proposal for a Peripheral Canal, a conveyance channel around the deteriorating San Francisco Bay Delta, became the focus of intense controversy. When environmentalists argued that it would divert too much water from the degraded Bay Delta, Brown proposed a constitutional amendment that purported to ensure the Delta's water quality and keep North Coast rivers wild and scenic forever. Even so, the Peripheral Canal proposal was soundly defeated in a 1982 statewide referendum, opposed by all sides in the water debate. The measure's defeat, the first for a major

---

percent of the peak 1967 level for highways and roads alone. The intertemporal comparison is problematic for the water sector, as data for early years are incomplete. These comparisons are for capital outlay only; noncapital outlay spending (for such functions as operations and maintenance) in these categories generally has risen steadily since the postwar era. When capital and noncapital outlay spending are combined, total spending for highways, roads, and mass transit in higher education has increased steadily since 1957. Total spending remained below peak postwar levels (for highways and roads alone) during the 1970s and 1980s but exceeded those levels by the 1990s.

water project since the 1920s, marked an end to the supply-side approach that had characterized state water policy (Hundley, 2001).

No such public outcry arose against college-building in the transitional period, but growing anti-tax sentiment among voters, combined with relatively flat enrollment rates until the late 1980s, helped usher in a period of lower investment and scaled-down expansion. More than eight times as many new campuses were established from 1945 to 1975 as from 1975 to 2000 (Douglass, 2002).

Growth Pressure Builds Again

The 1980s were a parallel to the years after World War II—a time during which growth pressures built to a critical stage. By the 1990s, policymakers faced a daunting set of challenges similar to those faced by postwar lawmakers: strain on existing facilities and planning challenges posed by new patterns of urban development and economic restructuring. Just as during the Brown era, these challenges provoked a shift in governance approaches.

California added more than 10 million new residents during the 1980s and 1990s, a population gain of 43 percent. Growth spilled to inland areas, but coastal areas also changed rapidly. As population pressure strained public facilities, changing patterns of urban development, related in particular to employment decentralization, raised planning challenges that traditional governance arrangements were not well-suited to address. The rate of job growth was higher than population growth during the 1980s and 1990s. Gains in suburban employment contributed to a steep rise in car use in spite of efforts to encourage mass transit as an alternative, and more complex commuting and travel patterns complicated transportation planning in metropolitan areas.

In another parallel with postwar developments, education became a major policy concern by the late 1980s because of climbing enrollments and underlying issues related to economic restructuring. The labor market has changed in recent decades with the rise of a knowledge-based economy, global competition, and the decline of manufacturing jobs. As higher education became an increasingly important determinant for securing well-paid employment, income inequality among workers also widened (Reed, 1999).

The basic character of these challenges is reminiscent of the postwar era. However, the state also has changed dramatically since then, and many of the changes make it harder to aggressively pursue new public investments.

The state's population has grown more diverse. In 1970, non-Hispanic whites constituted 77 percent of the state's population, but by 2000, they were 47 percent, and by 2025, they are projected to form about 32 percent to 35 percent (California Department of Finance, 1999, 2004a). This trend is even more pronounced among the state's college-going age group. By 2025, non-Hispanic whites are expected to constitute only one-quarter (27%) of 18 to 24-year-olds, while Hispanics are expected to constitute half (California Department of Finance, 2004a).

The policymaking environment has grown more complex. Governance is complicated by multiple state, local, and regional infrastructure agencies, often organized on a single-function basis. At the state level in 1960, there were 22 state departments; now there are 11 agencies, 79 departments, and over 300 boards and commissions (Neumann and Whittington, 2000; California Performance Review Commission, 2004). At the local level, an indication of complexity is the number of special districts—single-purpose governing units that provide services such as water, sewers, utilities, and public transit. Special districts rose especially rapidly in number during the postwar period; by 2002 there were more than 2,800 (U.S. Census Bureau, 2002b).

Many more private and nonprofit interest groups also seek a seat at the table today when the state makes development decisions—groups that range from environmentalists to neighborhood organizations to labor and business representatives. Policymaking is more contested, as activists have made increasing use of such tools as local and state voter initiatives and litigation to press for various causes.

Governments today also face higher costs and tighter fiscal and environmental constraints than in the past. Costs have risen substantially for land, materials and labor, and environmental and community mitigation. For example, the average ratio of annual inflation-adjusted capital outlay expenditures to each new road mile added in the United States was more than three times higher during the 1990s than during the early 1960s (Hanak and Barbour, 2005).

Meanwhile, Californians' commitment to environmental protection remains strong (Baldassare, 2004a). As development has extended outward, environmental and economic goals have come into sharp conflict in some areas, for example, where new development impinges on precious remaining natural habitat on the urban fringe, and as regional planners struggle to meet state and federal air quality mandates in spite of rapidly rising car use. As remaining sources of water pollution also increasingly have been traced to farmers, urban dwellers, and local land-use practices, the nexus between transportation, land use, and the environment has grown more problematic.

Fiscal constraint also has increased conflict among local governments and between the state and local governments. As revenues were squeezed after the passage of Proposition 13, local governments pursued policies to maximize fiscal returns, including skewing land-use policies to favor certain development such as retail sales (Lewis and Barbour, 1999). In an atmosphere of competition and constraint, regional policy coordination is difficult, although many local policies have effects beyond local borders. The relationship between local governments and the state also grew strained in recent years as the state government reduced local funding during budget crises.

Attitudes about growth and government also have changed since the postwar era. As Mark Baldassare and Jon Cohen discuss in Chapter 8, Californians are more likely to feel pessimistic about growth and also about government's ability to address their needs effectively (see also Baldassare, 2000, 2002a, 2004a). To limit governmental spending and discretion, voters made increasing use of state and local ballot initiatives during the 1980s and 1990s. Examples include successful efforts to mandate certain levels of education spending, to subject local tax increases to a supermajority vote, and to limit the number of terms state legislators may serve. At the local level, voters reacted to growth-related problems by the late 1980s by passing hundreds of local growth-control measures across the state; local ballot activity subsided somewhat by the

1990s, but it continues to influence development activity (Glickfeld, Graymer, and Morrison, 1987; Fulton et al., 2000).

Moving Beyond Bricks and Mortar

In a tightening vise of higher costs, growing demand for services, and fiscal and environmental constraints, administrators and planners in specific policy domains considered new strategies by the 1990s. Planners shifted their priority from building new physical capacity as the principal method for meeting future infrastructure needs. They sought instead to encourage more efficient use of existing systems and resources. The great state plans of the Brown era, and the governing institutions that implemented them, were revisited or revised, no longer considered suitable for contemporary needs. In particular, the top-down, single-function, engineering-driven approach to planning that was a hallmark of the Brown era is now increasingly viewed as ineffective as two needs have become more urgent: the need to consider policy tradeoffs and the need to reintegrate growth management (for land use, infrastructure, and the environment) at an efficient scale matching natural and social systems—often the bioregional and metropolitan scales.

Transportation

Transportation governance was fundamentally altered in the early 1990s in response to fiscal constraint and policy confusion. Traditional methods for accommodating travel demand were being questioned. A doubling of real per capita funding on transit capital outlay in California from 1972 to 1992 had failed to reverse the tide of increasing car use during the 1980s, and transit lost share to single-occupancy car use for commutes in most metropolitan areas (a trend that reversed slightly the following decade) (de Alth and Rueben, 2005; U.S. Census Bureau, decennial). Highway expansion was also viewed skeptically as a means to reduce congestion: Research suggested that as long as drivers desire more mobility than can be accommodated by an existing roadway system, increases in capacity may be quickly consumed as travelers shift from alternative modes or routes, and as land development responds to new road supply (Hansen and Huang, 1997; Cervero, 2003). Meanwhile, many of California's metropolitan areas were in violation of clean air standards, with automobile emissions a major factor.

In this context, funding and programming authority was pushed downward to regional and local agencies. California's Transportation Blueprint for the 21st Century, endorsed by state voters in 1990, designated transportation agencies in the state's 32 urbanized counties to oversee a program to reduce congestion and improve integrated planning for land use, transportation, and air quality. The federal government adopted a similar approach but empowered regional (metropolitan) rather than county agencies. Congress passed the Intermodal Surface Transportation Efficiency Act (ISTEA) in 1991; this legislation required that regional agencies take the lead in long-range planning and address potentially conflicting transportation and environmental policy goals (as did its sequel, passed in 1998). ISTEA also allowed about half of all federal funds to be used flexibly across program categories (Lewis and Sprague, 1997). California's Senate Bill 45, passed in 1997, completed the state's devolution by giving regional agencies responsibility for programming all federal and state funds for capital improvements in metropolitan areas. Numerous funding categories were combined into more flexible block grants. However, with funds allocated based on county shares (by population and lane miles), the regional planning role was somewhat undermined in multicounty areas (Innes and Gruber, 2001). County-level authority also was enhanced by optional "self-help" county sales tax measures. In recent years this source has accounted for one-third of local funding for transportation in the state (Legislative Analyst's Office, 2000a).

This new governance system promotes greater flexibility, strategic management, and policy integration at a regional scale. Regional agencies have devised innovative techniques blending transit with highway spending and demand-side with supply-side strategies. For example, they have combined HOV highway lane designation with peak-period toll lane pricing for single-occupant vehicles and have initiated Bus Rapid Transit service, a cheaper alternative to rail (Legislative Analyst's Office, 2000b). Regional agencies use performance measures to systematically examine alternatives in relation to cost-benefit, mobility, environmental, equity, and other objectives (Hanak and Barbour, 2005).

"Smart growth" strategies reflect greater integration of transportation with land-use planning. In all the state's major metropolitan areas, performance modeling is used to test not just alternative transportation program scenarios but also land-use scenarios. In the San Diego, San Francisco Bay, and Los Angeles areas, smart growth land-use plans were adopted as the basis of recent long-range transportation plans, in effect committing the local governments that ratify the plans to denser development. Some transportation funds also were provided to encourage implementation.[4]

However, the obstacles to success in the new system are also formidable. County and regional transportation agencies are essentially confederations of local governments, local transit providers, and the state department of transportation.[5] Although federal and state laws may mandate regional plans, the governmental agencies that compile and adopt them are not accountable at a regional scale to voters or to many specific performance mandates. Facing fiscal constraint, local governments may find it difficult to set aside parochial self-interest in favor of the "regional good." So-called regional plans sometimes resemble stapled-together lists of priorities of multiple jurisdictions more than clearly articulated regional strategies (California Transportation Commission, 2002). This parochial tendency is reinforced by the system of transportation funding, which also emphasizes jurisdictional equity. For example, with transit funds distributed to counties based on track or vehicle mileage or population rather than ridership, suburban systems receive deeper subsidies per transit rider than more heavily patronized

---

[4]In the San Diego area, the recently adopted Regional Comprehensive Plan commits $25 million in transportation funds over five years for localities that adopt supportive land-use policies. The half-cent sales tax for transportation passed in November 2004 includes $250 million over 40 years for local infrastructure improvements integrating land-use and transportation objectives and $850 million for environmental mitigation including acquiring and maintaining regional natural habitat preserves. The Sacramento area regional transportation plan commits $500 million over 23 years for smart growth community grants, whereas in the San Francisco Bay Area, $27 million annually is targeted for projects integrating transportation and land use or encouraging high-density housing near transit.

[5]In most of the state's major metropolitan areas, designated agencies are COGs, voluntary organizations of local governments that tend to operate on a one-government, one-vote basis.

central city systems, which are often strapped for funds (Taylor, 1991; Wachs, 1997; Garrett and Taylor, 1999). If transit funds were geared instead to promote regional efficiency, congested commuter corridors and highly used central city systems might be prioritized. Smart growth programs also are somewhat undermined by conflicting state policies. For example, environmental review requirements focused at the project level tend to deter infill development, and fiscal constraint and uncertainty render it difficult to provide infrastructure to support infill.

The state can fortify this system by providing policy focus and institutional support for regional planning. For example, it could implement performance-oriented policy mandates at the regional scale, restructure governing arrangements of Councils of Government, allocate regional transportation funds on a competitive basis for performance-oriented objectives, or allow regions to raise gas taxes to fund coordinated transportation and land-use investments. It could also enhance planning stability and efficient use of resources with a shift to a transportation revenue system based more on growth-indexed user fees (such as by increasing the gas tax or introducing a fee on vehicle miles traveled). In addition to providing revenue predictability, transportation economists widely agree that higher user fees would encourage efficiency by assessing drivers more of the full social costs of their vehicle use (Taylor, Weinstein, and Wachs, 2001; Wachs, 2003b). Similarly, reforms are needed to overcome current fiscal and regulatory land use incentives that work against regional coordination. For example, more incentives could be targeted toward land development that is oriented to regional transportation needs.

Water

Like transportation planning, water policymaking during the 1990s underwent a governance transformation. Federal law had established new water quality standards and mandated that the needs of a new constituency—wildlife and plants—be accommodated. By the 1990s, a new bioregional approach to regulation emerged, through such measures as health and environmental standards developed for bodies of water (Mazmanian and Kraft, 1999; Ruffolo, 1999). A severe drought from 1987 to 1992 brought matters to a head especially in the San Francisco

Bay Delta, a 700-square-mile region that, in addition to being the largest wetland habitat in the western United States, also forms the hub of California's two largest water distribution systems (the SWP and CVP). As localities enforced conservation measures while some fish species neared extinction, calls for greater coordination and more efficient water use emerged (Landy, Susman, and Knopman, 1998; Hundley, 2001).

To address Delta water concerns, the state and federal governments organized CALFED in the early 1990s, a collaborative effort among federal, state, and local agencies and other stakeholders. When development of an implementation plan became protracted, Governor Gray Davis and U.S. Interior Secretary Bruce Babbitt helped fashion a compromise by 2000. The first phase of an ambitious 30-year plan called for a range of measures, including conservation, Delta restoration, the elimination of barriers to water transfers, groundwater management, levee maintenance, a state Environmental Water Account to protect endangered species, and the raising of dams. Water costs were meant to reflect, as much as possible, the principle of "beneficiary pays" (Martin, 1999; Vogel, 1999; Lewis and Clemings, 1999; Hundley, 2001; McClurg, 2004).

Like its predecessor, the SWP, CALFED aims to meet and balance long-term water needs among competing users across the state. But its approach reflects important changes in the planning landscape. Rather than an engineering-driven bureaucracy intent on building a "big piece of plumbing," CALFED is a consensus-building and planning institution whose aim is to manage demand through negotiation as well as to increase supply. Ultimately, it aims to create an integrated, more efficient system to address environmental needs along with the needs of other users. But in spite of its collaborative approach, controversy resurfaced when the program quickly ran short of funds. By 2004, with federal support lagging and little progress made on implementing the beneficiary pays principle, conflicts erupted over side deals negotiated by some participants with state and federal agencies. Reminiscent of postwar dilemmas, observers looked to the governor to help resolve the conflicts (Boxall, 2004; Leavenworth, 2004b). The governance challenges parallel those in transportation, suggesting that collaborative arrangements are vulnerable without coordinated state programs and fiscal incentives to support them.

Southern California experienced similar controversies. During the drought of the early 1990s, the federal government threatened to enforce legal limits on use of Colorado River water, limits that California has traditionally exceeded by up to 20 percent (Brackman and Erie, 2002). Faced with this looming constraint, Southern California water agencies entered protracted negotiations, resolved in 1999 only after Governor Davis and Interior Secretary Babbitt intervened. California agreed to reduce its use to the legal limits over 15 years through water transfers to the urban sector and conservation in the agricultural sector through methods such as land fallowing, canal seepage recovery, desalination, groundwater banking, and "conjunctive use"—the purchasing of supplies for storage underground as reserves against times of need (Totten, 2004). When talks broke down again in 2003, the U.S. Department of the Interior forced a resolution by cutting California's allotment of Colorado River water (Krist, 2003).

A regional approach to integrated water management also has been promoted at a smaller scale through state support for regional groundwater basin and (surface) watershed management initiatives.[6] Collaborative initiatives have produced innovative approaches linking water quality, supply, and land use. However, observers conclude that they work best as a supplement to traditional regulatory approaches and

---

[6]A 1992 law (AB 3030) provided a systematic procedure for local agencies to develop groundwater management plans. This policy was strengthened in 2002 with passage of SB 1938, conditioning receipt of state funds for construction of groundwater projects on clearly defined objectives and monitoring protocols for groundwater levels, water quality, and subsidence. The Integrated Watershed Management Program, established in 2002, facilitates watershed-level planning for quality and supply reliability. The Integrated Regional Water Management Planning Act of 2002 authorized regional multipurpose water management planning and directed DWR to target grants and loans to help promote it. Bonds passed in 2000 and 2002 (Propositions 13, 40, and 50) allocated over $2 billion for regional management and watershed protection programs. Related measures that strengthen the connection between water and land-use planning include SB 610, passed in 2001, which requires that new residential development projects of more than 500 units demonstrate availability of adequate water supplies. SB 221, passed the same year, imposes a similar requirement at the point of subdivision map approval.

that local government land-use practices are critical to success (Kenney et al., 2000; River Network, 1999).

Just as in the transportation sector, efforts to encourage efficiency and coordination have not been limited to new governance arrangements but also rely on innovative demand-management and supply-side techniques for enhancing capacity. For example, a series of steps in the 1990s helped establish water markets in California, in which supplies are traded among willing purchasers and sellers (Hanak, 2003). Conservation is another technique aggressively being pursued by coastal water districts through programs such as promoting low-flush toilets and water recycling. Innovative supply-side solutions include conjunctive use; more than 65 water agencies in the state operate groundwater recharge programs (Totten, 2004). However, full implementation of conjunctive use may require more concerted state groundwater regulation. Systematic conjunctive use programs are difficult without adequate information and monitoring of groundwater quality and levels. Furthermore, groundwater concerns also complicate water marketing, as many worry that farmers may sell surface water and pump groundwater in its place. With many groundwater basins in the state already being overdrafted, the threat of critical land subsidence problems could worsen (Hundley, 2001; Totten, 2004).

Thus, California has been moving incrementally toward a more coordinated system of water planning that better allocates costs and benefits and integrates policymaking within and across regions and for environmental and economic needs. Such goals are evident in the recent draft update to the State Water Plan, which aims to integrate large- and small-scale regional plans and programs (California Department of Water Resources, 2004). The plan relies on a stakeholder agreement process and, as with transportation planning, on performance modeling of numerous management scenarios with varying assumptions for urban and rural land use, industrial activity, conservation efforts, and other factors.

Just as in transportation, however, the obstacles to effective governance are substantial. A more coordinated system must overcome institutional fragmentation, as thousands of local water districts still operate relatively independently across the state. And as in transportation, agreements reached through voluntary collaboration may be easier to reach in theory than to implement in practice. Thorny questions also persist about how to allocate costs for environmental water needs.

How can the state government strengthen water policy? As in transportation, state reforms should provide a coherent policy, governance, and fiscal framework of incentives and (when required) mandates to promote coordination and efficiency. Groundwater regulations and outcome-oriented performance standards could be strengthened to help provide focus for regional plans. Fiscal responsibilities must be clarified, for example, by resolving how to apply the beneficiary pays principle. Support could be increased for regional management initiatives that promote state objectives. The role of state leaders in brokering major water deals also will remain critical. Today, the long-term stability of water planning relies on commitment from multiple stakeholders to resolve conflicts in an ongoing, coordinated way. State leaders should avoid the temptation to broker side deals with some parties for the sake of political expediency and should focus instead on ensuring the viability of collaborative processes.

Higher Education

For decades, higher education planning was an orderly process, but the early 1990s were a turning point. A severe state budget crunch led to student fee increases and enrollment caps, and a flurry of reports in the late 1990s and early 2000s raised concerns about capacity and access.[7] In the early 2000s, student fees were increased sharply again, and expected enrollments dropped because of fee hikes and course cancellations. In early 2004, over 7,000 qualified applicants were initially denied admission to UC and CSU. Although funding was later

---

[7]See for example, California Postsecondary Education Commission (1995a, 1995b, 1999, 2000); California Higher Education Policy Center (CHEPC) (1996); Benjamin and Carroll (1998); California Education Roundtable (1998); Breneman (1998); Legislative Analyst's Office (1999, 2004g); California Citizens Commission on Higher Education (CCCHE) (1999); Little Hoover Commission (2000b); Dowall and Whittington (2003); Murphy (2004); and Shulock (2004).

restored in the state budget, this was the first such violation of the access tenets of the state's Master Plan since 1960.

Critics have charged that the Master Plan's inflexibility has made new solutions to these problems difficult to implement. The tripartite structure suited the state when it embodied the social consensus on which the original Master Plan was founded. Higher subsidies per student for the "high quality" institutions—in particular the University of California system—were justified based on its research role (which supports economic growth) and because of the equity and access provisions of the Master Plan. Its promise of equal opportunity was articulated when a more homogenous population was believed to have equal access to resources, so that ascension through the tiered levels of the higher education system would be based on choice and merit.

Various demographic and economic changes may be eroding these assumptions. College-going, transfer, and graduation rates vary considerably across racial and ethnic groups. They are particularly low for Latinos, African Americans, and Native Americans. Along with rising student fees, these patterns have raised concerns about the promise of economic opportunity through postsecondary education. Preserving quality is also a concern and has raised a host of questions. Given the role of research institutions in supporting California's knowledge-based industries, should they be given funding priority? Or should more funds be targeted to community colleges, which play a growing role in educating the workforce? The largest such system in the nation, CCC is expected to enroll 67 percent of new students from 2002 to 2012 (California Department of Finance, 2003c), but the system also faces pressure to provide remedial education, improve lagging transfer rates, and meet the growing demand for two-year terminal vocational and academic programs. In balancing these objectives with more limited funds, the CCCs will face complex tradeoffs between access and quality.

Today, basic elements of the Master Plan are being reconsidered or reframed. There are some common themes in recent proposals:

- Ensuring budgetary stability (such as through increasing student fees and offsetting financial aid for needy students to help preserve equity goals).

- Enhancing productivity (such as through varying fees or prioritizing access by education level and profession and through performance standards for institutions and learners).
- Enhancing efficiency (such as through varying fees to encourage rapid graduation rates, streamlining the transfer function, redirecting students from high-cost to lower-cost institutions, expanding existing campuses rather than building new ones, and instituting year-round operations).

Proposals for governance reform also are promoted, such as regional coordination among K–12 and higher education institutions to better address student and workforce needs, and more centralized management of the CCC system.

Reflecting many of these concerns, the legislature's Joint Committee to Develop a Master Plan for Education released a proposal to revise the Master Plan in 2002. It recommends greater linkages with K–12, more centralized governance of the CCC and K–12 systems, greater collaboration among segments through means such as expanding joint doctoral programs and cross-segmental instruction, development of an accountability system, strengthening of the transfer function, and greater use of alternative facilities. Governor Schwarzenegger's recently released *California Performance Review* picked up on many of these proposals, calling for consolidating education policy from preschool through postgraduate level, reorienting the educational system to meet the needs of the labor market, implementing performance-based accountability standards, streamlining transfer requirements, establishing CCC enrollment priorities, and permitting CCCs to offer bachelor's degrees. Governance for CCC and K–12 would be consolidated, with the powers of the CCC Board of Governors transferred to the state community college chancellor, who would report to the governor's education secretary. This arrangement would substantially alter the governance system of the Master Plan, creating, in essence, a unified K–14 system while retaining governing autonomy for the UC and CSU systems.

Leadership from the state government is needed to ensure that the Master Plan does not collapse without a new structure to take its place. The challenge, as in the other sectors, is to step back from traditional assumptions about functional and jurisdictional boundaries to consider needs that cross those boundaries. In education particularly, the basic goals of the system need to be clarified before proper governance arrangements can be implemented. Governor Schwarzenegger's proposals take a step in this direction, articulating not just a reoriented governance system but also a new vision for the goals and priorities of the system itself.

New Calls for Reform

As these discussions indicate, reforms in transportation, water, and environmental governance have reoriented decisionmaking arrangements to address new realities. Planning authority has been devolved to more collaborative, often regional decision processes. A major objective is to reintegrate local land-use planning with other growth policy areas, and a collaborative approach to governance allows that without usurping local government prerogatives. This approach is politically expedient in a state with a strong tradition of local control.

However, although collaborative approaches may be politically expedient, they tend to be ineffective if they lack clear policy goals or if they are undermined by conflicting incentives or mandates. As it stands, the new collaborative approach is grafted onto a system whose fundamental lines of authority and responsibility remain unchanged; and the extent to which policymaking has been altered should not be exaggerated. State departments are still organized largely on a single-function basis, land use is still a prerogative of local governments, and very little regulatory or revenue-raising authority is vested in regional governmental bodies.

California lacks a coordinated policy framework to support growth management. This shortcoming is evident, for example, in the absence of clear objectives and priorities guiding regional transportation planning, the sometimes conflicting mandates and fiscal incentives that shape local land-use policy, and the lack of a clear regulatory framework for groundwater management. Many funding and governing incentives still deter a comprehensive focus on problems and solutions defined regionally or statewide—from the structure of COG governance and transportation funding allocations, to decentralized governance of much water policymaking, to the set-in-stone quality of segmental boundaries in higher education. As a result, gains from recent governance reforms often have been limited or ephemeral.

Perhaps the clearest steps toward establishing a more unified state and regional growth policy framework involve the development of system performance measures. In all the sectors studied in this chapter, state and regional agencies made some progress during the 1990s in developing objective, performance-oriented measures of program outcomes. These measures allow tradeoffs to be modeled among complex goals and alternatives and help provide focus for planning and accountability in more collaborative governance frameworks. However, effective implementation of performance *standards* (as opposed to measures) can ultimately emerge only as part of a more strategic, coordinated state approach to growth management.

Many observers have concluded that a more strategic approach to state investment is needed.[8] In response to these concerns, a few incremental steps have been taken at the state level to promote integrated investment planning. In 1999, a new requirement was established for the governor to submit an annual five-year capital improvement plan, but the first two editions, released in 2002 and 2003, generally failed to clarify overarching priorities (Legislative Analyst's Office, 2002d). In 2002, Assembly Bill 857 was passed, requiring that state agencies develop consistent planning and spending priorities based on a set of smart growth principles—promoting infill development, protecting environmental and agricultural resources, and encouraging efficient development patterns. It remains to be seen whether these policy goals will be translated into effective program mandates.

In 2004, Governor Schwarzenegger's *California Performance Review* was released, containing more than 1,000 specific recommendations for improving efficiency in state government. Many align with our own—from increasing vehicle user fees, to developing better system performance measures and accountability standards, to promoting regional water planning and better integration of plans for land use, infrastructure, and environmental protection. The report also called for

---

[8]See the citations in footnote 1 of this chapter.

consolidating state administration, including establishing a new Infrastructure Department that would consolidate 32 programs in six sectors (water; energy; housing, building, and construction, including for schools; transportation; telecommunications; and boating and waterways). The inclusion of housing programs expands the traditional definition of state infrastructure. To facilitate more strategic, integrated planning, three oversight divisions would operate across the six sectoral divisions to integrate planning, programming, research and development, and financing. It is too early to know which of these proposals will receive support from the administration and legislature. However, the scope and emphasis of the proposed reforms underscore the central message of this chapter—that broad governance and fiscal reform is necessary to guide public investment policy.

Toward 2025: The Governance Challenges of Public Investment

California is now potentially at a point of departure in its approach to infrastructure governance as important as that of the Pat Brown era. Although the state faces critical long-term infrastructure challenges, the solutions of the past—in particular, large-scale facilities expansion—are less feasible now. The following nine trends make it highly unlikely that another Pat Brown figure will lead the state in that direction. The overall theme that emerges is the increased level of *complexity* in state and local policymaking.

1. *The decline of confidence in government.* Not unique to California, residents tend to view government and politicians with distrust and suspicion. Residents are mildly more positive about their city and county governments but even at that level they believe that officials waste a significant proportion of revenues (Baldassare, 2004b, p. 24). Politically, therefore, today's elected leaders are on a considerably tighter leash than were Governors Earl Warren or Pat Brown and are unlikely to expend sizable amounts of political capital on major (and potentially controversial) infrastructure projects. Even the current popular governor may be constrained in what he can

accomplish; his appeal during the campaign rested in part on promises to restrain the power of politicians and entrenched interests in Sacramento.

2. *Increased use of the popular initiative.* The wave of citizen activism and anti-government criticism of the 1960s and 1970s found its institutional expression in the increased use of voter initiatives, many of which sought to bypass public officials in the policymaking process or to limit their power and discretion (Silva, 2000). Compared to the postwar era, deals cut with college presidents, water users, and elite state commissions are now more vulnerable to end-runs by aggrieved interests resorting to the direct democracy process. At the local level, too, efforts by local officials to coordinate planning with neighboring jurisdictions may be undone by voter-led ballot measures.

3. *Reduced potential for "entrepreneurial" state policy leadership.* A corollary of the above two trends is the reduced capacity of state policymakers to craft visionary solutions to California's infrastructure problems. Term limits and staff reductions (brought about by a voter initiative) limit the legislature's capacity to build substantive expertise in such areas as transportation or higher education. Likewise, gerrymandered districts and political polarization in the legislature impede "middle way" solutions that could appeal to Californians across partisan and regional divisions.

4. *More interests at the table.* Governance today is complicated by multiple state, regional, and local agencies—many of them with single functions and still insulated from public scrutiny. Interest groups and so-called stakeholder organizations (a term that did not exist during the Brown era) also have proliferated in recent decades, and many have full-time staffs and lobbyists in Sacramento. This trend has complicated the deal-making necessary to change infrastructure policies.

5. *Fiscal constraints.* In a state that is now much more built-up, the costs of constructing and improving public facilities are far higher than in the Brown era. Furthermore, voters have constrained government's ability to raise revenue. In this environment, governments have often focused on the need to meet basic funding needs of operational services, turning capital facilities into a luxury accessible only in years of bounty.

6. *Reduced federal funding for bricks-and-mortar investment.* For most of U.S. history, Congress lavished substantial attention on "internal improvements" such as dams and highways. The rise of federal programs geared toward assistance to individuals (Social Security, Medicare and Medicaid, welfare, and assistance to the disabled, among others) has shifted the federal budget increasingly toward transfer payments and away from physical infrastructure. Although federal infrastructure spending recovered in the 1980s and 1990s, federal involvement has splintered into new areas (such as homeland security equipment, and more emphasis on mass transit facilities). Moreover, federal infrastructure programs have faced the same cost-escalation pressures as have state programs, leaving little room for major new building programs.

7. *Devolution and concern with regional and local control.* As the federal and state governments seemed to disengage from grand approaches to infrastructure provision—in part because of contentious local disputes that spilled into state and national policy arenas—local governments, regional agencies, and more ad-hoc public-private assemblages increasingly stepped into the policymaking void. Federal and state policymakers sympathetic to devolution, or wary of centralized responsibility, have often funded, enabled, or encouraged such tendencies, notably through such efforts as Senate Bill 45 and CALFED. Any would-be Pat Brown in California would need to work in careful partnership with these decentralized policy processes and be

comfortable with the lack of direct state control over many investment decisions.

8. *Disjuncture between the electorate and the population as a whole.* In recent decades, a noticeable difference has emerged between the state's relatively young, increasingly foreign-born, and majority nonwhite population and the state's registered voters, who are older, predominantly native-born, and nearly 70 percent non-Hispanic white (Citrin and Highton, 2002). During the postwar era, in contrast, there was less of a demographic divide between voters and the general public; and overall rates of voter participation were higher. The current disjuncture highlights the challenges of state and local leaders building consensus around a collective vision of serving Californians' future needs.

9. *Confusion about goals for growth-planning and investment.* As Mark Baldassare and Jon Cohen show, Californians of all political stripes, ages, and racial/ethnic backgrounds tend to feel pessimistic about growth and governments' ability to plan for the future. Voters demonstrate a continued willingness to issue bonds or increase taxes for such purposes as schools, transportation, open space, housing, and water projects, but they feel more comfortable if funding is carefully targeted. This trend may reflect a desire to regain a lost sense of control over the shape of future growth, but it also hampers the ability of elected leaders to craft comprehensive dialogues about the shape of future growth in the state. Growth planning is now a complicated balancing act among multiple, sometimes conflicting goals and objectives for efficiency, equity, quality of life, and environmental protection. Although some decisionmaking frameworks have emerged in which such deliberation can occur, they are not widely known, and Californians still indicate substantial confusion and disagreement about how the state should prepare for its future.

Infrastructure Governance in a Mature State

The transition from an approach emphasizing massive statewide engineering projects to a broader consideration of the costs and effects of potential investments across metropolitan areas ultimately seems a healthy one in a mature state. Complexity can hamper decisionmaking, but effective collaborative arrangements may balance policy objectives and state, regional, and local needs and concerns more effectively than either imposed top-down solutions or fragmented, laissez-faire localism. The protections now offered to environmental values, community self-determination, mitigation of the harms of projects, and fiscal restraint can be carried to excessive lengths in some instances, but they are also values that most Californians seem likely to embrace, at least in general terms. In any case, there is no putting the genie of policy complexity back into the bottle. Moreover, we suspect that the reasons for such complexity have much to do with democratic values of inclusiveness and full debate.

Given these challenges and constraints, what can state leaders do to set a more deliberate course toward meeting future needs? First, consider those models that help point a way forward. In the midst of all the current obstacles outlined in this chapter, new governance frameworks have emerged that reestablish deliberative, comprehensive decisionmaking on growth. Although they may not look like the great infrastructure engineering plans of the past, processes such as CALFED are, in their own way, equally impressive in scope and impact. As the vice president of the Metropolitan Water District of Southern California recently noted, "Though they are messy and difficult, participatory collaborative processes such as CALFED are the only way we are getting anything done in the state" (Quinn, 2004).

Second, consider the basic elements that make these models work. Leaders now must often secure political agreements not on how to allocate *more* services and facilities but on how beneficiaries of state services can make do with *less*. A basic incentive for participation in collaborative arrangements today is mutual gains through more efficient use of facilities or resources. Stakeholders are drawn to the negotiating table not just by the promise of new facilities but also often by the potential for gaining predictability in service delivery and regulation and by reducing transaction costs and regulatory requirements through a more deliberate and coordinated approach to conflict resolution. Government leadership is critical in helping align incentives and in mediating the allocation of costs and risks to support effective processes and outcomes.

Rather than being based on one-time political agreements for single-purpose blueprints meant to address public works needs for several decades, the new models are more apt to rely on gaining political support for stable, pluralistic, ongoing decision processes. We are not suggesting that long-range investment plans are less important today than in the past or that all cooperative planning processes will be ongoing. However, given the policymaking environment of constraint and complexity, today's plans are more likely to require periodic reevaluation. The goal is to accomplish this in a coordinated way rather than through defaulting to conflict and short-term crisis management. In spite of its weaknesses, California's transportation planning system provides the state's most well-developed model for such a purpose. By providing clear rules and incentives to guide a stable *process* of ongoing intergovernmental planning coordination, it institutionalizes the development of long-range yet evolving (regularly updated) investment plans. However, although the transportation sector succeeds at keeping stakeholders at the table, it still lacks sufficient policy focus to produce plans with clear, regionally oriented objectives.

Effective state reforms for public investment should accomplish three interrelated goals: align incentives and costs (responsibility and authority), provide a policy focus, and foster strategic, coordinated decisionmaking processes for implementation. At the level of state departments and agencies, reforms can be more mandate-driven. The state government can clarify growth policy goals and priorities, translate them into quantifiable outcome-oriented policy objectives, and require more integrated planning to model alternative program scenarios. State investments and program priorities then should be made congruent with this strategic planning process.

However, the state also needs to foster more strategic, coordinated planning *across* levels of government and, in particular, within regions. A more coherent approach by the state toward its own investment policies will help greatly in this endeavor. Even without intergovernmental planning, the state can promote preferred regional outcomes through more strategic targeting of its own investments and by aligning fiscal incentives. Similarly, ensuring greater funding stability would help stabilize planning processes and possibly make them less contentious. Going further, quantifiable growth policy objectives also could be used as the basis for new mandates or preferential grants or loans to local and regional agencies that aim to meet the standards. Even further, state incentives might be made available on a regional basis contingent on collaborative development of regional growth plans that further state priorities.

Models for this sort of strategy exist. In particular, the new approach to environmental regulation that emerged by the 1990s emphasizes a clear policy focus coupled with collaborative implementation at a bioregional scale. Programs such as ISTEA (in conjunction with the Clean Air Act) and watershed initiatives focus regional planning on attaining clear health and environmental standards, but implementation is left to collaborative processes among multiple actors. These programs helped propel many of the collaborative planning innovations of the past decade, especially because they relied on building closer links with local land-use and infrastructure planning.[9]

Today, the state is less in need of new large-scale physical infrastructure systems than coordinated governance and fiscal systems to help guide strategic investment. Specific reforms to establish a clearer framework might include the following:

---

[9]Other states have gone further in applying this approach to policy areas other than environmental protection. For example, a transportation planning rule passed in Oregon in 1991 mandated that regional plans work to reduce congestion and per capita vehicle miles traveled and that local governments orient land-use designations and densities to support multiple transportation modes, infill development, and a jobs-housing balance. Along with other growth policies and programs, including urban growth boundaries and protections for agricultural land, the new transportation rule prompted a dramatic shift in Portland's approach to development (Calthorpe and Fulton, 2000).

- Establishing performance-oriented state growth objectives to guide state and regional plans and investments;
- Reconsidering the governing arrangements of regional transportation agencies;
- Establishing incentives for local governments—through tax base sharing, tax increment financing, targeted grants, loans, or mandate relief—to promote state and regional growth objectives and neutralize the adverse fiscal consequences of land-use policies that promote the objectives;
- Raising gasoline taxes and other user fees to better align costs and benefits;
- Providing regional revenue-raising authority, contingent upon and linked to coordinated capital investment and land-use plans;
- Integrating local government planning requirements and the California Environmental Quality Act to promote more "up-front" consideration of the large-scale environmental effects of development choices;
- Strengthening groundwater management regulation;
- Resolving how the beneficiary pays principle is interpreted and implemented;
- Setting performance goals for institutions of higher education and students; and
- Promoting cooperation across higher education institutions within each region, with a focus on emerging needs of the labor market.

Also key to effective growth planning will be to acknowledge and address voter skepticism and desire for fiscal constraint. Strategies might aim to promote more comprehensive dialogue and debate on integrated investment plans, while also respecting voters' expressed preferences for local control, intergovernmental cooperation, and targeted investment. In spite of certain drawbacks, ballot and bond measures on new investment and development often form the most effective forums for dialogue and deliberation on growth concerns. One way to incorporate voters in integrated investment decisions would be to authorize regional revenue-raising authority, subject to voter approval, to fund coordinated environmental and infrastructure improvement plans. Such plans might include parks and open space along with transportation improvements and incentives to local governments to orient land use toward regional goals and objectives.

Given fiscal and political pressures and constraints, lawmakers face a substantial incentive to ignore long-term fiscal and governance concerns in favor of short-term political victories or because they are busy "putting out fires." However, the price of political expediency is rising. Meeting infrastructure needs will require concerted governance and fiscal reforms that may not be as dramatic as grand facilities programs of the past but could be just as far-reaching. State leaders must meet this challenge if future quality of life is to be fostered thoughtfully and not by default. Postwar policymakers rose to a similar challenge, adapting governance and fiscal arrangements to meet changing needs. Should we ask less from our leaders today?

7. Understanding Equitable Infrastructure Investment for California

Manuel Pastor, Jr., and Deborah Reed[1]

All Californians rely on public infrastructure. It brings the water we drink, the energy that lights our homes, the classrooms where our children are taught, and the roads that take us to work. Public infrastructure provides a building block for education, health, and economic opportunity. Perhaps because of the importance of infrastructure in improving quality of life and opportunity, there has been a growing policy emphasis on equitable infrastructure investments. Indeed, state law clarifies the intent of infrastructure planning priorities to "promote equity, strengthen the economy, protect the environment, and promote public health and safety" (Assembly Bill 857, Chapter 1016, Statutes of 2002).

Infrastructure, by its nature, is not distributed equally across communities. Transit service tends to be better in densely populated urban areas where it is efficient to provide. Roads and highways are less expensive and less congested in rural areas. Whereas purely equal investments may not be attainable or even desirable, a notion of "fair treatment" underlies equitable approaches. For example, Senate Bill 115 (1999) calls for "the fair treatment of people of all races, cultures, and incomes with respect to the development, adoption, implementation and enforcement of environmental laws and policies." More generally, the concept of equity can apply to comparisons across any social groups such as those defined by region, income, gender, race, ethnicity, or age. However, in the context of existing inequalities, equitable investment

---

[1]For a fuller discussion of the issues raised in this chapter, see the occasional paper *Understanding Equitable Infrastructure Investment for California* (Pastor and Reed, 2005), available at www.ca2025.org.

policies often refer particularly to low-income and minority communities. For the California Department of Transportation (Caltrans), for example, the "policy goal of promoting fair treatment . . . means ensuring that low-income and minority communities receive an equitable distribution of the benefits of transportation activities without suffering disproportionate adverse impacts" (California Department of Transportation, 2003c).

Equitable infrastructure investment is a multidimensional concept (see PolicyLink, 2005). It often concerns equitable access to the benefits of infrastructure, such as in the Caltrans policy or equitable access to funding resources, such as California's Critically Overcrowded School Facilities program, which creates a priority allocation of state bond funds for facility needs in districts with overcrowded schools. Equitable financing considers whether revenue sources place disproportionate burden on some groups. The Legislative Analyst's Office (2001), for example, has proposed a financing policy for school facilities that takes into account a community's ability to pay. Equity considerations may involve the broader consequences of infrastructure investments, such as Caltrans programs to abate adverse environmental impacts or the Alameda Corridor Transportation Authority's efforts to create local jobs as part of a rail project. Equitable investment also involves participation in decisionmaking, such as Caltrans planning grants to projects that "Identify and engage low income and minority communities early in the transportation planning process" (California Department of Transportation, 2004b).

Recognizing the complex and multidimensional nature of equitable investment, this chapter is intended as a conceptual framework rather than an exhaustive study of infrastructure and equity. We seek to frame the infrastructure equity issues facing the state rather than to prescribe specific policies the state should follow. Whereas we focus our discussion on the equity issues in infrastructure investments, we recognize that policy considerations must take into account a wider range of goals. We begin with rationales for equitable infrastructure investment. We then consider key infrastructure equity issues and related policy in transportation, school facilities, higher education, and environmental justice. Finally, we outline broad components that shape the future of infrastructure equity. We maintain that equity should be an integral part of the vision for California as the state plans and invests for the future.

Infrastructure, Opportunity, and Equitable Growth

The first rationale for equitable infrastructure is that it can create opportunities for communities that have been left behind by California's economic growth. Low-income families have not shared equally in economic growth in California and in the United States. Infrastructure investments play a role in shaping economic growth and, through more equitable investments, infrastructure can improve opportunities for low-income families and communities.

This rationale takes on more importance when we consider the income patterns in California over the last several decades. In 2002, incomes of low-income families were lower in real terms than incomes of similar families in 1969 (Figure 7.1). Over the same period, incomes of

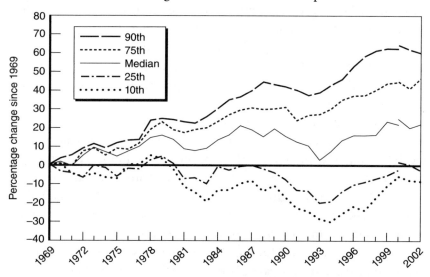

SOURCE: Reed (2004) from the March Current Population Survey, 1970–2003.
NOTES: Income is adjusted for family size and for inflation (to 2002 dollars). Because of a change in the survey methodology, two estimates are provided for 2000.

Figure 7.1—Percentage Change in California Family Income Relative to 1969 by Income Percentile, 1969–2002

middle-income families showed a 22 percent gain, and families at the high end of the distribution showed a 60 percent increase. One primary driver of this income pattern has been the growing value of education in the California labor market. California workers with a college education have seen their earnings rise, whereas those with a high school education have lower earnings today than did similar workers three decades ago (Reed, 1999, 2004; Reed and Cheng, 2003).

The provision of school facilities, a key infrastructure investment, creates educational and thus economic opportunities. Building and maintaining quality K–12 facilities support children's learning. As we will describe below, there are critical facilities deficits in some California communities, particularly in schools that serve low-income, Latino, and African American children. Furthermore, poor facilities likely limit the ability of these schools to attract highly qualified teachers. A survey of California teachers found that poor school facilities were an important factor in teachers' decisions about where to teach (Harris, 2002). In the area of higher education, facilities challenges include deferred maintenance and growing enrollments. Improving poor and overcrowded K–12 school facilities and expanding capacity in higher education will likely improve educational opportunities for low-income children and youth.

Highways are another form of infrastructure investment that shapes the pattern of economic opportunity. In a recent survey, scholars ranked the federal highway program as the most important influence on the American metropolis (Fishman, 1999). By facilitating movement between distant areas, highways spur economic and population growth in areas outside the central cities. Other federal policies have also fueled suburbanization. In the same survey, the second-ranked influence on suburbia was the Federal Housing Administration's low-down-payment, long-term, fixed-rate mortgage. Between 1945 and 1965, these mortgages were restricted to newer housing, mostly on the suburban fringe. Although federal funds have also targeted inner city revitalization, their effects have been comparatively minor (Dreier, Molenkopf, and Swanstrom, 2001; Pastor et al., 2000; Wolch, Pastor, and Dreier, 2004).

State and local policy has also directed economic activity away from the state's urban areas. Faced with limited property tax revenues after the passage of Proposition 13 in 1978, many California cities have adopted land-use policies designed to promote retail and raise local sales tax revenue. Insofar as this "fiscalization of land use" has pushed residential development beyond city limits, it has led to sprawl and may exacerbate spatial mismatches between jobs and housing (Lewis and Barbour, 1999; Little Hoover Commission, 2002). In addition, educational policy has not been able to redress the large differences in quality between schools that serve central city neighborhoods and those that serve suburban neighborhoods (Betts, Rueben, and Danenberg, 2000; Sonstelie, Brunner, and Ardon, 2000). As a result, many young families with the means to do so have moved to the suburbs, as have many employers. Between 1990 and 2003, total nonfarm employment in Los Angeles County fell by 3.5 percent but grew by 21.6 percent in Orange County and by 52.6 percent in the Riverside–San Bernardino area.

In light of this pattern, many analysts have concluded that, on balance, suburbanization has worsened social equity (Orfield, 1997). The pattern of residential and economic growth in outlying areas has coincided with a concentration of low-income families, as well as Latino, African American, and Asian families, in more densely populated areas and central cities (Figure 7.2). Thus, investments in highway infrastructure and other public policies have contributed to a "spatial mismatch" between urban areas with high concentrations of low-income and minority residents and outlying areas with strong job growth (Kain, 1992). In the California context, Raphael (1997), for example, shows that African American males in the San Francisco Bay Area tend to live in areas with weak or negative employment growth and that differential access to employment explains up to 50 percent of the neighborhood employment rate differences between white and African American youths. Similarly, Pastor and Marcelli (2000) gauge the difference between a neighborhood's skill base and the educational requirements of proximate employment for Los Angeles County and find a downward effect on wages for full-time male workers, especially African Americans.

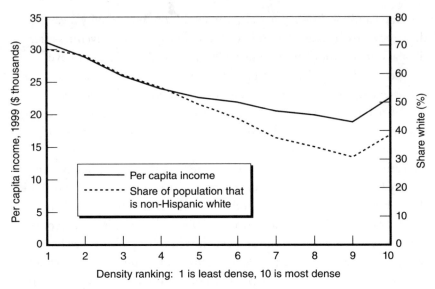

Density ranking: 1 is least dense, 10 is most dense

SOURCE: Author's calculations from 2000 census data.

NOTES: Density is measured by persons per square mile of residential land and is divided into deciles. Analysis is based on census tracts.

Figure 7.2—Neighborhood Density, Income, and Race in California, 2000

One infrastructure-based approach to bridging the spatial divide is to expand transit routes from central cities to suburbs. The federal Job Access Reverse Commute (JARC) program was established in 1998 to address the transportation challenges of low-income workers including reverse commutes from cities to suburbs. The JARC program has not been comprehensively evaluated (Multisystems, 2003), but research for California finds that improving job accessibility for transit users significantly augments the employment prospects of low-skill workers without cars in San Francisco and Los Angeles (Kawabata, 2002; see also Blumenberg, 2002).

Another approach to improving opportunities in central cities is to promote economic development in low-income communities. Infrastructure investments could play a role in attracting employers, for example, by providing better road conditions and transit for the movement of goods, workers, and consumers (California Department of Transportation, 2003c). Improved schools and open space infrastructure could help attract and retain higher-income families which, in turn, might promote further economic development. One concern with this approach is that a wave of "gentrification" could displace current residents (Wyly and Hammell, 2000). Thus, refocusing investment on central cities in an equitable fashion might also require policies and tools to limit or ameliorate the effects of displacement (McCulloch, 2001). Another concern with development in central cities is that it not further exacerbate pollution and other adverse environmental conditions. We return to this concern below in a section on "environmental justice."

The expanding trade infrastructure in Los Angeles is an example of infrastructure projects that, proponents argue, will create jobs that are well suited to the educational and skill levels of Southern California's existing labor force. Traditionally, that labor force has relied on manufacturing jobs, but that sector has been shrinking rapidly since 1990 (Los Angeles County Economic Development Corp., 2004). SCAG is looking to jobs in the logistics industry, in which training is often provided on-the-job, to provide wage structures in which workers can move up to mid-wage jobs. However, furthering trade in Southern California could have adverse consequences for mid-wage manufacturing employment because of crowded roads and rails and increased foreign competition for local firms (Haveman and Hummels, 2004).

The discussion in this section illustrates the complex equity consequences, intended and unintended, of infrastructure investments. Our intent is not to argue that any specific investment is good or bad for equity but rather that infrastructure is a public choice that helps structure the nature of educational and employment opportunities in a region and that these critical decisions should be made against a backdrop of increasing income inequality and with equity in mind.

Infrastructure Equity, Growth, and Fiscal Efficiency

The notion of strengthening infrastructure investments in the neediest communities and in low-income, central city communities may raise concerns about whether these investments will come at the expense of other communities. Our second rationale for these investments is that they may actually promote broader economic growth in a cost-effective manner. The evidence for this claim comes from a variety of findings emerging in the research literature. Taken together, these lines of research suggest that, in some circumstances, equitable infrastructure investments may promote broader growth and fiscal efficiency.

Comparative studies of economic growth across nations have found that countries with lower income inequality tend to have more economic growth (see Thorbecke and Charumilind, 2002, for a review of this research). Research comparing regions across the United States has found that reducing gaps in the distribution of income is associated with improvements in regional growth (Voith, 1998; Pastor et al., 2000). This regional research also concludes that investments that lead to reduced poverty in central cities may actually promote regionwide growth, thus providing broad benefits. Other work indicates that the stability of city finances affects the economic well-being of surrounding areas (Haughwout and Inman, 2002).

The potential for broad economic gains from improving conditions in central cities has been of recent interest to private business leaders. Johnson (2002b) maintains that enlightened self-interest has driven business leaders to tackle inner city problems and that doing so has become a strategic imperative in the global marketplace. In Charlotte, for example, business leaders focused on highway, rail, and airport infrastructure that would position their city as the anchor of a regional distribution system and ensure that the urban core would not hollow out (Pastor et al., 2000). The Bay Area Council, a leading business group in the San Francisco area, has identified poverty as one of the top five challenges to doing business in that region. The council is taking steps to encourage business investment in impoverished communities partly to develop market opportunities but also because of a sense that fuller inclusion of low-income workers and families in the regional economy will improve the business climate.

Another line of research studies the advantages of investing in densely populated areas—sometimes described as a form of "smart growth." Investments in dense areas are likely to be equity-enhancing because low-income families tend to live in dense communities. For example, scenario models for the San Francisco Bay Area find that smart growth strategies of focusing investments in dense areas yield an increase in housing and jobs in impoverished communities (Association of Bay Area Governments, 2002).

Proponents of the sort of smart growth investments that could improve equity also suggest that there are positive impacts on fiscal efficiency. Muro and Puentes (2004) argue that a more compact style of development over the period 2000–2025 could reduce road-building costs at the national level by nearly 12 percent, save 6 percent on water and sewer spending, and save 4 percent on annual spending for operations and service. For these and other reasons, Michigan Governor Jennifer Granhold has created a statewide leadership council on land use, arguing that the current approach to infrastructure investment supports sprawl and impedes the efficient provision of public services.

An emerging literature is considering whether smart growth investments will foster economic growth. Conceptually, the hypothesis is that with dense development, businesses are located closer to consumers and closer to each other, and this closeness will lead to gains from greater specialization, division of labor, and lower input prices. Several studies suggest that such "economies of agglomeration" tend to support aggregate growth (Boarnett, 1998; Haughwout, 1999; but see also Garreau, 1991). Decentralized infrastructure, in contrast, may forgo these agglomeration opportunities (Ciccone and Hall, 1996; Cervero, 2000; and Anthony, 2004). Nelson and Peterman (2000) conclude that regions that employ growth-management techniques saw a gain in their share of income relative to other regions, controlling for other factors that affect growth.

But if more compact growth and central city development is more efficient than urban sprawl, why do more metropolitan regions not choose it? One answer lies in the split between private and public costs. Whereas compact development might be better for the metropolitan region or state as a whole, building in outlying areas is often easier and more profitable for developers. Reversing this incentive structure has been the logic behind Maryland's smart growth initiative, which seeks to reduce or eliminate state infrastructure spending outside designated "Priority Funding Areas." A newly adopted proposal in Contra Costa County also restricts funding for new roads to areas within an existing urban area.

Taken together, these lines of research highlight the potential economic advantages of promoting equity. The research on smart-growth-type investments in dense areas has not generally been conceived in an equity framework. However, given the demographic profiles of California's dense areas, these infrastructure investments could also promote equity for low-income and minority residents.

Equity and Political Consensus

A third rationale for promoting equity in infrastructure investments is that equity may help build the political consensus required for large public projects. Basic political logic suggests that investments with broad benefits have more popular appeal. Beyond the simple logic of broad benefits, perceived inequities in the costs and benefits of public investments may erode public support, with literature from the field of experimental economics suggesting that potential deals, even ones with mutual gains, can be derailed by perceptions of extreme inequity (Guth, 1988). Because the empirical work around the potential role for equity in promoting political consensus is still in its infancy, we illustrate our point with two case studies from Southern California: the Nueva Azalea power plant and the Alameda Corridor.

In 2000, California's energy crisis created considerable pressure to expand the power grid quickly. Sunlaw Energy approached the city of South Gate with plans to build a natural-gas-powered power plant, poetically named Nueva Azalea. To assuage fears about air pollution, the company promised to use a new pollution-control system that had been deployed only in mini-generators. Because this was to be the first test of this technology at that scale, many environmentalists supported the project, as did the county's central labor council. The combined support of environmentalists, labor unions, and business interests seemed to make the project a political as well as an economic winner.

Some community members and city leaders of South Gate, however, were less enthusiastic. They argued that a new plant, no matter how clean, was too large a burden in a community that already hosted numerous pollution-emitting facilities as well as heavy truck traffic from both its own industrial sites and a nearby freeway. Eager to move forward, Sunlaw Energy proposed a citywide referendum and underwrote a campaign that included ads, community picnics, and a float in the city's Christmas parade. In the end, however, roughly two out of three city voters opposed the project, and the company withdrew its plans (Martin, 2001a, 2001b).

Why was the plant defeated? The overriding issue for voters was equity. They were persuaded that the solution to a general problem—namely, a statewide shortage of electricity—would impose disproportionate costs on their community. Indeed, they rejected what might have been a win-win outcome, as the plan's failure left in place a truck terminal and its associated diesel emissions. Still, the perceived sense of inequity drove both public sentiment and eventually decisionmaking.

In contrast to the Nueva Azalea case, the development of the Alameda Corridor shows how incorporating community concerns facilitated progress on public infrastructure and secured a broader distribution of its benefits. Originally conceived in the 1980s, the Alameda Corridor is a high-speed, below-grade rail line designed to transport goods from the Los Angeles ports to transfer stations and then to consumers in the rest of the country. Proponents argued that the project would have long-term positive environmental impacts in poorer areas of the Los Angeles region, primarily because rail traffic was causing truck delays at nearly 200 grade crossings and thereby increasing air pollution (Erie, 2004, p. 151).

However, the project raised equity issues that focused mostly on job creation. The project was of particular interest because the corridor ran through the "rust belt" area of Los Angeles, whose shrinking manufacturing base had worsened employment prospects for low- and mid-skilled workers. Moreover, those worsening prospects were associated, both statistically and in the popular mind, with the international trade that the corridor was meant to facilitate (Pastor, 2001). Proponents predicted that the investment would generate 10,000 construction jobs and at least 70,000 new jobs throughout the United States in trade-related industries, but many officials in the cities adjoining the corridor were concerned that their constituents would not fill those jobs. They filed a 1995 lawsuit (dismissed in 1996) centering on environmental and other concerns, but the underlying tensions arose because the Alameda Corridor project had, in the words of UCLA planning professor Goetz Wolff, "no explicit linkages between the construction of the corridor and actual job creation and business development in the corridor cities" (Ohland, 1995).

The Alameda Corridor Transportation Authority sought to defuse the tensions by working with developers, municipalities, and community groups to allocate 30 percent of the total hours on the project to new hires. One such community group was the Alameda Corridor Jobs Coalition, a group that was initially spearheaded by a church-based community development corporation and eventually included 60 community and labor organizations spanning 11 cities. Once demands were heard and negotiated, conflicts gave rise to consent and collaboration, including a key role for the community organizations in terms of recruitment of residents for the new training and employment programs. In the end, the project was completed on time, under budget, and with an impressive level of community and municipal support. As noted above, SCAG is now arguing for expanded trade infrastructure, not only because it will facilitate growth but also because it will create jobs that are well suited to the region's workforce. Again, there are reasonable disputes as to whether the SCAG strategy will worsen environmental disparities or come at the cost of other manufacturing jobs, but the fact that SCAG leaders are now explicitly including equity considerations when proposing new infrastructure suggests that lessons around the benefits of community inclusion have been incorporated into their thinking.

Equity Issues in California's Large Infrastructure Sectors

With these three rationales in mind, we turn to equity issues in the state's largest infrastructure sectors: transportation, K–12 school facilities, higher education, and water. In addition, we discuss environmental justice issues because of their importance as an infrastructure equity concern. We describe equity-related policies within each infrastructure sector and document major equity concerns, relying primarily on existing studies. We do not provide a comprehensive analysis of equity measures in each sector. Such analysis is highly valuable and might allow for measurement of the degree of progress toward equity, comparisons between regions and across states, and broad evaluation of specific policies intended to improve equity. However, in light of the paucity of available data and the breadth of equity issues that we seek to address, our discussion is based on equity measurements and concerns raised by existing studies.

Transportation

We begin with transportation, a key infrastructure investment that has shaped economic development and helps determine economic opportunities. The policy context for transportation has been formed by a series of federal policies mandating equitable investments. Title VI of the 1964 Civil Rights Act requires that the Federal Highway Administration and the Federal Transit Administration ensure that any programs and agencies that receive their financial assistance do not exclude, deny benefits, or discriminate on the basis of race, color, national origin, age, sex, disability, or religion. The Federal-Aid Highway Act of 1970 requires equitable treatment of communities affected by transportation projects including effects on residences, businesses, the tax base, and other resources. In 1994, President Clinton signed an executive order for environmental justice mandating that federal agencies address "disproportionately high and adverse human health or environmental effects . . . on minority populations and low-income populations." In 1997, the U.S. Department of Transportation issued an order explicitly extending the environmental justice issues beyond health and environment to include community economic vitality, employment effects, and displacement.

All state and metropolitan transportation agencies receive federal funding and are bound by these federal mandates. Studies by these agencies as well as independent researchers generally find that public transit service tends to be better in low-income and minority neighborhoods (Metropolitan Transportation Commission or MTC, 2001; Center for Urban Transportation Research, 1998). One reason for this is that these groups are more likely to live in densely populated urban areas, which lend themselves to efficient public transit. A fuller analysis of equity concerns would compare transit service between high-income and low-income neighborhoods that were similarly situated in dense, urban areas. Furthermore, analysis should consider whether transit service is sufficient to meet the needs of low-income neighborhoods whose residents have limited access to vehicles. For example, a recent study found limited transit access to health facilities and supermarkets for low-income communities in the San Francisco Bay Area (Transportation and Land Use Coalition of the Bay Area et al., 2002).

In the area of public transit, an important equity concern is whether expensive public investments serve high- and low-income communities equally. Two commuter rail projects—the extension of Bay Area Rapid Transit to the San Francisco Airport and the extension of the Metro Gold Line in Los Angeles—have absorbed a large portion of federal transit money coming to California. For low-wage transit riders who do not commute to a central business district, bus systems are often more useful than commuter rail. For example, the NAACP Legal Defense Fund filed a high-profile civil rights lawsuit against Los Angeles County's Metropolitan Transportation Authority (MTA) on behalf of a group called the Bus Riders' Union (BRU). The BRU argued that rail commuters, representing only 6 percent of the overall public transit ridership, were receiving 70 percent of the MTA's spending (Pastor et al., 2000, p. 61). Some have argued that investments in commuter rail can actually increase the time and money costs of existing transit users when bus lines are eliminated (Garrett and Taylor, 1999; DeLong, 1998). On the other hand, commuter rail can also have positive equity impacts; for example, the Pasadena to Los Angeles commuter rail runs through the heavily immigrant neighborhood of Highland Park and offers residents convenient access to employment and retail in the downtowns of both Pasadena and Los Angeles.

Current policy tends to focus on an equitable distribution of transportation funds across regions, such that suburban transit operators have been highly favored on a per capita ridership basis (Taylor, 1991, 1992). Recent efforts to use "system performance measurement" techniques that prioritize transit needs may be more likely to lead to more equitable transit investments. Additionally, transit-oriented development strategies, such as MTC's Transportation for Livable Communities program, support mixed-used and affordable housing developments such as the Fruitvale station in Oakland—an example of how a transit hub can be turned into a local development opportunity.

The tradeoff between highway and public transit investments also raises equity concerns (Sanchez, Stolz, and Ma, 2003). Because higher-income people are more likely to own and drive cars, the concern is that highway investments disproportionately serve their needs. Furthermore, the general emphasis on driving has disproportionately adverse effects on low-income and minority communities. Urban highways are more likely to be located in low-income residential neighborhoods and vehicle emissions are a major source of ground-level ozone that can cause asthma. Indeed, inner city children have the highest rates for asthma prevalence, hospitalization, and mortality (Centers for Disease Control and Prevention, 1995).

On the finance side, federal and state fuel taxes collected at the pump are a major source of transportation funding for highways, roads, and transit. Some have argued that fuel taxes are regressive because low-income drivers pay a higher share of income per mile driven. However, low-income people tend to drive few miles, and fuel taxes make up a lower share of household expenditures for low-income families (Poterba, 1991). Local sales taxes, a major source of funding for transportation, are regressive because low-income families spend a higher share of their income on taxed items. Other user fees, such as toll roads, also create equity concerns because they typically do not consider users' ability to pay and are thus likely to be regressive and potentially limit access. The Legislative Analyst's Office (1998c) suggests measures for subsidizing low-income drivers. Nevertheless, the benefits of toll roads may be widespread including less congestion on traditional roads as well as potential for tolls to be used for general road improvements.

School Facilities

Although equitable educational investments are critical for increasing economic opportunities for disadvantaged populations, California schools that serve low-income, African American, and Latino students tend to have lower-quality resources, including more uncertified teachers and curricula that offer fewer college preparatory courses per student (Reed, 2005; Betts, Rueben, and Danenberg, 2000). The evidence on school facilities shows a similar pattern. Overall, 17 percent of California public school students are in critically overcrowded schools, which the California Department of Education (CDE) defines as those with more than 90 students per usable acre for high schools and middle schools or more than 115 students for elementary schools. About 5 percent of white students are enrolled in such schools whereas the comparable figure for African American, Latino, and low-income students is about 25 percent (Table 7.1). The problem is particularly acute in the Los Angeles Unified School District, where almost 80 percent of students are in critically overcrowded schools.

As a measure of overcrowding, number of students per usable acre is not ideal because *classroom* crowding can occur in schools with acres devoted to fields or large common areas. However, comprehensive data

Table 7.1

Critically Overcrowded and Multitrack School Facilities in California, 2003

	% in Critically Overcrowded Schools	% in Critically Overcrowded or Multitrack Schools
All	17	24
White	5	11
Latino	25	34
Filipino	14	20
Other Asian	14	19
African American	24	34
Pacific Islander	12	20
American Indian	6	12
Multirace	6	12
Students on meal program	25	35
Los Angeles Unified	79	80

SOURCE: Authors' calculations from data provided by the California Department of Education.

on classroom overcrowding are not available for California schools. As an alternative, we examined the use of multitrack scheduling, which allows schools to enroll more students by staggering student vacations throughout the year. Statewide, 24 percent of students are in schools that are either critically overcrowded or have multitrack schedules. Among white students, the share is 11 percent; the comparable figure for Latino, African American, and low-income students is close to 35 percent.

Schools also differ in the quality and upkeep of facilities as well as in the provision of specific facilities, including computers, Internet access, libraries, laboratories and other specialized classrooms (e.g., woodshop), and sports and exercise facilities. Although the CDE has data for some of these facilities, such as computer availability, there are no systematic data that would support a comprehensive equity study of school facilities.

The plaintiffs in *Williams vs. California*, a class-action lawsuit filed in San Francisco Superior Court in May 2000, argued that schools in low-income communities and communities of color are more likely to have extremely hot or cold classrooms, unkempt or inadequate bathroom facilities, and unrepaired and hazardous facilities such as broken windows, vermin infestations, leaky roofs, or mold. In settling the case in August 2004, the state agreed to funding for emergency repairs and a facilities assessment for schools with low academic performance as well as the development of further facilities guidelines, assessments, and funds.

Local bonds remain a major source of school facilities funding, and under this system, a district with high property values can raise substantially more revenue than a low-wealth district, even with the same tax rate. With a 0.06 percent tax rate (the maximum allowed on any single ballot), school districts with rich property tax bases can raise an average of $1,340 per student, whereas the lowest-wealth districts can raise an average of $106 per student (Legislative Analyst's Office, 2001). To address this, the LAO has suggested an "ability-to-pay adjustment program" whereby the state would make up the difference between a district's maximum potential revenue (calculated from the property tax base) and a set standard for local financing of school capital.

Recent state bonds providing $21.4 billion for K–12 schools have several equitable aspects. First, they are paid back through California's progressive state taxes. Second, they spread out the payment over future populations, which will also benefit from the investment, and thereby promote intergenerational equity. Third, school districts can reduce or eliminate the need for a local contribution, which most state bonds require, based on hardship conditions. Fourth, the bonds set aside over $4 billion to target critically overcrowded schools, allowing for preliminary apportionment in advance of meeting all state regulations. Preliminary apportionment, as opposed to "first come, first served" allocation, improves equity for schools in urban areas because of the lengthy time required to find suitable land for new construction.

Despite these virtues, there remains concern that the state bond funds will not be allocated to address the most critical school facilities needs. For example, PolicyLink and MALDEF (2005) estimate that addressing current overcrowding would cost approximately two to four times more than the current allocation of $4.1 billion. In addition to overcrowding, schools need to address repair, renovation, and modernization issues for which there is no system in place to assess priorities and target school facilities most in need. Almost $9 billion in state bond revenue is allocated to new school construction related to growth. Many growing districts face substantial facilities challenges, but it is important to ensure that this policy does not put the needs of "projected" neighborhoods yet to materialize above those of students already in schools with inadequate facilities. In addition, almost $5 billion is allocated to projects that were already in the pipeline in 2002 but do not necessarily represent the neediest schools.

Perhaps the most fundamental barrier to an equitable distribution of school bond funds is the lack of a comprehensive school facilities assessment. The state simply does not have the information to compare schools and identify the greatest facility needs. Several recent reports have called for a statewide inventory and prioritization of need, including the Legislative Analyst's Office (2001), the Little Hoover Commission (2000a), the Joint Legislative Committee to Develop a Master Plan for Education (2002), and PolicyLink and MALDEF (2005). It is too early to tell the extent to which these issues will be addressed by new guidelines, assessments, reporting, and complaint procedures put in place by the Williams settlement.

Higher Education

As David Neumark shows in Chapter 3, with economic forecasts suggesting that the demand for skilled workers will continue to rise, a college education is especially important to economic opportunities in California's labor market. In addition to preparing a more qualified workforce, increased educational attainment can reduce income gaps, especially for Latinos, who are substantially less likely than other racial and ethnic groups in California to advance into higher education. Over the next decade, higher education facilities must address a backlog of deferred maintenance as well as expand to accommodate growing enrollment. As the children of baby boomers reach college age and college participation rates continue to improve, this will produce a "Tidal Wave II" of new college enrollments.

Recent state bond measures provide almost $4 billion for higher education facilities. The situation for CCC has improved dramatically since the passage of Proposition 39, which decreased the supermajority requirement for local school bonds from two-thirds to 55 percent. Since that time, voters have passed about $9.1 billion in local bonds for CCC. One equity issue is whether these funds are available to the community colleges with the greatest facilities needs. About half of community college districts have passed local bonds since 2000, but we know of no analysis that compares bond financing with facility needs at the local level. If low-wealth districts are indeed less able to raise adequate funds through local bonds, the state should consider prioritizing these districts in the allocation of state bond funds.

Several strategies look beyond simply increasing funding to focus on using existing capacity more efficiently. One option is to increase the use of current facilities during summer (Legislative Analyst's Office, 1999). If adopted, such a policy must ensure that low-income students who work during summers are not penalized. Furthermore, financial aid programs would need to consider the greater per year expenses and diminished work opportunities and perhaps provide incentives for accelerated studies. Another strategy is to encourage students to move through the system faster (Dowall and Whittington, 2003). To encourage students to finish within four years, the UC system could follow the University of North Carolina by increasing fees for extended enrollment. However, these additional fees may be disproportionately borne by low-income students who work while attending university as well as by those who require remedial coursework. A scholarship linked to degree progress could relieve the need to work as well as promote four-year graduation.

Distance learning is another strategy that helps relieve facilities constraints. The term refers to courses that can be taken without traveling to traditional classrooms, usually by using the Internet. The CSU system in particular has been moving toward distance learning approaches. Distance learning increases accessibility by allowing students to complete their coursework conveniently, but concerns about the quality of instruction remain. Although many distance learning courses offer real-time interaction with instructors and other students, they do not compare well with traditional courses in this area. In addition, low-income and minority students in California may have less access to the technology (e.g., a home computer) as well as less experience with the technology (Fairlie, 2003).

Another way to increase the efficiency of the higher education system is to rely more heavily on the CCCs for lower-division instruction. This strategy would reduce per student facility and operating costs. One concern with this approach is whether it would adversely affect the traditional CCC student body, which has a relatively higher proportion of low-income, Latino, and African American students. The CCCs have a broad mission to provide workforce training, vocational or occupational education, and remedial education. From an equity perspective, it is important that an increased role for CCCs in lower-division instruction not put at risk these other functions. In addition, there are concerns about whether the CCC is adequately successful in its transfer function (California Postsecondary Education Commission, 2002; Shulock and Moore, 2004). If the transfer function is not successful, it creates a challenge to the Master Plan's promise of access and affordability in postsecondary education.

A final equity issue concerns the location of higher education institutions. A local college is likely to promote educational attainment in nearby neighborhoods, lead to job growth, and attract educated workers who can facilitate further economic growth. For example, the potential for regional economic development inspired the siting of the next UC campus in Merced (University Committee of Merced, 1997).

To meet the access, quality, and affordability goals of the Master Plan, the state's higher education system must expand. The capital funds for facilities appear to be in place for the next few years, although they may not be available to the neediest CCC districts. In this current period of fiscal crisis, financing operating costs may constitute the major challenge to access to public higher education (Hayward et al., 2004).

Water Supply and Quality

The passage of Proposition 50 in November 2002 authorized the sale of $3.44 billion in bonds for water-related programs and affirmed a commitment to "provide a safe, clean, affordable, and sufficient water supply." To meet these goals in all communities requires consideration of several equity issues.

A widespread approach to water conservation and pricing is "demand management," whereby consumers face price incentives to reduce water use. Because water is a basic human need, access and affordability are critical. To ensure both, many California water districts use block pricing to keep prices low for the first units consumed by a household and raise prices as consumption increases (Hanak, 2005). Another approach to ensuring affordability for basic usage is to offer discounts for low-income or medically needy populations, as found in other utilities. Such lifeline discounts could be creatively combined with block-rate pricing to provide affordability in the context of incentives to save water.

Another equity issue concerns the development of water markets, which allocate water to users willing to pay the highest rate. When selling water leads to fallowing land, communities may face job loss, lower sales of services and other goods, and reduced local tax revenue. Because the source communities tend to be in high-poverty, largely Latino, rural regions of the state, these so-called "third party" issues have social equity components. Although there is no comprehensive state policy to mitigate the impact on communities, several recent water deals provide examples of agreements that include earmarked funds to benefit the source communities. Examples include the Palo Verde Irrigation

District (selling to the Metropolitan Water District of Southern California) and the Imperial Irrigation District (selling to San Diego).

One major issue facing California is drinking water contamination. The most common contaminant identified as exceeding maximum levels is arsenic, which is associated with lung and bladder cancer. Problems with arsenic are concentrated in communities that use wells. Data on the affected communities are not currently available, but many believe that they are typically small, rural communities, which tend to have greater shares of low-income and Latino residents. With new federal standards, these communities are faced with expensive arsenic clean-up projects.

For low-income communities, especially those faced with arsenic clean-up or major system upgrades, financing may pose a significant problem. Small communities may be most at risk, especially in the area of wastewater treatment, which is particularly expensive when implemented at a small scale. State and federal programs do offer support for water in low-income communities, however, and the state Revolving Fund gives higher priority for drinking water systems. The U.S. Department of Agriculture provides targeted financial assistance to rural communities for drinking water and wastewater. California also has a small grants program for wastewater systems.

More could be done, however. The Legislative Analyst's Office (2004h) suggests consideration of legislation that would target Proposition 50 bond funding to water systems in disadvantaged communities. In addition to aid for low-income and high-need communities, the federal and state government could offer subsidies directly to ratepayers in low-income households (Congressional Budget Office, 2002). This approach would support low-income households living in communities where most ratepayers could afford higher costs without subsidizing high-income ratepayers in low-income communities.

Community participation and representation in water resource management appear to be particularly poor. In some agricultural areas, landowners alone elect the board members of special water districts (California Senate Local Government Committee, 2003). The Latino Issues Forum (2003) has noted that of 68 regional water quality control board members, only one is Latino and only 11 are minorities. In Rialto, where the poverty rate is 20 percent, the Santa Ana Regional

Water Control Board held a closed-door hearing and rescinded its own order to have polluters pay for clean-up of perchlorate, an industrial contaminant. A clean-up settlement has been reached with only one of 30 responsible parties (Jahagirdar, 2003).

Looking toward 2025, California's population growth will continue to increase demand for drinking water and wastewater services. At the same time, the demand for water for environmental purposes is also expected to grow. These demand pressures, combined with the need to address system upgrades and contamination, will force water prices upward. As prices rise, it will become increasingly important to address water affordability for low-income families and small communities.

Environmental Justice

How does California perform on measures of the equitable distribution of the environmental burdens of a modern society? National studies have given mixed answers, with some showing patterns of inequity and others providing little evidence of significant disparity (Anderton et al., 1994a, 1994b; Been, 1995; Bowen, 2001; and Lester, Allen, and Hill, 2000). In contrast, California studies consistently find evidence of disparities. For example, one study in Los Angeles County found that African Americans were about 50 percent more likely than whites to be living in neighborhoods directly proximate to hazardous waste treatment storage, transfer, and disposal facilities. Latinos were twice as likely as whites to be living near these facilities. These differences diminished but did not disappear when other factors, such as population density and even local land use, were taken into account (Boer et al., 1997). The disparities appear to be due to disproportionate siting of facilities in minority neighborhoods rather than to the move-in of minorities to neighborhoods that became affordable after facilities were sited (Pastor, Sadd, and Hipp, 2001).

Another study of Southern California found that relative to whites, African Americans were a third more likely and Latinos were twice as likely to be living in a neighborhood with a facility that emits high-priority pollutants listed in the federal Toxic Release Inventory. The racial differences in exposure persisted even when controlling for income, land use, and manufacturing presence (Sadd et al., 1999). Statewide analysis using recent census and environmental data finds that relative to whites, African Americans were one-third more likely and Latinos were two-thirds more likely to be living within one mile of a facility reporting toxic air emissions. Disparities diminished but still persisted when controlling for homeownership, population density, and whether the community is rural or urban (Pastor, Sadd, and Morello-Frosch, 2004).

Some air toxins result from the location of private industries and public facilities, but much of this risk is from vehicular sources, and the implications for freeway construction are significant. A study of Southern California ranked neighborhoods by cancer risk from all airborne toxics. The authors found that whites made up roughly two-thirds of the population in the least risky third of census tracts, whereas in the riskiest third of tracts, two-thirds of the population was African American, Asian, or Latino (Morello-Frosch, Pastor, and Sadd, 2001). Even after controlling for income differences, African Americans, Latinos, and Asians generally faced a 15 to 25 percent higher risk of cancer from airborne toxins.

Perhaps because of the substantial evidence of environmental injustice in California, the state has recently become a leader in environmental justice legislation. Senate Bill 115, signed into law in 1999, required that the California Environmental Protection Agency (Cal/EPA) and related agencies administer and enforce programs in a way that "ensures fair treatment." Cal EPA Secretary Terry Tamminen (who was just appointed to serve as Governor Schwarzenegger's Cabinet Secretary) recently announced an action plan to address four priority areas: precautionary approaches to limit adverse environmental impacts, reduction of cumulative health impacts, development of community capacity and public participation, and ensuring environmental justice considerations in the Governor's Environmental Action Plan (California Environmental Protection Agency, 2004). At least seven other pieces of legislation have raised environmental justice concerns, and several focused on landfills and other solid waste facilities (Bonorris, 2004). Other legislation has aimed to ensure that schools are not built too close to freeways and other busy roads, particularly in light of research suggesting a connection between exposure to heavy traffic and respiratory problems, including the triggering of asthma attacks. Caltrans has had an environmental justice policy since 2001. New legislation is in the works to require that landfill operators analyze the impacts of their facilities in terms of cumulative risk imposed on nearby communities, at least when considering expansion of current operations.

Environmental justice considerations can be particularly challenging because many projects provide broad regional economic benefits but also cause sharp, localized environmental degradation. In these cases, planners may seek to compensate the community with the creation of new employment opportunities and other economic development. But environmental costs have a high degree of uncertainty and potentially severe personal costs. For example, diesel fumes increase the risk of cancer and respiratory disease, but the probabilities are not well understood and depend on individual biology as well as actual levels of pollution. In some cases, the harm done by contaminants is not discovered until years later (as was the case with asbestos). The Nueva Azalea plant in South Gate is an illustrative example of a project that was rejected largely on the grounds that it might exacerbate cumulative exposure and worsen the state of environmental inequity, despite a significant amount of promised employment and economic compensation.

In the face of these challenging tradeoffs, ensuring environmental justice may require new strategies. One possibility is to require community participation and engagement in infrastructure decisions when a project is expected to exacerbate existing environmental inequalities. Another possibility is to require a publicly available environmental justice analysis for infrastructure projects. Alternatively, environmental quality could be regulated as a binding constraint rather than traded for economic opportunities.

What Will It Take to Improve Equity by 2025?

In this section, we consider the forces shaping the future of infrastructure equity and the broad policy directions that would promote more equitable investment. In particular, we address five components of equitable infrastructure investment: equity-based infrastructure assessment, equitable funding, community participation, innovative integrated policies, and public will and leadership.

Equity-Based Infrastructure Assessment

If infrastructure investments are to target the communities with the greatest needs, California must develop a strategy for assessing needs. Since 2002–03, the governor has been required to present a statewide five-year infrastructure plan, but that plan has not been clear on how priorities were implemented within or across departments; and some departments lack the basic data from which to assess needs (Legislative Analyst's Office, 2003a; State of California, 2004). State law clarifies the intent of planning priorities to "promote equity, strengthen the economy, protect the environment, and promote public health and safety in the state" (Assembly Bill 857, Chapter 1016, Statutes of 2002). These priorities were to be implemented with the 2004 five-year infrastructure plan, which was put on hold by the current administration. It remains to be seen how the state plan will promote equity, but substantial infrastructure investment also occurs at the local level, and thus evaluation of priorities would need to go beyond the state plan (Center for the Continuing Study of the California Economy, 1999).

Equitable Funding

Most infrastructure investment is funded through bonds. Bonds have equitable aspects including that payments are spread over future generations who will be the users of today's new infrastructure. Furthermore, general obligation bonds are paid back through California's progressive state taxes. Recent school bonds further promote equity by prioritizing critically overcrowded schools. However, as the case of schools facilities illustrates, bond funding can be unstable and delayed until problems become acute. In contrast to bonds, sales tax add-ons, such as those used to finance local transportation projects, are regressive because low-income families tend to spend a larger share of their income on taxed items.

User fees have been gaining momentum in California and elsewhere. The advantage of user fees is that a higher burden of the cost of provision is borne by those who use the infrastructure services. However, user fees are sometimes regressive and may create barriers to access to important infrastructure services. For example, substantial growth in transit fares could limit access to jobs, health services, and other amenities for some poor families (Rice, 2004). In principle, this concern could be addressed by combining higher user fees with expanded subsidies for low-income families. For example, the Legislative Analyst's Office (1998c) suggests toll subsidies for low-income drivers. Fee increases for higher education could be combined with increased financial aid, perhaps even reducing the costs for low-income families to below today's levels. However, this approach could also diminish popular support for the subsidy, especially among those who must pay more for the same service. As with user fees, impact fees for new homes pay for infrastructure including sewage lines, roads, and schools, but they also increase the cost of new homes. One strategy to promote equity is to reduce or remove the impact fee for affordable housing projects.

In October 2003, California voters rejected Proposition 53 to create an infrastructure fund from general revenue fund transfers. This initiative would have provided a "reliable and significant source of funds for state infrastructure needs" (Legislative Analyst's Office, 2003a) and it would have required that half of the fund be allocated to local government infrastructure. This type of funding would provide a way to move forward on the highest-priority projects and to coordinate state and local priorities.

Community Participation

Developing investments equitably also requires seeking participation in decisionmaking from affected groups. Infrastructure investments inherently involve tough choices about how to allocate resources and how to weigh opportunities and costs that can be hard to quantify. Federal statutes, which apply particularly in the case of transportation because of the high degree of federal funding, require opportunities for community input (U.S. Department of Transportation, 2002). Public involvement is also a part of Caltrans policies and the California Environmental Quality Act.

Because infrastructure planning tends to be a long and technical process, full community participation may entail proactive policies on the part of public agencies, including both innovative research and investments in improving the technical capacities of community groups

(Pastor et al., 2004; O'Rourke and Macy, 2003). For example, the Metropolitan Transportation Commission provides grants to community organizations to co-sponsor workshops on its major regional *Transportation 2030* plan. As the Alameda Corridor example shows, those who worry that community voices may disrupt a smoothly running technical process should consider the importance of consensus and other benefits from effective participation.

Integrated Policies and Approaches

In the previous section, we described policy efforts within specific infrastructure sectors, but many policies address equity issues across infrastructure areas. For example, cooperation at the regional level is an approach to growth planning that potentially leads to more equitable infrastructure development and financing (Pastor et al., 2000). Regional cooperation can reduce the concentration of poverty by opening up affordable housing possibilities throughout the region. Regional approaches to development can seek to locate employment opportunities, community colleges, shopping, and other amenities near underserved populations or near transit hubs. Regional tax-sharing schemes can allow for more equitable sharing of the costs of public investments.

To increase financing for infrastructure and development projects in disadvantaged communities, State Treasurer Phil Angelides has launched the "Double Bottom Line" initiative to direct state investment programs and pension investments into needy communities. The first bottom line is fiduciary responsibility to ensure a strong rate of return (with limited risk) on taxpayer and pensioner investments. The second bottom line is to invest in broadening economic opportunities in low-income communities. The plan calls for investment of over $8 billion in pension and state program investment funds toward economic growth and development in California communities. Thus far, the plan has led to investments in affordable housing, home mortgages, community development, and private businesses in underserved communities (California State Treasurer, 2004b).

Another integrated approach is to provide incentives or remove barriers for local development plans when the plans address equity concerns. An example of providing incentives is the Metropolitan Transportation Commission's program to provide transit funding to cities and counties that address housing affordability issues. An approach to removing barriers is reduction of the voter threshold for new local infrastructure resources (special taxes and bonds) from two-thirds to 55 percent when projects provide for a balanced mix of investments in neighborhoods and transportation, affordable housing, open space, and general infrastructure. By lowering the voter requirements and by requiring that various constituencies work together to form a comprehensive, balanced plan, these constitutional amendments would help local communities to address infrastructure equity concerns (PolicyLink, 2003).

Another approach would be to add a "Social Impact Review" (akin to an Environment Impact Report) to public infrastructure projects above a certain size (Pastor et al., 2000; Gross, 2002). Such reports would help ensure that equity considerations were integrated into the decisionmaking process for large public investments in infrastructure.

Public Will and Leadership

Public will is an important component of any successful major infrastructure effort. According to the PPIC Statewide Survey, Californians are attuned to the equity issues that accompany these efforts. When asked whether school facilities in low-income and minority neighborhoods are more likely to be in need of repair and replacement, 72 percent of adults said "yes" (see Chapter 8). When asked whether school districts in low-income and minority neighborhoods should receive more public funding for school facilities, even if it means less funding for other school districts, 56 percent of respondents said "yes" (Table 7.2). Republicans were the only group strongly opposed to this approach, with 37 percent responding "yes" and 57 percent responding "no." Of adults who said that school facilities in low-income and minority neighborhood were more in need of repair and replacement, 67 percent agreed with more public funding for these districts.

Table 7.2

Californians' Willingness to Provide Public Funding, 2004

	School Facilities			Roads and Transportation		
	Yes (%)	No (%)	Do Not Know (%)	Yes (%)	No (%)	Do Not Know (%)
All adults	56	38	6	49	44	7
Registered voters	53	41	6	46	47	7
Likely voters	52	43	5	45	49	6
Regions						
Central Valley	47	48	5	40	55	5
San Francisco Bay Area	60	33	7	50	43	7
Los Angeles County	64	30	6	57	36	7
Orange and San Diego Counties	52	41	7	45	48	7
Inland Empire	51	45	4	49	47	4
Party registration						
Democrat	62	31	7	55	37	8
Republican	37	57	6	33	62	5
Independent	58	39	3	52	43	5
Self-identified ideology						
Liberal	67	27	6	60	34	6
Moderate	54	38	8	44	49	7
Conservative	48	46	6	43	51	6
Age						
18 to 34	62	34	4	55	39	6
35 to 54	54	39	7	47	47	6
55 and older	49	41	10	43	48	9
Race and ethnicity						
White	48	46	6	39	54	7
Latino	67	27	6	62	31	7
Asian	59	30	11	50	36	14
African American	67	28	5	66	30	4
Noncitizen	72	21	7	59	33	8
Education						
High school or less	58	35	7	53	39	8
Some college	50	42	8	45	48	7
College graduate	58	37	5	47	47	6
Annual income						
<$40,000	60	31	9	55	36	9
$40,000 to $79,999	55	40	5	48	47	5
$80,000 or more	51	46	3	41	55	4
Has children	56	39	5	50	45	5
Does not have children	55	37	8	47	44	9

SOURCE: PPIC Statewide Survey, 2004. See Baldassare (2004c).

For roads and transportation infrastructure, 61 percent of adults responded that low-income and minority neighborhoods had worse conditions (see Chapter 8; see also Baldassare, 2002a, 2002b). When asked whether low-income and minority neighborhoods should receive more public funding for roads and other transportation infrastructure, even if it means less funding for projects in other neighborhoods, 49 percent of respondents said "yes" and 44 percent said "no." Among likely voters, only 45 percent said "yes." Liberals, African Americans, and Latinos favored more funding, whereas most Central Valley respondents, Republicans, conservatives, and whites were opposed. However, of those who said that transportation infrastructure was worse in these neighborhoods, 65 percent agreed with more public funding.

These findings suggest that Californians favor equitable funding more for school facilities than for transportation infrastructure. This preference may reflect a willingness to invest more equitably in sectors that have a clear effect on broad opportunities. They may also suggest that the supermajority requirement for local bonds may very well impede infrastructure investments that address equity concerns aside from K–14 schools.

In his account of California's recent political and economic history, *Paradise Lost*, Peter Schrag (1998) wonders whether older, whiter, wealthier voters will share a sense a common destiny with younger, minority, and poorer future residents. Consistent with this, the Statewide Survey data suggest that willingness to invest more in low-income and minority communities is highest among the youngest cohorts and declines with age (Table 7.2). Spending trends provide mixed evidence on this issue. Until the mid-1990s, public investment had indeed declined as demographic diversity increased. However, in more recent years, public investment as measured by capital outlays is similar in real, per capita terms to levels of the 1960s, when the state was far less racially and ethnically diverse. Furthermore, there has been a shift in capital outlays away from transportation and toward education. This shift and the recent passage of over $21 billion in new statewide bonds for K–12 school facilities demonstrate that Californians are willing to make large capital investments in children.

Promoting equity is not simply a matter of following current public will—there is a crucial role for leaders to take on the hard task of elevating equity as a concern for policy. Throughout the state, public officials and local leaders are working to reform policy, create an economic vision for low-income areas, and promote investments in disadvantaged communities. The task of connecting people across generations and regions into a sense of common destiny requires leaders willing to provide a vision.

Conclusion

Is California on a path that will lead to equitable infrastructure investments? Equity and environmental justice have emerged as major themes in infrastructure policy, but it remains to be seen how these new policies will be implemented and whether the cumulative effects will be substantial. We believe that several structural impediments to addressing equity issues persist. First, there is only limited evaluation of infrastructure needs, and investment decisions are not generally linked to meeting the most urgent needs. Second, the projected future budget gap and the unstable nature of past infrastructure financing create challenges for addressing equity priorities. Finally, we must enhance the ability of low-income and minority communities to participate in decisions about infrastructure investments that affect them.

Moving on all these fronts will require public will and public leadership. In particular, we must weave a political narrative that connects Californians across generations, regions, and economic and ethnic divisions. We believe that addressing equity and interconnection can be part of that new narrative, and that it is both possible and imperative to do this as the state plans for its next 20 years.

8. Public Opinion: Californians' Views of the Present, the Future, Governance, and Policy Options

Mark Baldassare and Jonathan Cohen[1]

Californians face unprecedented growth-related challenges that could seriously erode their quality of life and economic well-being over the next two decades. Between now and 2025, California's population is expected to grow by 10 million residents. That growth, in turn, will alter the state's economy, racial and ethnic makeup, and regional balance. It is by no means clear that the state is prepared to finance and deliver the basic infrastructure required by this growth or to ensure that unequal access to such infrastructure will not be magnified. Any outcomes, of course, will depend on the public's willingness to pressure the state's leadership to take actions and to support policies that improve the state's prospects.

Does the public realize that this growth and change are on the way? In the late 1990s, a time of giddy optimism about the state's economic and fiscal conditions, our public opinion research indicated that the public was largely unaware of the dimensions of this projected growth and its implications for roads, school facilities, water, and other infrastructure projects. Even so, most residents believed that current problems would worsen. Later, the gubernatorial recall reflected a profound distrust of state government, and the state's persistent budget deficits led state policymakers to postpone critical discussions about California's future. The election of Governor Schwarzenegger restored

[1]This chapter draws on the PPIC Statewide Survey, which benefited from the research and writing of Eliana Kaimowitz, Renatta DeFever, and Kimberly Curry (see Baldassare, 2004b).

some trust in the state's chief executive, but confidence in state government's ability to solve problems has remained low. Thus, we reexamine the public's views about the future in a different and unique historical context.

This chapter presents the results of a PPIC Statewide Survey undertaken for this volume. Conducted in May 2004 with a sample of 2,506 adults, the survey focused on four issues:

- Public perceptions of present conditions;
- Perceptions of the future;
- Attitudes toward governance; and
- Attitudes toward policy options.

Reaching consensus on current conditions, predictions, and policy preferences is of considerable importance, and we therefore devote much of our analysis to these questions. We also analyze similarities and differences in responses across the major regions of the state, racial and ethnic groups, voter status, party affiliation, and other demographic factors. When possible, we contrast the 2004 survey with the findings from the 1999 survey to see whether attitudes about the future have correlated with changes in political and economic circumstances.

To refine the ideas and questions in this survey, we conducted focus group research in Fresno, Los Angeles, and the San Francisco Bay Area throughout 2003 and 2004. We also expanded the survey sample size from its typical large base (from 2,000 to 2,500 adults) and expanded the bilingual survey approach to interviewing in five languages (Chinese, English, Korean, Spanish, and Vietnamese) to better reflect the opinions of diverse groups.

Current Conditions

"It's the economy," could well be the motto of Californians in the early years of the new millennium. When asked to name the most important issue facing the state today, 29 percent of adult Californians placed the economy, jobs, and unemployment at the top of the list. In comparison, 11 percent mentioned gasoline prices, 10 percent cited the state budget and taxes, and 8 percent said education and schools. Our survey in June 2003 found that a similar share (31%) named economic issues as the most important issue facing California. In September 1999, however, only 3 percent named jobs and the economy as their top issue. In the spring 2004 survey, economic issues ranked higher in the San Francisco Bay Area (38%) than elsewhere (Table 8.1).

The degree of concern about economic issues varied significantly across racial and ethnic groups. Forty-one percent of African Americans thought that economic issues were paramount, but only 26 percent of whites thought so. Asians (35%) and Latinos (32%) fell between whites and African Americans on this question (Table 8.2).

We also asked whether the state was headed in the right or wrong direction. Californians were evenly divided on this question: 44 percent of residents said that things in California were generally going in the right direction, 44 percent said the opposite, and 12 percent were uncertain. State residents were significantly more optimistic than they had been a year earlier. The June 2003 survey found that only 30 percent of adults said that things were moving in the right direction. However, respondents were even more optimistic in September 1999 when 61 percent held that view.

Table 8.1

Most Important Issue by Region
(responses in percent)

"What do you think is the most important issue facing people in California today?" (top five mentions)

			Region			
	All Adults	Central Valley	San Francisco Bay Area	Los Angeles	Orange/ San Diego	Inland Empire
Economy, jobs, unemployment	29	27	38	30	23	27
Gasoline prices	11	9	7	13	15	13
State budget, deficit, taxes	10	17	11	6	10	10
Education, schools	8	8	13	6	9	8
Immigration, illegal immigration	5	4	3	6	8	8

Table 8.2

Most Important Issue by Race/Ethnicity
(responses in percent)

*"What do you think is the most important issue facing
people in California today?" (top five mentions)*

| | | Race/Ethnicity | | | |
	All Adults	Asian	African American	Latino	White
Economy, jobs, unemployment	29	35	41	32	26
Gasoline prices	11	14	13	13	10
State budget, deficit, taxes	10	7	8	3	15
Education, schools	8	10	6	6	9
Immigration, illegal immigration	5	2	2	5	6

There were significant differences across regions and population groups on this question. Large shares of residents in the Central Valley (46%), Orange County and San Diego (50%), and the Inland Empire (50%) thought the state was headed in the right direction, but pluralities in the San Francisco Bay Area (48%) and Los Angeles (46%) believed that the state was headed in the wrong direction. There was a sharp partisan divide on this question, as well, with Republicans (59%) expressing more confidence than Democrats (36%). As Table 8.3 indicates, whites were more optimistic than Asians, Latinos, and African Americans about the state's direction. Homeowners were more optimistic than renters (47% versus 38%), and men were more optimistic than women (48% versus 39%).

When asked to rate the seriousness of certain conditions in their own regions of the state, most Californians said that affordable housing (67%) and traffic congestion on freeways and major roads (63%) were big problems. Many residents also cited the quality of education in K–12 public schools (44%), the lack of well-paying jobs (42%), and air pollution (39%) as big problems in their regions. Since the May 2001 survey, there has been a sharp increase in the proportion of state residents who mention housing affordability (47% to 67%), job opportunities (29% to 42%), and air pollution (30% to 39%) as big regional

Table 8.3

Overall Direction by Race/Ethnicity
(responses in percent)

*"Do you think things in California are generally going
in the right direction or the wrong direction?"*

| | All Adults | Race/Ethnicity | | | |
		Asian	African American	Latino	White
Right direction	44	40	27	39	49
Wrong direction	44	39	59	51	39
Do not know	12	21	14	10	12

problems. In contrast, there has been little change in perceptions of traffic congestion (60% to 63%).

Again, attitudes varied across regions (Table 8.4). Concerns about affordable housing were highest in the San Francisco Bay Area (76%), Orange County and San Diego (75%), and Los Angeles (68%).

Table 8.4

Perceived Regional Problems by Region
(responses in percent)

"How big a problem is____in your part of California?"

| | All Adults | Region | | | | |
		Central Valley	San Francisco Bay Area	Los Angeles	Orange/ San Diego	Inland Empire
Availability of housing that you can afford	67	51	76	68	75	60
Traffic congestion on freeways and major roads	63	43	63	78	70	64
Quality of education in K–12 public schools	44	41	53	46	39	38
Lack of opportunities for well-paying jobs	42	44	41	44	32	38
Air pollution	39	54	23	53	29	47

Nearly eight in 10 Los Angeles residents said that traffic was a big problem in their part of California, compared to only 43 percent of Central Valley residents. Most residents in the San Francisco Bay Area (53%) thought that public education had reached that level, whereas only 38 percent of Inland Empire residents thought so. Across regions, significant percentages rated the lack of well-paying job opportunities as a big problem; a higher proportion of Central Valley and Los Angeles residents (both 44%) held that view, compared to 32 percent of Orange County and San Diego residents. More than half (53%) of Los Angeles residents cited air pollution as a big problem, but only 23 percent of Bay Area residents did so.

Attitudes about some of these issues varied significantly across racial and ethnic groups (Table 8.5). Most African Americans (61%) thought that K–12 public education in their regions was a big problem, compared to 45 percent of whites, 42 percent of Asians, and 36 percent of Latinos. Majorities of African Americans (58%) and Latinos (54%) also cited the lack of opportunities for well-paying jobs, compared to 42 percent of Asians and 33 percent of whites. Lower-income and less-educated Californians were much more likely than those with higher

Table 8.5

Perceived Regional Problems by Race/Ethnicity
(responses in percent)

"How big a problem is____in your part of California?"

| | | Race/Ethnicity | | | |
	All Adults	Asian	African American	Latino	White
Availability of housing that you can afford	67	62	77	67	67
Traffic congestion on freeways and major roads	63	57	64	59	65
Quality of education in K–12 public schools	44	42	61	36	45
Lack of opportunities for well-paying jobs	42	42	58	54	33
Air pollution	39	31	46	49	33

incomes or a college education to think that jobs were a big problem. Nearly half of Latinos (49%) and 46 percent of African Americans cited air pollution as a big problem, compared to 33 percent of whites and 31 percent of Asians.

Are residential conditions unequal? Most Californians thought that low-income and minority neighborhoods in their regions were more likely than other neighborhoods to have poor public facilities (Table 8.6). Although majorities across demographic groups and regions agreed with that view, African Americans (90%) were much more likely than Asians (77%), Latinos (72%), and whites (69%) to hold it. Likewise, Los Angeles residents (80%) were the most likely to say that this type of inequity exists, followed by residents in San Francisco (75%), Orange County and San Diego (71%), the Central Valley (67%), and the Inland Empire (63%).

Although the numbers were slightly lower, similar patterns held for perceptions of road and other infrastructure equity. About 61 percent of residents said that low-income and minority neighborhoods in their regions were more likely than others to have roads and other infrastructure in need of repair and replacement. Again, answers varied along regional as well as racial and ethnic lines (Table 8.7). Two-thirds

Table 8.6

Local School Perceptions by Race/Ethnicity
(responses in percent)

"Are low-income and minority neighborhoods more likely than other neighborhoods in your region to have school facilities that are in need of repair and replacement?"

| | All Adults | Race/Ethnicity | | | |
		Asian	African American	Latino	White
Yes	72	77	90	72	69
No	21	12	9	20	24
Do not know	7	11	1	8	7

Table 8.7

Local Transportation Perceptions by Race/Ethnicity
(responses in percent)

*"Do you think that low-income and minority neighborhoods are
more likely than other neighborhoods in your region to have roads
and other transportation infrastructure that are in
need of repair and replacement?"*

	All Adults	Race/Ethnicity			
		Asian	African American	Latino	White
Yes	61	63	86	64	56
No	32	24	13	31	37
Do not know	7	13	1	5	7

of Los Angeles residents noted these inequities, as did majorities in the San Francisco Bay Area (64%), Orange County and San Diego (60%), the Inland Empire (60%), and the Central Valley (59%) regions.

Californians were divided on the issue of state spending on roads and infrastructure projects. Just under half (49%) said that they would rather pay higher taxes and have the state government spend more money for roads and other infrastructure projects, whereas 43 percent said the opposite. A solid majority of Democrats (60%) would rather pay higher taxes and spend more on infrastructure projects, and 50 percent of Republicans would rather pay lower taxes and have the government spend less. Differences across racial and ethnic lines were modest (Table 8.8).

The Future

Few Californians were aware that the state's population was about 35 million people; only 16 percent placed it in the 30 million to 39 million range. According to PPIC projections, the state will have between 43 million and 48 million residents by 2025, but when asked what the state's population might be in that year, only 13 percent of respondents expected the state's population to be in the 40 million to 49 million range in 2025 (Table 8.9). This pattern resembled that of five years ago.

Table 8.8

Tax and Spending Preference by Political Group
(responses in percent)

"Which of the following statements do you agree with more:"

	All Adults	Party Registration			Likely Voters
		Dem.	Rep.	Ind.	
I'd rather pay higher taxes and have the state government spend more money for roads and other infrastructure projects	49	60	42	52	54
I'd rather pay lower taxes and have the state government spend less money for roads and other infrastructure projects	43	35	50	42	39
Do not know	8	5	8	6	7

Table 8.9

Perceptions of California's Population
(responses in percent)

"What do you think the state of California's population is today—in millions?" and "Could you please tell me what you think the state of California's population will be about 20 years from now—in millions?"

	California Population Today	California Population in 2025
Under 10 million	16	8
10–19 million	13	9
20–29 million	13	9
30–39 million	16	8
40–49 million	4	13
Over 50 million	11	27
Do not know	27	26

When told that the state would add another 10 million residents between now and 2025, six in 10 said it would be a bad thing for them and their families, and only 14 percent considered it a good thing (Table 8.10). Whites (66%) were the most likely and Latinos (46%) the least likely to be pessimistic, but pluralities across all political and demographic groups were unenthusiastic about population growth. Earlier surveys—even those conducted when the economy was strong and the state had a budget surplus—showed similar results.

Today's most important issue seems to influence residents' perceptions of what the future holds. The economy, jobs, and unemployment top the list of most important issues in both 2004 and 2025. Across the state, nearly one in four residents said that these economic issues will be the most important in 2025, whereas 10 percent or less mentioned others issues, such as housing (10%), environment and pollution (8%), population growth and development (8%), water quality and availability (7%), or education (5%).

Economic issues were the top future concern in every region, but other important issues showed some regional variation. San Francisco Bay Area residents were more likely than others to express concern about the environment and pollution in 2025 (12%). Residents of the Orange

Table 8.10

Perceptions of Future Growth by Race/Ethnicity
(responses in percent)

"Between now and 2025, California's population is estimated to increase by 10 million people from 35 to 45 million. On balance, do you think this population growth is a good thing or a bad thing or does it make no difference to you and your family?"

| | All Adults | Race/Ethnicity | | | |
		Asian	African American	Latino	White
Good thing	14	18	11	20	12
Bad thing	59	54	58	46	66
No difference	23	23	26	30	19
Do not know	4	5	5	4	3

County and San Diego (12%), the San Francisco Bay Area (11%), and Los Angeles (11%) were nearly twice as likely as Central Valley (6%) or Inland Empire (6%) residents to express concern about future housing costs and availability. Orange County and San Diego residents were the most concerned about immigration (8%). About one in three Asians, African Americans, and Latinos—but only 18 percent of whites—said that the economy, jobs, and unemployment would be the biggest issues facing California in 2025 (Table 8.11). Whites (11%) were much more likely than Asians (3%), African Americans (3%), or Latinos (2%) to name water quality and availability as the most important issue in 2025.

In general, Californians were pessimistic about the future quality of life in their state. Nearly half (49%) thought that the state will be a worse place to live in 2025 than it is now; one-quarter said it will be a better place, and one-fifth said there will be no change (Table 8.12). Five years ago, 43 percent thought it would be a worse place and a similar 25 percent expected it to become a better place by 2025. Levels of pessimism were similar across regions but varied across racial and ethnic groups. Whites (57%) were more likely than African Americans

Table 8.11

Most Important Issue in 2025 by Race/Ethnicity
(responses in percent)

"What do you think will be the most important issue facing people in California in the year 2025?"(top 6 mentions)

	All Adults	Race/Ethnicity			
		Asian	African American	Latino	White
Economy, jobs, unemployment	24	32	33	33	18
Housing costs, housing availability	10	12	15	8	10
Environment, pollution	8	6	3	4	11
Population growth and development	8	8	8	8	8
Water quality and availability	7	3	3	2	11
Education, schools	5	5	7	5	5

Table 8.12

Overall Conditions in 2025 by Race/Ethnicity
(responses in percent)

*"Overall, do you think that in 2025 California will be a
better place to live than it is now or a worse place to
live than it is now or will there be no change?"*

| | All Adults | Race/Ethnicity | | | |
		Asian	African American	Latino	White
Better place	25	31	25	31	21
Worse place	49	34	49	39	57
No change	20	24	18	24	17
Do not know	6	11	8	6	5

(49%), Latinos (39%), and Asians (34%) to say that the state will
become a worse place to live in 20 years. Residents with and without
children at home were equally pessimistic, but pessimism increased with
education and income.

What should be done to plan for the state's future? About one-third
of residents said that the state should focus on improving jobs and the
economy. Slightly less (30%) cited improved roads, schools, and water
systems, and smaller shares mentioned environmental protection (16%)
and creating a more equal society (9%). By far the top priority for
Asians, African Americans, and Latinos is improving jobs and the
economy; whites were the least likely to mention those issues as well as
creating a more equal society. Whites were also the most likely to
mention roads, schools, and water systems (Table 8.13).

Statewide, pluralities said that their regions will be worse places to
live in 2025 than they are now. Inland Empire residents were the most
optimistic; almost one in four predicted an overall improvement in their
region. Once again, there were significant racial and ethnic differences
(Table 8.14). More than half of whites (52%) were pessimistic,
compared to 30 percent of Asians, 45 percent of African Americans, and
41 percent of Latinos. Asians were the most likely to say that their part
of California will be a better place to live in 2025 than it is now.

Table 8.13

Most Important Priority by Race/Ethnicity
(responses in percent)

*"In planning for the expected population growth between now
and 2025, what do you think should be the state's
most important priority?"*

| | All Adults | Race/Ethnicity | | | |
		Asian	African American	Latino	White
Improving jobs and the economy	34	47	41	37	30
Providing roads, schools, water systems	30	24	19	26	35
Protecting the environment	16	10	9	16	17
Creating a more equal society	9	10	15	12	6
Something else *(specify)*	9	6	16	7	10
Do not know	2	3	0	2	2

Table 8.14

Regional Conditions in 2025 by Race/Ethnicity
(responses in percent)

*"Do you think that in 2025 your part of California will be a better place
to live than it is now or a worse place to live than it is
now or will there be no change?"*

| | All Adults | Race/Ethnicity | | | |
		Asian	African American	Latino	White
Better place	18	25	21	22	14
Worse place	46	30	45	41	52
No change	33	38	33	32	32
Do not know	3	7	1	5	2

Overall, Californians were split over the future of K–12 education and good job opportunities in their regions. Five years ago, they were more optimistic about both issues, with 63 percent predicting an improved public school system and 60 percent expecting improved job opportunities and economic conditions over a 20-year span. Inland Empire residents were more optimistic than residents elsewhere, but regional differences were relatively small (Table 8.15).

There were slightly greater differences across racial and ethnic groups on the questions of public education and job opportunities. A majority of Latinos (55%) believed that the public education system in their part of California will improve, whereas most African Americans (56%), whites (51%), and a plurality of Asians (44%) said that K–12 public education will worsen (Table 8.16). Most African Americans (59%) and Latinos (52%) were also pessimistic about future job opportunities and economic conditions, whereas pluralities of whites (47%) and Asians (45%) expected these conditions to improve. In general, residents with

Table 8.15

Perceptions of Jobs and Schools by Region
(responses in percent)

"Please tell me which is more likely to happen in your part of California."

			Region			
	All Adults	Central Valley	San Francisco Bay Area	Los Angeles	Orange/ San Diego	Inland Empire
The public education system will						
Improve	45	46	39	47	43	52
Get worse	46	46	51	45	48	40
Job opportunities and economic conditions will						
Improve	44	46	46	40	43	53
Get worse	47	48	44	51	47	41

Table 8.16

Perceptions of Jobs and Schools by Race/Ethnicity
(responses in percent)

*"Please tell me which is more likely to happen in
your part of California."*

	All Adults	Race/Ethnicity			
		Asian	African American	Latino	White
The public education system will					
Improve	45	36	38	55	43
Get worse	46	44	56	34	51
Job opportunities and economic conditions will					
Improve	44	45	38	41	47
Get worse	47	34	59	52	45

high incomes and high levels of education were pessimistic about schools but optimistic about the economic conditions.

On other issues that were currently viewed as major regional problems, most residents expected conditions to go from bad to worse (Table 8.17). Large majorities of state residents said that the availability of affordable housing (78%) and traffic conditions (81%) will worsen in their part of California between now and 2025, and this pessimism was shared across regions. Seven in 10 residents (69%) said that air quality will grow worse by 2025.

Although majorities in all racial and ethnic groups thought that air quality will worsen, this view was expressed more often among African Americans (75%) and Latinos (74%) than among whites (67%) and Asians (64%). Racial and ethnic differences were smaller on the issue of housing affordability and traffic conditions. Younger residents were more likely than others to say that air quality will worsen, and pessimism about traffic and housing increased with income and education (Table 8.18).

Table 8.17

Perceptions of Traffic, Air Quality, and Housing by Region
(responses in percent)

*"Please tell me which is more likely to happen in
your part of California."*

		Region				
	All Adults	Central Valley	San Francisco Bay Area	Los Angeles	Orange/ San Diego	Inland Empire
The air quality will						
Improve	23	16	26	24	27	21
Get worse	69	79	65	71	65	74
The availability of affordable housing will						
Improve	18	17	14	18	16	23
Get worse	78	80	80	78	79	73
Traffic conditions on freeways and major roads will						
Improve	15	11	18	14	14	17
Get worse	81	86	77	83	82	82

Governance

When asked who should make important decisions on growth issues, most residents (73%) said that local voters should do so at the ballot box. Preferences for direct democracy were more common in Orange County, San Diego, the Central Valley, and the Inland Empire than they were in the San Francisco Bay Area (Table 8.19). Most African Americans (81%), Asians and whites (73%), and Latinos (71%) also preferred that approach. There were no significant differences between Democrats (73%), Republicans (77%), and Independents (75%) on this question, although support for local direct democracy increased somewhat with income and education.

Table 8.18

Perceptions of Traffic, Air Quality, and Housing by Race/Ethnicity
(responses in percent)

"Please tell me which is more likely to happen in your part of California."

	All Adults	Race/Ethnicity			
		Asian	African American	Latino	White
The air quality will					
Improve	23	22	20	20	25
Get worse	69	64	75	74	67
The availability of affordable housing will					
Improve	18	19	20	18	16
Get worse	78	70	79	78	79
Traffic conditions on freeways and major roads will					
Improve	15	16	20	21	11
Get worse	81	74	79	75	86

Residents lacked confidence in their local government's ability to plan for future growth. Only 15 percent of Californians said that they have a great deal of confidence in their local governments to plan for the future; Orange County and San Diego residents (11%) were the least confident, compared to 17 percent of their Los Angeles counterparts. Confidence was higher among Latinos (19%) than whites, African Americans, and Asians (all 13%) and lower among Independents than Republicans and Democrats (Table 8.20).

The state government also received low ratings on this point. Twelve percent of residents had a great deal of confidence that it could effectively plan for the state's future, 46 percent had only some confidence, and 40 percent had very little or no confidence. Across the state, Inland Empire residents were the most likely (18%) and San Francisco Bay Area residents the least likely (7%) to express a great deal of confidence in the state government (Table 8.21). Those with at least

Table 8.19

Local Growth Decisions by Region
(responses in percent)

"Who should make important decisions on growth issues?"

			Region			
	All Adults	Central Valley	San Francisco Bay Area	Los Angeles	Orange/ San Diego	Inland Empire
Local voters should make the important decisions at the ballot box	73	76	66	73	77	74
Local elected officials should provide leadership and make the most important decisions	23	21	30	22	22	22
Do not know	4	3	4	5	1	4

Table 8.20

Confidence in Local Government by Political Group
(responses in percent)

"How much confidence do you have in your local government's abilities to plan for growth and the future in your region?"

	All Adults	Party Registration			Likely Voters
		Dem.	Rep.	Ind.	
A great deal	15	13	15	10	13
Only some	47	53	49	44	52
Very little	28	25	26	31	27
None at all	8	7	9	14	8
Do not know	2	2	1	1	0

some college education or in higher-income brackets were somewhat more confident than others.

As further evidence of a lack of confidence in state government officials, only 35 percent of California residents approved of the

Table 8.21

Confidence in State Government by Region
(responses in percent)

*"How much confidence do you have in the state government's
ability to plan for the state's future and growth?"*

			Region			
	All Adults	Central Valley	San Francisco Bay Area	Los Angeles	Orange/ San Diego	Inland Empire
A great deal	12	12	7	14	12	18
Only some	46	48	45	46	47	42
Very little	31	30	36	30	31	29
None at all	9	8	11	8	9	8
Do not know	2	2	1	2	1	3

legislature's handling of the plans for the future, and 54 percent of likely voters disapproved. With the exception of Bay Area residents, who were more dubious than their counterparts elsewhere, there were virtually no partisan or regional differences on this question. Among Latinos, 46 percent approved of the legislature's plans, whereas only 31 percent of respondents from other racial and ethnic backgrounds expressed positive ratings.

In comparison, the highly popular governor at the time of this survey was a major source of optimism. Most Californians (55%) said they approved of Arnold Schwarzenegger's plans and policies for California's future, including 82 percent of Republicans, 56 percent of Independents, and 46 percent of Democrats (Table 8.22). Majorities in most regions approved of his approach with the exception of the San Francisco Bay Area (48%). As for racial and ethnic differences, whites (65%) and Asians (58%) were more likely than African Americans (44%) and Latinos (38%) to approve. The governor's ratings increased with age, education, and income.

Table 8.22

Governor's Approval Ratings by Political Group
(responses in percent)

*"Do you approve or disapprove of the way that Governor Schwarzenegger
is handling plans and policies for California's future?"*

	All Adults	Party Registration			Likely Voters
		Dem.	Rep.	Ind.	
Approve	55	46	82	56	61
Disapprove	30	39	8	31	26
Do not know	15	15	10	13	13

Californians see themselves as having a limited role in growth planning today. One in eight Californians said that they had been involved a lot in discussions about the issues in planning for the future in their part of California. In comparison, 58 percent of Californians had little or no involvement. Seventeen percent of African Americans and 14 percent of whites said they had discussed such issues, compared to 9 percent of Latinos and only 3 percent of Asians (Table 8.23). Participation also tended to increase with education, income, and years at one's residence, but there were no significant differences across regions.

Table 8.23

Civic Involvement in Planning Decisions by Race/Ethnicity
(responses in percent)

*"How much have you been involved in discussions about the
issues in planning for the future in your part of California?"*

	All Adults	Race/Ethnicity			
		Asian	African American	Latino	White
A lot	12	3	17	9	14
Only some	30	31	28	22	34
Very little	32	34	33	33	31
Not at all	26	32	22	36	21

Many Californians would like to be more involved in such discussions, however. Overall, one in four Californians would like to be involved a lot, and 41 percent said they would like to be involved only to some degree. Almost a third said they would like very little or no involvement. There were no significant variations across regions or partisan differences on this question, although interest increased with education and varied by race and ethnicity (Table 8.24). Those who lacked confidence in their local government's ability to plan or who thought that the state was going in the wrong direction were more likely to express interest in these discussions.

Table 8.24

Preferences for Civic Involvement by Race/Ethnicity
(responses in percent)

"How much would you like to be involved in discussions about the issues in planning for the future in your part of California?"

	All Adults	Race/Ethnicity			
		Asian	African American	Latino	White
A lot	25	16	35	27	23
Only some	41	45	40	35	45
Very little	20	27	16	22	20
Not at all	12	11	8	16	11
Do not know	2	1	1	0	1

Policy Options

Although most Californians we surveyed were not engaged in local planning discussions, they had strong opinions about what the state must do to plan for the future. Most (85%) named three types of infrastructure projects—school facilities (40%), surface transportation (24%), and water systems (21%)—as their top priorities. Large pluralities of African Americans (58%), Latinos (48%), and Asians (41%) thought that school facilities should be the top priority for state infrastructure funds, but whites were more evenly divided between schools (35%), surface transportation (29%), and water systems (24%).

Democrats (44%) and Independents (43%) were more likely than Republicans (32%) to favor funding for school facilities. Republicans were almost equally split between surface transportation (30%) and school facilities (32%). Half of those ages 18 to 34 gave top priority to school facilities, compared to only a quarter of those ages 55 and older. About half of Californians with children chose school facilities as the top priority, whereas those without children showed significantly less support (34%).

Within the realm of transportation, however, Californians were not of one mind when it came to funding priorities. Almost half (49%) listed road-oriented projects, including freeways and highways (32%), local streets and roads (10%), and carpool lanes (7%). A slightly smaller portion gave priority to transit-oriented solutions, including light rail systems (31%) and public bus systems (13%). Pluralities of Orange County and San Diego (38%) and Inland Empire (37%) residents gave priority to freeways and highways, but similar shares in the San Francisco Bay Area (38%) and Central Valley (34%) preferred light rail systems (Table 8.25). Los Angeles residents were evenly divided between these

Table 8.25

Transportation Priority by Region
(responses in percent)

"What type of surface transportation project do you think should have the top priority for public funding as your part of California gets ready for the growth that is expected by 2025?"

		Region				
	All Adults	Central Valley	San Francisco Bay Area	Los Angeles	Orange/ San Diego	Inland Empire
Freeways and highways	32	28	26	33	38	37
Light rail system	31	34	38	31	28	23
Public bus system	13	12	16	12	12	13
Local streets and roads	10	12	7	11	6	13
Carpool lanes	7	5	5	9	8	6
Something else (*specify*)	4	6	6	3	4	4
Do not know	3	3	2	1	4	4

two modes. Overall, a narrow plurality of urban residents preferred to fund light rail in their areas (32%), and a similarly small plurality of suburbanites preferred spending on highways and roads (34%).

There were also differences in transportation preferences among racial, ethnic, and political groups. Whites (39%) were much more likely than Asians (28%), African Americans (24%), and Latinos (16%) to prefer funding for light rail, but 21 percent of African Americans, 19 percent of Latinos, and 16 percent of Asians thought that the public bus system should have the top priority for public funding. Republicans were more likely than Democrats to prefer funding for freeways and highways (41% versus 26%), and Democrats were more likely than Republicans to prefer funding light rail systems (38% versus 30%).

We also asked a series of tradeoff questions to understand how Californians were thinking through the state's planning issues. In each, respondents were asked to choose between two proposed strategies to address the top priorities for public funding of infrastructure projects. There was considerable consensus that the state should focus on expanding mass transit and making more efficient use of existing freeways and highways (67%) rather than building more freeways and highways (30%). Majorities in each region held this view (Table 8.26). Democrats (73%) expressed more support than Republicans (59%), and whites (79%) were more supportive than Latinos (61%). Support was highest in the San Francisco Bay Area, whereas residents of the Inland Empire preferred new freeways and highways.

When asked to choose between two policy options for preparing the state's education system for 2025, a majority of Californians (55%) preferred strategies to use existing public education facilities more efficiently (Table 8.27). Another 42 percent thought that we should focus on building more schools and universities. Whites (36%) and Asians (38%) were less likely than Latinos (52%) and African Americans (47%) to support new school construction. The preference for more building was lowest in the San Francisco Bay Area. Democrats (40%) and Republicans (36%) express similar support for more building.

Table 8.26

Transportation Tradeoffs by Region
(responses in percent)

*"Which one comes closest to your views about planning
for 2025 in your part of California?"*

			Region			
	All Adults	Central Valley	San Francisco Bay Area	Los Angeles	Orange/ San Diego	Inland Empire
We should focus on expanding mass transit and more efficient use of freeways and highways	67	66	75	64	66	59
We should focus on building more freeways and highways	30	31	23	33	32	38
Do not know	3	3	2	3	2	3

Table 8.27

School Facility Tradeoffs by Region
(responses in percent)

*"Which one comes closest to your views about planning for
2025 in your part of California?"*

			Region			
	All Adults	Central Valley	San Francisco Bay Area	Los Angeles	Orange/ San Diego	Inland Empire
We should focus on repairs and renovation, year-round schools, and other strategies to more efficiently use the existing public education facilities	55	52	62	52	52	52
We should focus on building more public schools and universities	42	45	34	45	42	46
Do not know	3	3	4	3	6	2

As in transportation and education, Californians preferred demand-management strategies for water systems rather than new construction projects in their region (Table 8.28). Fifty-five percent preferred more efficient use of the current water supply, whereas 41 percent would rather build new water storage systems and increase the water supply. Again, the San Francisco Bay Area was the region with the highest level of support for increased efficiency (62%), whereas public support for new water storage systems was highest in the Inland Empire (47%). A majority across all racial and ethnic groups chose water conservation over building new water systems (Asians, 61%; African Americans, 53%; Latinos, 58%; whites, 53%). There were also partisan differences, with most Democrats (58%) favoring water conservation and a majority of Republicans (51%) supporting the building of new water systems. Younger Californians were more likely than older Californians to favor

Table 8.28

Water Facility Tradeoffs by Region
(responses in percent)

"Which one comes closest to your views about planning for 2025 in your part of California?"

			Region			
	All Adults	Central Valley	San Francisco Bay Area	Los Angeles	Orange/ San Diego	Inland Empire
We should focus on water conservation, user allocation, pricing, and other strategies to more efficiently use the current water supply	55	53	62	55	51	51
We should focus on building new water storage systems and increasing the water supply	41	43	33	41	45	47
Do not know	4	4	5	4	4	2

efficiency: 60 percent of 18 to 34 year olds preferred more efficient use of existing supplies, compared to 50 percent of those ages 55 and older.

Another important policy consideration is the extent to which state government should be involved in local planning. When asked about the state's role, about six in 10 Californians believed that the state government should provide guidelines for local land use and development as opposed to leaving land-use decision to localities. Los Angeles residents and Democrats were somewhat more likely to favor this position, as were majorities in each region (Table 8.29) and in each racial and ethnic group (Asians, 64%; African Americans, 63%; Latinos, 62%; whites, 53%). Public support for state land-use guidelines decreased somewhat with age and income. Renters were only somewhat more likely than homeowners to favor state growth guidelines (62% versus 53%).

Californians also had strong opinions about whether and how local governments should work together. Nearly eight in 10 Californians (77%) preferred that local governments work together to form a

Table 8.29

State Government Involvement by Region
(responses in percent)

"Please tell me which statement comes closer to your views."

			Region			
	All Adults	Central Valley	San Francisco Bay Area	Los Angeles	Orange/ San Diego	Inland Empire
The state government should provide guidelines for local land use and development	57	51	59	63	53	60
The state government should not be involved in local land use and development	37	43	36	31	40	37
Do not know	6	6	5	6	7	3

common regional plan. Large majorities favored this view in each party and region (Table 8.30) as well as each age, educational, and racial and ethnic group.

The public's attitudes toward current spending and tax increases will also shape policy choices on planning for the future. A majority of Californians (60%) and likely voters (67%) thought that local government lacked adequate funding for roads, school facilities, and other infrastructure projects. Democrats (70%) were somewhat more likely than Republicans (62%) to hold this view (Table 8.31). Pluralities across regions agreed that their local governments did not have adequate funding. San Francisco Bay Area residents (66%) were the most likely and Los Angelenos (56%) the least likely to say that local government lacked adequate funding. California residents who had incomes over $40,000 (66%), a college education (68%), and who were white (67%) were more likely than their counterparts to say that their local governments had inadequate funding for infrastructure projects.

Table 8.30

Local Government Involvement by Region
(responses in percent)

"Please tell me which statement comes closer to your views."

			Region			
	All Adults	Central Valley	San Francisco Bay Area	Los Angeles	Orange/ San Diego	Inland Empire
Local governments should work together and have a common regional plan	77	78	82	78	74	78
Local governments should work independently and each have its own local plan	20	19	16	20	23	20
Do not know	3	3	2	2	3	2

Table 8.31

Perceptions of Local Government Funding by Political Group
(responses in percent)

"Do you think local government does or does not have adequate funding for the roads, school facilities, and other infrastructure projects that are needed to prepare for future growth in your part of California?"

	All Adults	Party Registration			Likely Voters
		Dem.	Rep.	Ind.	
Does have adequate funding	33	25	32	33	28
Does *not* have adequate funding	60	70	62	61	67
Do not know	7	5	6	6	5

Would Californians support tax increases to prepare for future growth? A solid majority of likely voters (66%) said they would vote to increase the local sales tax for roads and public transit projects by one half-cent for 20 years. (In California, such local special taxes require a two-thirds vote to pass.) Democrats (73%) and Independents (70%) were more likely than Republicans (58%) to support that approach. Latinos (76%) were more likely than residents of any other racial or ethnic group to support a measure of this type. Sixty-six percent of whites and lower percentages of Asian and African Americans (both 59%) said they would vote yes on this measure. Across regions, 66 percent or more of all adults and at least six in 10 likely voters would support this local sales tax increase. There were no significant differences across gender, age, or educational groups or across regions on this issue. However, support for this local transportation sales tax measure declined at higher-income levels. For building and improving local school facilities, the overall majority was even stronger: 72 percent said they would vote yes on a 20-year bond measure to pay for school construction and renovation projects in their local school district.

Residents were more divided, however, when asked whether they would support disproportionate funding for these low-income and minority neighborhoods to alleviate infrastructure deficiencies. Overall, 56 percent of California adults thought that these neighborhoods should receive more public funding for school facilities even if it meant less funding for other school districts; 38 percent say they should not. Large percentages of Latinos and African Americans (both 67%) and Asians (59%) supported that approach for school facilities, but only 48 percent of whites did so (Table 8.32). Party divisions were even more important. Sixty-two percent of Democrats favored disproportionate funding for disadvantaged neighborhoods, compared to only 37 percent of Republicans. Most residents in Los Angeles (64%) and the San Francisco Bay Area (60%) favored this approach, whereas other regions were less supportive.

Of the 56 percent who thought that low-income and minority neighborhoods were more likely than other neighborhoods in their region to have school facilities in need of repair, two-thirds believed that these neighborhoods should receive more public funding even at the expense of other neighborhoods. In contrast, two-thirds of Californians viewed low-income and minority neighborhoods as more likely than others to have roads and other transportation infrastructure in need of repair and replacement, yet they were more evenly divided (49% versus 44%) when asked if these neighborhoods should receive more public funding for roads and other transportation projects. Los Angeles (57%) was the only region where more than half of residents thought that low-income neighborhoods should receive more funding. Whites (54%)

Table 8.32

Preferences for Local School Funding by Race/Ethnicity
(responses in percent)

"Should school districts in low-income and minority neighborhoods receive more public funding for school facilities even if it means less funding for other school districts?"

	All Adults	Race/Ethnicity			
		Asian	African American	Latino	White
Yes	56	59	67	67	48
No	38	30	28	27	46
Do not know	6	11	5	6	6

were not supportive of weighted funding formulas for this purpose, whereas African Americans (66%), Latinos (62%), and Asians (50%) viewed it more favorably (Table 8.33). There was also a partisan divide: Fifty-five percent of Democrats thought that low-income and minority neighborhoods should receive more public funding for this purpose, whereas 33 percent of Republicans held this view. Among the 61 percent of residents who believed that low-income and minority neighborhoods were more likely than others to have road and other transportation deficiencies, 65 percent agreed that such neighborhoods should receive higher public funding even at the expense of others.

Table 8.33

Preferences for Local Transportation Funding by Race/Ethnicity
(responses in percent)

"Should low-income and minority neighborhoods receive more public funding for roads and other transportation infrastructure even if it means less funding for projects in other neighborhoods?"

	All Adults	Asian	African American	Latino	White
Yes	49	50	66	62	39
No	44	36	30	31	54
Do not know	7	14	4	7	7

Conclusion

Much has changed since 1999, the last time we asked Californians to evaluate the state's future. At that time, the state's economy was booming, and the doomsayers who had given California up for dead in the early 1990s were proven wrong. Although Californians in 1999 overwhelmingly believed that their state was headed in the right direction and expected the good economic times to continue, they still worried about the future. Most expected that current problems—such as traffic congestion, crime rates, an income gap between the rich and the poor, and environmental pollution—could only go from bad to worse. Many believed that the best days were behind them, and that the state would never be able to catch up with the rapid population growth and immigration facing the state and plan for a better tomorrow. But they also hoped that schools and job conditions would continue to improve because the economy was strong and the state's coffers were overflowing with public funds.

What gave the public a dim view of the state's future? Many Californians had the nagging feeling that the state's leadership was not up to the challenges that were ahead. Every survey that we conducted in the late 1990s found that many voters did not trust their state government to act efficiently and responsively. This distrust ran deep and helped explain their desire to resolve important issues though initiatives at the ballot box (see Schrag, 1998; Sears and Citrin, 1982; Clark and Inglehart, 1998; Cain and Gerber, 2001; Broder, 2000; Bowler and Donovan, 1998).

That was then, and this is now. No sooner did the new millennium begin than a host of new problems emerged—some confirming the doubts that were present about California's readiness for the future. The high-tech boom went into a tailspin in late 2000 and, with it, the promise of job creation, budget surpluses, and extra funding for public projects without raising taxes. The state began to experience power brownouts in 2001 that many attributed to market manipulation made possible by a flawed state law to deregulate the electricity industry. The terrorist strike in September 2001 officially ended one of the longest periods of U.S. peace and prosperity and launched the war on terror. By 2002, the state's budget deficit had grown and partisan gridlock prevented the governor and legislature from passing a balanced budget on time. That same year, the state's gubernatorial election set a record for the most campaign spending and lowest turnout in state history, and the daily blitz of negative advertising took its toll on an already cynical California public (Baldassare et al., 2004). For the winner of that contest, the new year and 2003 brought more history-making bad news: a record state budget deficit, more gridlock over spending and taxes, record low approval ratings for the governor and state legislature, and the first-ever recall election of a California governor.

When we checked the pulse of Californians in the May 2004 survey, Governor Schwarzenegger had been in office for six months. He was enjoying high approval ratings, and there was a rebound in confidence in the overall direction of the state and improvement in ratings of the state's economy. Still, the mood of the state fell far short of the optimism that was pervasive in the late 1990s. The public had not shed its lingering doubts about the government's ability to perform, and voter distrust was still high.

Today, population pressures and economic uncertainties continue to cloud the state's future. Residents rank jobs and the economy among their chief concerns, both now and over the next two decades. For this reason, they believe that improving the state's economy and job opportunities takes precedence over roads, infrastructure, and environmental protection in planning for growth. Yet there is little doubt that residents regard growth-related problems—such as traffic congestion, air pollution, and housing affordability—as a threat to their quality of life.

Although the facts about population trends are not widely known, the public's reactions to population projections—both statewide and regionally—are strongly negative. Indeed, today's problems are expected to get worse, and the hopes for improving conditions have diminished in the past five years. There is an overwhelming belief that air quality, traffic congestion, and housing affordability will worsen and only muted optimism that we will see improving schools and job opportunities. Most Californians believe that the government lacks the resources to fund roads, schools, and other infrastructure projects that are needed to plan for the future. Moreover, a tiny minority of those sampled is confident that state and local government can rise to the challenge. Their one glimmer of hope at the time of the survey was their new governor.

What type of planning should and could take place as Californians prepare for 2025? Residents agree that the emphasis should be on school facilities, surface transportation, and water systems. They also seem resigned to the fact that the era of big projects in California's history is long gone. Rather than looking to massive highway projects, new public universities, and new water systems, they favor more efficient uses of existing infrastructure. The public believes that the state, working in concert with local governments to develop regional plans, can provide a better blueprint for housing and transportation—one that can ensure jobs, economic vitality, and a decent quality of life for local communities. With certain assurances that their money will be put to appropriate uses, the majority seems willing to invest in the future by increasing taxes and spending for schools, roads, and what they define as deserving purposes.

Other complex issues must also be addressed in any future plans. Immigration and other demographic trends have transformed California into a majority-minority state, and the gap between the rich and the poor has been growing (Reed, Haber, and Mameesh, 1996; Reed, 1999; Reyes, 2001). Most Californians perceive inequalities in roads, schools, and other infrastructure. However, public support for diminishing these disparities—for example, by investing disproportionately in low-income and minority neighborhoods—is more tepid. Yet, without careful planning, current inequities could be locked in for decades or even exacerbated. The challenge of reaching consensus in a state as large and diverse as California is also a roadblock to future planning. Regional, racial and ethnic, and partisan divisions sometimes lead to disparate solutions to current problems—even when everyone acknowledges these problems explicitly.

Last but not least is the task of restoring the public's trust and confidence in government at all levels in California. A concerted effort will be needed to bridge the gap between the people and their government. In our system, voters will have the final say in many of the important policy decisions that shape the future of the state. It is therefore essential to engage the public in a way that informs the decisions they will be asked to make at the ballot box.

Appendix: Survey Methodology

The findings in this chapter are based on a telephone survey of 2,506 California adult residents interviewed between May 24 and June 8, 2004. Interviewing took place on weekday nights and weekend days, using a computer-generated random sample of telephone numbers that ensured that both listed and unlisted telephone numbers were called. All telephone exchanges in California were eligible for calling. Telephone numbers in the survey sample were called up to six times to increase the likelihood of reaching eligible households. Once a household was reached, an adult respondent (age 18 or older) was randomly chosen for interviewing by using the "last birthday method" to avoid biases in age and gender. Each interview took an average of 19 minutes to complete. Interviewing was conducted in English, Spanish, Chinese, Korean, or Vietnamese. This choice of languages is because Spanish is the dominant non-English language in the state, and the three Asian languages account for most of the non-English speaking Asian adults in California. Casa Hispana translated the survey into Spanish. Schulman, Ronca & Bucuvalas, Inc., translated the survey into Chinese, Korean, and Vietnamese and conducted the telephone interviewing.

We used recent U.S. Census and state figures to compare the demographic characteristics of the survey sample with characteristics of California's adult population. The survey sample was closely comparable to the census and state figures on dimensions such as age, gender, and geographic distribution. The survey data in this report were statistically weighted to account for any demographic differences.

The sampling error for the total sample of 2,506 adults is ± 2 percent at the 95 percent confidence level. This means that 95 times out of 100, the results will be within 2 percentage points of what they would be if all adults in California were interviewed. The sampling error for subgroups is larger. The sampling error for the 1,868 registered voters is ± 2.3 percent. The sampling error for the 1,284 likely voters is ± 3 percent. Sampling error is only one type of error to which surveys are subject. Results may also be affected by such factors as wording, question order, and survey timing.

Throughout the report, we refer to five geographic regions. "Central Valley" includes Butte, Colusa, El Dorado, Fresno, Glenn, Kern, Kings, Madera, Merced, Placer, Sacramento, San Joaquin, Shasta, Stanislaus, Sutter, Tehama, Tulare, Yolo, and Yuba Counties. "San Francisco Bay Area" includes Alameda, Contra Costa, Marin, Napa, San Francisco, San Mateo, Santa Clara, Solano, and Sonoma Counties. "Los Angeles" refers to Los Angeles County, "Inland Empire" includes Riverside and San Bernardino Counties, and "Orange County and San Diego" refers to Orange and San Diego Counties. These five regions were chosen for analysis because they are the major population centers of the state, accounting for approximately 90 percent of the state population.

We present specific results for respondents in the four self-identified racial/ethnic groups of Asian, African American, Latino, and white. We did not include the "other" racial/ethnic category because of small sample size. We also compare the opinions of registered Democrats, Republicans, and Independents. The "Independents" category includes only those who are registered to vote as "decline to state." We also analyze the responses of "likely" voters who are the most likely to frequently participate in the state's elections based on their responses to a series of questions on past voting, level of political interests, and intentions to vote.

We used earlier PPIC Statewide Surveys to compare trends over time in California, such as the December 1999 survey that asked residents for their perceptions of California's future and population trends, and a May 2001 survey that asked about the impacts of recent population growth on the state's social and economic conditions (Baldassare, 1999, 2001). We also rely on the survey analysis and interpretation in Baldassare (2000, 2002a).

Bibliography

Altshuler, Alan, and David Luberoff, *Mega-Projects: The Changing Politics of Urban Public Investment*, Brookings Institution Press, Washington, D.C., and Lincoln Institute of Land Policy, Cambridge, Massachusetts, 2003.

American Water Works Association Water Industry Technical Action Fund, *Dawn of the Replacement Era: Reinvesting in Drinking Water Infrastructure*, Denver, Colorado, May 2001.

Anderton, D. L., A. B. Anderson, J. M. Oakes, and M. R. Fraser, "Environmental Equity: The Demographics of Dumping," *Demography*, Vol. 31, No. 2, 1994a, pp. 229–248.

Anderton, D. L., A. B. Anderson, R. H. Rossi, J. M. Oakes, M. R. Fraser, E. W. Weber, and E. J. Calabrese, "Hazardous Waste Facilities: Environmental Equity Issues in Metropolitan Areas," *Evaluation Review*, Vol. 18, 1994b, pp. 123–140.

Anthony, Jerry, "Do State Growth Management Regulations Reduce Sprawl?" *Urban Affairs Review*, Vol. 39, No. 3, 2004, pp. 376–397.

Aschauer, David Alan, "Does Public Expenditure Crowd Out Private Capital?" *Journal of Monetary Economics*, Vol. 24, No. 2, September 1989a, pp. 171–188.

Aschauer, David Alan, "Is Public Expenditure Productive?" *Journal of Monetary Economics*, Vol. 23, No. 2, March 1989b, pp. 177–200.

Association of Bay Area Governments, *Smart Growth Strategy, Regional Livability Footprint Project: Shaping the Future of the Nine-County Bay Area*, Oakland, California, 2002.

Association of Bay Area Governments, *Forecasts for the San Francisco Bay Area to the Year 2030: Projections 2003*, Oakland, California, 2003.

Baldassare, Mark, PPIC Statewide Survey, *Californians and Their Government Series*, Public Policy Institute of California, San Francisco, California, December 1999.

Baldassare, Mark, *California in the New Millennium: The Changing Social and Political Landscape,* Public Policy Institute of California, San Francisco, California, 2000.

Baldassare, Mark, PPIC Statewide Survey, *Special Survey on Growth,* Public Policy Institute of California, San Francisco, California, May 2001.

Baldassare, Mark, *PPIC Statewide Survey: Special Survey on Land Use,* Public Policy Institute of California, San Francisco, California, November 2002a.

Baldassare, Mark, *PPIC Statewide Survey: Special Survey on the Environment,* Public Policy Institute of California, San Francisco, California, June 2002b.

Baldassare, Mark, *A California State of Mind: The Conflicted Voter in a Changing World,* Public Policy Institute of California, San Francisco, California, 2002c.

Baldassare, Mark, *PPIC Statewide Survey: Special Survey on Californians and the Environment,* Public Policy Institute of California, San Francisco, California, July 2004a.

Baldassare, Mark, *PPIC Statewide Survey: Special Survey on the California State Budget,* Public Policy Institute of California, San Francisco, California, May 2004b.

Baldassare, Mark, *PPIC Statewide Survey: Special Survey on Californians and the Future,* (for the California 2025 project), Public Policy Institute of California, San Francisco, California, August 2004c.

Baldassare, Mark, Bruce Cain, D. E. Apollonio, and Jonathan Cohen, *The Season of Our Discontent: Voters' Views on California Elections,* Public Policy Institute of California, San Francisco, California, 2004.

Barbour, Elisa, and Paul G. Lewis, *California Comes of Age: Governing Institutions, Planning, and Public Investment,* Occasional Paper, Public Policy Institute of California, San Francisco, California, 2005.

Barro, Robert J., "Education as a Determinant of Economic Growth," in Edward P. Lazear, ed., *Education in the Twenty-First Century,* Hoover Institution, Stanford University, Palo Alto, California, 2002, pp. 9–24.

Been, Vicki, "Analyzing Evidence of Environmental Justice," *Journal of Land Use and Environmental Law,* Vol. 11, Fall 1995, pp. 1–37.

Benjamin, Roger, and Stephen J. Carroll, *Breaking the Social Contract: The Fiscal Crisis in California Higher Education,* RAND Corporation, Santa Monica, California, 1998.

Berman, Jay M., "Industry Output and Employment Projections to 2010," *Monthly Labor Review,* November 2001, pp. 39–56.

Betts, Julian, *The Changing Role of Education in the California Labor Market,* Public Policy Institute of California, San Francisco, California, September 2000.

Betts, Julian R., Kim S. Rueben, and Anne Danenberg, *Equal Resources, Equal Outcomes? The Distribution of School Resources and Student Achievement in California,* Public Policy Institute of California, San Francisco, California, February 2000.

Black and Veatch, *California Water Charge Survey,* Irvine, California, 2003.

Blackburn, McKinley, and David Neumark, "Unobserved Ability, Efficiency Wages, and Interindustry Wage Differentials," *Quarterly Journal of Economics,* Vol. 107, No. 4, November 1992, pp. 1421–1436.

Blumenberg, Evelyn, "Planning for the Transportation Needs of Welfare Participants," *Journal of Planning, Education and Research,* Vol. 22, No. 2, 2002, pp. 152–163.

Boarnet, Marlon G., "Spillovers and the Locational Effects of Public Infrastructure," *Journal of Regional Science,* Vol. 38, No. 3, 1998, pp. 381–400.

Boer, Tom J., Manuel Pastor, James L. Sadd, and Lori D. Snyder, "Is There Environmental Racism? The Demographics of Hazardous Waste in Los Angeles County," *Social Science Quarterly,* Vol. 78, No. 4, 1997, pp. 793–810.

Bonorris, Steven, *Environmental Justice for All: A Fifty-State Survey of Legislation, Policies, and Initiative,* Public Law Research Institute, Hastings College of the Law, University of California, San Francisco, California, 2004.

Bowen, William, *Environmental Justice Through Research-Based Decision-Making,* Garland Publishing, New York, New York, 2001.

Bowler, Shaun, and Todd Donovan, *Demanding Choices: Opinion, Voting, and Direct Democracy,* University of Michigan Press, Ann Arbor, Michigan, 1998.

Boxall, Bettina, "Water Accord Said to Be in Peril," *Los Angeles Times,* November 7, 2004.

Brackman, Harold, and Steven P. Erie, "California's Water Wars Enter a New Century," in Ali Modarres and Jerry Lubenow, eds., *California's Future in the Balance: Transportation, Housing/Land Use, Public Higher Education, and Water Four Decades Beyond the Pat Brown Era,* Edmund G. "Pat" Brown Institute of Public Affairs, California State University, Los Angeles, California, 2002.

Breneman, David W., *The Challenges Facing California Higher Education: A Memorandum to the Next Governor of California,* National Center for Public Policy and Higher Education, San Jose, California, September 1998.

Broder, David, *Democracy Derailed: Initiative Campaigns and the Power of Money,* Harcourt Brace, New York, New York, 2000.

Brunner, Eric J., and Kim Rueben, *Financing New School Construction and Modernization: Evidence from California,* Occasional Paper, Public Policy Institute of California, San Francisco, California, June 2001.

Cain, Bruce, and Elisabeth Gerber, eds., *California's Open/Blanket Primary: A Natural Experiment in Election Dynamics,* University of California Press, Berkeley, California, 2001.

CALFED, *CALFED Bay-Delta Program Finance Plan,* Sacramento, California, December 2004.

Calfee, John, and Clifford Winston, "The Value of Automobile Travel: Implications for Congestion Policy," *Journal of Public Economics,* Vol. 69, pp. 83–102, 1998.

California Air Resources Board and California Department of Health Services, *Report to the California Legislature: Environmental Health Conditions in California's Portable Classrooms,* Sacramento, California, June 12, 2003.

California Budget Project, *Budget Brief: CA's Public Investment Gap*, 1999, Sacramento, California, available at www.cbp.org/1999/bb990901.html.

California Business Roundtable, *Building a Legacy for the Next Generation*, Sacramento, California, 1998.

California Citizens Commission on Higher Education, *Toward a State of Learning: California Higher Education for the Twenty-First Century*, Sacramento, California, March 1999.

California Commission on Building for the 21st Century, *Invest for California—Strategic Planning for California's Future Prosperity and Quality of Life*, Sacramento, California, 2002.

California Department of Education, *J-200 Expenditure Data, 1959–2002*, various years, available at www.cde.ca.gov/ds/fd/fd/.

California Department of Education, *Year-Round Education: 2002–03 Statistics*, Sacramento, California, September 9, 2003.

California Department of Education, *School Facilities Fingertip Facts*, Sacramento, California, January 2004.

California Department of Finance, *Governor's Budget & Budget Summary*, Sacramento, California, 1962–63.

California Department of Finance, *Governor's Budget & Budget Summary*, Sacramento, California, 1967–68.

California Department of Finance, *Governor's Budget & Budget Summary*, Sacramento, California, 1998–99.

California Department of Finance, *County Population Projections with Age, Sex and Race/Ethnic Detail*, Sacramento, California, 1998.

California Department of Finance, *Governor's Budget & Budget Summary*, Sacramento, California, 2001–02.

California Department of Finance, *California Public K–12 Enrollment Projections by Ethnicity, 2003 Series*, Sacramento, California, October 2003a.

California Department of Finance, *California's Five Year Infrastructure Plan 2003*, Sacramento, California, March 2003b.

California Department of Finance, *California Public Postsecondary Enrollment Projections, 2003 Series,* Sacramento, California, November 2003c.

California Department of Finance, *A Review of the Department of Transportation's Storm Water Management Program,* Performance Review Unit, Sacramento, California, November 10, 2003d.

California Department of Finance, *Population Projections by Race/Ethnicity, Gender and Age for California and Its Counties 2000–2050,* Sacramento, California, May 2004a.

California Department of Finance, Demographic Research Unit, *Interim County Population Projections: Estimated July 1, 2000 and Projections for 2005, 2010, 2015, and 2020,* Sacramento, California, May 14, 2004b.

California Department of Finance, *California Public K–12 Enrollment and High School Graduate Projections by County, 2004 Series,* Sacramento, California, October 2004c.

California Department of Finance, *Governor's Budget & Budget Summary,* Sacramento, California, 2004–05.

California Department of Transportation, "California Transportation Plan 2003," draft, Sacramento, California, June 2003a.

California Department of Transportation, *California Motor Vehicle Stock, Travel and Fuel Forecast,* Sacramento, California, November 2003b.

California Department of Transportation, *Desk Guide: Environmental Justice in Transportation Planning and Investments,* Sacramento, California, 2003c.

California Department of Transportation, *Fact Sheet: Important Events in California's History,* n.d., available at www.dot.ca.gov/hq/paffairs/about/cthist.htm.

California Department of Transportation, http://www.dot.ca.gov/hq/tpp/offices/ote/socio-economic.htm, accessed April 8, 2004a.

California Department of Transportation, *Grant Program— Environmental Justice Context-Sensitive Planning for Communities,* Sacramento, California, 2004b.

California Department of Water Resources, *California Water Plan— Update 2004,* advisory committee review draft, Sacramento, California, June 7, 2004.

California Education Roundtable, *California at the Crossroads: Investing in Higher Education for California's Future*, Sacramento, California, November 1998.

California Employment Development Department, *Table 3.6: Occupational Employment Projections 2000–2010,* August 12, 2003, available at http://www.calmis.cahwnet.gov/FILE/OCCPROJ/Cal$TB6.XLS.

California Environmental Protection Agency, *Environmental Justice Action Plan,* Sacramento, California, 2004.

California Higher Education Policy Center, *Shared Responsibility: Strategies to Enhance Quality and Opportunity in California Higher Education,* June 1996.

California Legislative Joint Committee to Develop a Master Plan for Education, *California Master Plan for Education,* Sacramento, California, September 9, 2002.

California Performance Review Commission, *Government for the People for a Change,* Sacramento, California, August 3, 2004.

California Postsecondary Education Commission, *A Capacity for Growth: Enrollments, Resources, and Facilities for California Higher Education, 1993–94 to 2005–06,* Sacramento, California, 1995a.

California Postsecondary Education Commission, *The Challenge of the Century: Planning for Record Student Enrollment and Improved Outcomes in California Postsecondary Education,* Sacramento, California, 1995b.

California Postsecondary Education Commission, *A Bridge to the Future: Higher Education Planning for the Next Century,* Sacramento, California, September 1999.

California Postsecondary Education Commission, *Providing For Progress: California Higher Education Enrollment Demand and Resources Into the 21st Century,* Sacramento, California, February 2000.

California Postsecondary Education Commission, *Student Transfer in California Postsecondary Education*, Report 02-03, Sacramento, California, February 2002.

California Postsecondary Education Commission, *Fiscal Profiles 2002*, Sacramento, California, April 2003a.

California Postsecondary Education Commission, *Frequently Asked Questions Concerning Student Fees and Financial Aid at California's Public Colleges and Universities*, Sacramento, California, August 2003b.

California Postsecondary Education Commission, *Student Access, Institutional Capacity, and Public Higher Education Enrollment Demand, 2003–2013*, Sacramento, California, June 2004.

California Rebuild America Coalition, "Wastewater Collection and Treatment," policy brief, Sacramento, California, 2003.

California Senate Local Government Committee, *Integrity and Accountability: Exploring Special Districts' Governance*, Publication 1240-S, Sacramento, California, November 24, 2003.

California State Controller, *Counties Annual Report, Cities Annual Report, School Districts Annual Report, Special Districts Annual Report, Streets and Roads Annual Report, Transit Operators & Non-Transit Claimants Annual Report*, Sacramento, California, 1996–97, 1997–98, 1999–00, 2001–02.

California State Controller, Special District Data on Total Fixed Assets for 2001 and 2001, emailed from Alice Fong, August 9, 2004.

California State Treasurer, *Smart Investments: A Special Update of the California Debt Affordability Report*, Sacramento, California, June 1999.

California State Treasurer, *General Fund Supported Debt*, July 1, 2004a, available at www.treasurer.ca.gov/Bonds/gfdebt.pdf.

California State Treasurer, *Investment Initiatives: Ideas to Action*, Sacramento, California, September 2004b.

California State University, Office of the Chancellor, Press Release, "State Budget Agreement Restores Critical Funding for Higher Education," Long Beach, California, August 2, 2004.

California Transit Association and California Association for Coordinated Transportation, *California Public Transit: Report to the California Legislature and Governor Gray Davis*, Sacramento, California, March 1999.

California Transportation Commission, *Inventory of Ten-Year Funding Needs for California's Transportation Systems*, Sacramento, California, 1999.

California Transportation Commission, *Annual Report to the Legislature: Issues for 2002*, Sacramento, California, 2002.

Calthorpe, Peter, and William Fulton, *The Regional City: New Urbanism and the End of Sprawl*, Island Press, Washington, D.C., 2000.

Campbell, Paul R., *Population Projections for States by Age, Sex, Race, and Hispanic Origin: 1995 to 2025*, U.S. Bureau of the Census, Population Division, PPL-47, Washington, D.C., 1996.

Center for the Continuing Study of the California Economy, *Smart Public Investments for the California Economy: Information and Analysis for Infrastructure Planning*, Palo Alto, California, September 1999.

Center for the Continuing Study of the California Economy, *California Economic Growth, 2002 Edition*, Palo Alto, California, 2002.

Center for the Continuing Study of the California Economy, *California Economic Growth, 2003 Edition*, Palo Alto, California, 2003.

Center for Urban Transportation Research, *Public Transit in America: Findings from the 1995 Nationwide Personal Transportation Survey*, University of South Florida, Tampa, Florida, 1998.

Centers for Disease Control and Prevention, "Asthma—United States, 1982–1992," *Morbidity & Mortality Weekly Report*, Vol. 43, 1995, pp. 952–955.

Cervero, Robert, "Efficient Urbanization: Economic Performance and the Shape of the Metropolis," Lincoln Institute of Land Policy Working Paper, Cambridge, Massachusetts, 2000.

Cervero, Robert, "Are Induced-Travel Studies Inducing Bad Investments?" *Access*, University of California Transportation Center, Berkeley, California, No. 22, Spring, 2003.

Ciccone, Antonio, and Robert E. Hall, "Productivity and the Density of Economic Activity," *American Economic Review,* Vol. 86, No. 1, 1996, pp. 54–70.

Citrin, Jack, and Benjamin Highton, *How Race, Ethnicity, and Immigration Shape the California Electorate*, Public Policy Institute of California, San Francisco, California, 2002.

Clark, Terry N., and Ronald Inglehart, "The New Political Culture," in Terry Clark and Vincent Hoffman-Martinot, eds., *The New Political Culture*, Westview Press, Boulder, Colorado, 1998, pp. 9–72.

Congressional Budget Office, *Future Investment in Drinking Water and Wastewater Infrastructure,* Washington, D.C., November 2002.

Crane, Randall, Abel Valenzuela, Dan Chatman, Lisa Schweitzer, and Peter J. Wong, et al., *California Travel Trends and Demographics Study, Final Report,* Institute of Transportation Studies, University of California, Los Angeles, California, December 2002.

Deakin, Elizabeth "Transportation in California: The Coming Challenges," in Ali Modarres and Jerry Lubenow, eds., *California's Future in the Balance: Transportation, Housing/Land Use, Public Higher Education, and Water Four Decades Beyond the Pat Brown Era*, Edmund G. "Pat" Brown Institute of Public Affairs, California State University, Los Angeles, California, 2002.

de Alth, Shelley, and Kim Rueben, *Understanding Infrastructure Financing for California*, Occasional Paper, Public Policy Institute of California, San Francisco, California, 2005.

DeLong, J., *Myths of Light-Rail Transit*, Reason Public Policy Institute, Policy Study No. 244, Los Angeles, California, September 1998.

Denison, Edward F., *The Sources of Economic Growth in the United States and the Alternatives Before Us,* Supplementary Paper No. 13, Committee for Economic Development, New York, New York, 1962.

Douglass, John Aubrey, *The California Idea and American Higher Education*, Stanford University Press, Stanford, California, 2000.

Douglass, John Aubrey, "A Reflection and Prospectus on California Higher Education: The Beginning of a New History," in Ali Modarres and Jerry Lubenow, eds., *California's Future in the Balance: Transportation, Housing/Land Use, Public Higher Education, and Water*

Four Decades Beyond the Pat Brown Era, Edmund G. "Pat" Brown Institute of Public Affairs, California State University, Los Angeles, California, 2002.

Dowall, David, *California's Infrastructure Policy for the 21st Century: Issues and Opportunities*, Public Policy Institute of California, San Francisco, California, June 2001.

Dowall, David E., and Jan Whittington, *Making Room for the Future: Rebuilding California's Infrastructure*, Public Policy Institute of California, San Francisco, California, 2003.

Dreier, Peter, John Mollenkopf, and Todd Swanstrom, *Place Matters: Metropolitics for the Twenty-first Century,* University Press of Kansas, Lawrence, Kansas, 2001.

EdSource, *Portable School Buildings: Scourge, Saving Grace, or Just Part of the Solution*, Palo Alto, California, April 1998.

Erie, Steven P., *Globalizing L.A.: Trade, Infrastructure, and Regional Development,* Stanford University Press, Stanford, California, 2004.

Fairlie, Robert W., *Is There a Digital Divide? Ethnic and Racial Differences in Access to Technology and Possible Explanations,* Final Report to the University of California, Latino Policy Institute and California Policy Research Center, 2003, available at http://cjtc.ucsc.edu/docs/techreport5.pdf.

Fielding, Gordon J., "Transit in American Cities," in Susan Hanson, ed., *The Geography of Urban Transportation*, Guilford Press, New York, New York, 1995.

Fishman, Robert, *Bourgeois Utopias: The Rise and Fall of Suburbia*, Basic Books, New York, New York, 1987.

Fishman, Robert, "The American Metropolis at Century's End: Past and Future Influences," *Housing Facts and Findings,* Vol. 1, No. 4, Fannie Mae Foundation, Washington, D.C., 1999.

Fulton, William, Paul Shigley, Alicia Harrison, and Peter Sezzi, *Trends in Local Land Use Ballot Measures, 1986–2000*, Solimar Research Group, Ventura, California, October 2000.

Garreau, Joel, *Edge City: Life on the New Frontier*, Doubleday Publishing, New York, New York, 1991.

Garrett, M., and Brian Taylor, "Reconsidering Social Equity in Public Transit," *Berkeley Planning Journal,* Vol. 13, 1999, pp. 6–27.

Glickfeld, Madelyn, LeRoy Graymer, and Kerry Morrison, "Trends in Local Growth Control Ballot Measures in California," *UCLA Journal of Environmental Law and Policy,* Vol. 6, No. 2, 1987.

Goldman, Todd, Sam Corbett, and Martin Wachs, *Local Option Transportation Taxes in the United States*, Institute of Transportation Studies, University of California, Berkeley, California, 2001.

Griliches, Zvi, "Measuring Inputs in Agriculture: A Critical Survey," *Journal of Farm Economics*, Vol. 42, No. 5, December 1960, pp. 1411–1427.

Griliches, Zvi, "Notes on the Role of Education in Production Functions and Growth Accounting," in W. Lee Hansen, ed., *Education, Income, and Human Capital*, National Bureau of Economic Research, New York, New York, 1970, pp. 71–114.

Gross, Julian, with Greg Leroy and Madeline Janis-Aparicio, *Community Benefits Agreements: Making Development Projects Accountable,* Good Jobs First and the Los Angeles Alliance for a New Economy, 2002, available at http://www.laane.org/research/docs/CBAs.pdf.

Guth, W., "On the Behavioral Approach to Distributive Justice—A Theoretical and Empirical Investigation," in S. Maital, ed., *Applied Behavioral Economics,* Vol. II, Wheatsheaf, Brighton, United Kingdom, 1988.

Hanak, Ellen, *Who Should Be Allowed to Sell Water in California? Third-Party Issues and the Water Market*, Public Policy Institute of California, San Francisco, California, 2003.

Hanak, Ellen, *Water for Growth: California's New Frontier,* Public Policy Institute of California, San Francisco, California, 2005 (forthcoming).

Hanak, Ellen, and Elisa Barbour, *Sizing Up the Challenge: California's Infrastructure Needs and Tradeoffs*, Occasional Paper, Public Policy Institute of California, San Francisco, California, 2005.

Hansen, Marc, and Y. Huang, "Road Supply and Traffic in California Urban Areas," *Transportation Research A*, Vol. 31, 1997, pp. 205–218.

Harris, Louis, *A Survey of the Status of Equality of Public Education in California: A Survey of a Cross-Section of Public School Teachers,* March 2002, available at www.edfordemocracy.org.

Haughwout, Andrew, "State Infrastructure and the Geography of Employment," *Growth and Change,* Vol. 30, No. 4, Fall 1999, pp. 549–566.

Haughwout, Andrew F., and Robert P. Inman, "Should Suburbs Help Their Central City?" *Brookings-Wharton Papers on Urban Affairs,* 2002.

Haveman, Jon D., and David Hummels, *California's Global Gateways: Trends and Issues,* Public Policy Institute of California, San Francisco, California, 2004.

Hayward, Gerald C., Dennis Jones, Aims McGuiness, Jr., and Allene Timar, *Ensuring Access with Quality to California's Community Colleges,* National Center for Public Policy and Higher Education, San Jose, California, 2004.

Hill, Laura E., and Hans P. Johnson, *Understanding the Future of Californians' Fertility: The Role of Immigrants,* Public Policy Institute of California, San Francisco, California, 2002.

Hill, Laura E., and Joseph M. Hayes, "California's Newest Immigrants," *California Counts,* Vol. 5, No. 2, Public Policy Institute of California, San Francisco, California, November 2003.

Hise, Greg, *Magnetic Los Angeles: Planning the Twentieth-Century Metropolis,* Johns Hopkins University Press, Baltimore, Maryland, 1997.

Horrigan, Michael W., *Employment Projections to 2012: Concepts and Context,* Bureau of Labor Statistics, Washington, D.C., February 2004.

Hundley, Norris, Jr., *The Great Thirst: Californians and Water—A History,* University of California Press, Berkeley, California, 2001.

Innes, Judith, and Judith Gruber, *Bay Area Transportation Decision Making in the Wake of ISTEA: Planning Styles in Conflict in the Metropolitan Transportation Commission,* University of California Transportation Center, Berkeley, California, 2001.

Jaeger, David, "Reconciling the Old and New Census Bureau Education Questions: Recommendations for Researchers," *Journal of Business & Economic Statistics*, Vol. 15, No. 3, July 1997, pp. 300–309.

Jahagirdar, Sujatha, *Down the Drain: Six Case Studies of Groundwater Contamination That Are Wasting California's Water,* Environment California Research and Policy Center, Los Angeles, California, January 2003.

Johnson, Hans P., "A State of Diversity: Demographic Trends in California's Regions," *California Counts*, Vol. 3, No. 5, Public Policy Institute of California, San Francisco, California, May 2002a.

Johnson, James H., Jr., "A Conceptual Model for Enhancing Community Competitiveness in the New Economy," *Urban Affairs Review*, Vol. 37, No. 6, July 2002b.

Johnson, Hans P., "A Review of Population Projections for California," working paper, Public Policy Institute of California, San Francisco, California, 2005.

Johnson, Hans P., Laura Hill, and Mary Heim, "New Trends in Newborns: Fertility Rates and Patterns in California," *California Counts*, Vol. 3, No. 1, Public Policy Institute of California, San Francisco, California, August 2001.

Joint Legislative Committee to Develop a Master Plan for Education, *California Master Plan for Education*, Sacramento, California, September 9, 2002.

Jones, David W., Jr., *California's Freeway Era in Historical Perspective*, Institute of Transportation Studies, University of California, Berkeley, California, June 1989.

Kain, John F., "The Spatial Mismatch Hypothesis: Three Decades Later," *Housing Policy Debate*, Vol. 3, No. 2, 1992, pp. 371–459.

Kain, John F. "The Urban Transportation Problem: A Reexamination and Update," in Jose Gomez-Ibanez, William B. Tye, and Clifford Winston, eds., *Essays in Transportation Economics and Policy*, Brookings Institution Press, Washington, D.C., 1999.

Kawabata, Mizuki, *Access to Jobs: Transportation Barriers Faced by Low-Skilled Autoless Workers in U.S. Metropolitan Areas*, dissertation submitted to the Department of Urban Studies and Planning,

Massachusetts Institute of Technology, Cambridge, Massachusetts, 2002.

Kelejian, Harry H., and Dennis P. Robinson, "Infrastructure Productivity Estimation and Its Underlying Econometric Specifications: A Sensitivity Analysis," *Papers in Regional Science*, Vol. 76, No. 1, January 1997, pp. 115–131.

Kenney, Douglas S., Sean T. McAllister, William H. Caile, and Jason S. Peckham, *The New Watershed Source Book*, Natural Resources Law Center, University of Colorado School of Law, Boulder, Colorado, 2000.

Krist, John, "Salton Sea Pieces Missing from Water Transfer Puzzle," *California Planning and Development Report*, Solimar Research Group, Ventura, California, May 2003.

Landy, Marc K., Megan M. Susman, and Debra S. Knopman, *Civic Environmentalism in Action: A Field Guide to Regional and Local Initiatives*, Progressive Policy Institute, Washington, D.C., 1998.

Latino Issues Forum, *Promoting Quality, Equity and Latino Leadership in California Water Policy*, San Francisco, California, June 2003.

Leavenworth, Stuart, "Dire Warnings for Delta's Future. UCD Scientists Say the State Needs to Prepare for Likely Levee Failures," *Sacramento Bee*, October 5, 2004a.

Leavenworth, Stuart, "Major Shift Mapped for Delta Water," *Sacramento Bee*, September 26, 2004b.

Lee, Ronald, Timothy Miller, and Ryan Douglas Edwards, *The Growth and Aging of California's Population*, California Policy Research Center, University of California, Berkeley, California, 2003.

Legislative Analyst's Office, *A Primer on State Bonds*, Sacramento, California, February 1998a.

Legislative Analyst's Office, *Overhauling the State's Infrastructure Planning and Financing Process*, Sacramento, California, December 1998b.

Legislative Analyst's Office, *After the Transportation Blueprint: Developing and Funding an Efficient Transportation System*, Sacramento, California, March 5, 1998c.

Legislative Analyst's Office, *Year-Round Operation in Higher Education,* Sacramento, California, February 12, 1999.

Legislative Analyst's Office, *California Travels: Financing Our Transportation,* Sacramento, California May 2000a.

Legislative Analyst's Office, *HOV Lanes in California: Are They Achieving Their Goals?,* Sacramento, California, January 7, 2000b.

Legislative Analyst's Office, *A New Blueprint for California School Facility Finance,* Sacramento, California, May 2001.

Legislative Analyst's Office, *Water Special Districts: A Look at Governance and Public Participation,* Sacramento, California, March 2002a.

Legislative Analyst's Office, *Proposition 42 Analysis,* Sacramento, California, March 2002b.

Legislative Analyst's Office, *A Commuter's Dilemma: Extra Cash or Free Parking?* Sacramento, California, March 19, 2002c.

Legislative Analyst's Office, *A Review of the 2002 California Infrastructure Plan,* Sacramento, California, December 19, 2002d.

Legislative Analyst's Office, *Building Standards in Higher Education,* Sacramento, California, January 2002e.

Legislative Analyst's Office, *California Infrastructure Plan,* Sacramento, California, February 19, 2003a.

Legislative Analyst's Office, *A Primer: Assembly Constitutional Amendment 11,* Sacramento, California, February 2003b.

Legislative Analyst's Office, *Analysis of the 2004–05 Budget Bill,* "Capital Outlay Overview," Sacramento, California, February 2004a.

Legislative Analyst's Office, latest debt service ratio projections, emailed from Brad Williams, December 2004b.

Legislative Analyst's Office, *Funding UC Research Facilities,* Sacramento, California, June 2004c.

Legislative Analyst's Office, *Higher Education: Answers to Frequently Asked Questions, What Has Been Happening to Community College Access?* Sacramento, California, May 2004d.

Legislative Analyst's Office, *Analysis of the 2004–05 Budget Bill: Department of Transportation (2660),* Sacramento, California, February 2004e.

Legislative Analyst's Office, *Analysis of the 2004–05 Budget Bill, Funding for Transportation Programs*, Sacramento, California, February 2004f.

Legislative Analyst's Office, *Analysis of the 2004–05 Budget Bill, Intersegmental: Student Fees*, Sacramento, California, February 2004g.

Legislative Analyst's Office, *Funding Eligibility of Private Water Companies*, Sacramento, California, 2004h.

Lester, James P., David W. Allen, and Kelly M. Hill, *Environmental Injustice in the United States: Myths and Realities*, Westview Press, Boulder, Colorado, 2000.

Lewis, Mike, and Russell Clemings, "Long-Sought Delta Water Plan Issued," *Fresno Bee*, June 26, 1999.

Lewis, Paul G., and Mary Sprague, *Federal Transportation Policy and the Role of Metropolitan Planning Organizations in California*, Public Policy Institute of California, San Francisco, California, 1997.

Lewis, Paul G., and Elisa Barbour, *California Cities and the Local Sales Tax*, Public Policy Institute of California, San Francisco, California, 1999.

Little Hoover Commission, *To Build a Better School*, Sacramento, California, February 2000a.

Little Hoover Commission, *Open Doors and Open Minds: Improving Access and Quality in California's Community Colleges*, Sacramento, California, March 2000b.

Little Hoover Commission, *Rebuilding the Dream: Solving California's Housing Crisis*, Sacramento, California, May 2002.

Los Angeles County Economic Development Corp., *Manufacturing in Southern California, April 2004 Update*, Economic Information and Research Department, Los Angeles, California, 2004.

Martin, Glen, "Divvying Up Our Water," *San Francisco Chronicle*, June 25, 1999.

Martin, Hugo. "Proposed South Gate Power Plant Faces Fierce Opposition," *Los Angeles Times*, January 10, 2001a.

Martin, Hugo, "Firm Drops Plan for South Gate Generator," *Los Angeles Times*, March 9, 2001b.

Mazmanian, Daniel A., and Michael E. Kraft, "The Three Epochs of the Environmental Movement," in Daniel A. Mazmanian and Michael E. Kraft, eds., *Toward Sustainable Communities: Transition and Transformation in Environmental Policy*, Massachusetts Institute of Technology Press, Cambridge, Massachusetts, 1999.

McClurg, Sue, *A Briefing on the Bay-Delta and CALFED*, Water Education Foundation, Sacramento, California, March 2004.

McCulloch, Heather, with Lisa Robinson, "Sharing the Wealth: Resident Ownership Mechanisms," PolicyLink, Oakland, California, 2001.

Metropolitan Forum Project, *What If: New Schools, Better Neighborhoods, More Livable Communities*, Los Angeles, California, 1999.

Metropolitan Transportation Commission, *The 2001 Regional Transportation Plan: Equity Analysis and Environmental Justice Report*, Oakland, California, 2001.

Morello-Frosch, Rachel, Manuel Pastor, and James Sadd, "Environmental Justice and Southern California's 'Riskscape': The Distribution of Air Toxics Exposures and Health Risks among Diverse Communities," *Urban Affairs Review*, Vol. 36, No. 4, March 2001.

Multisystems, *JARC Reporting Issues: An Examination of Current Job Access Reverse Commute (JARC) Program Evaluation Efforts*, U.S. Department of Transportation, Washington, D.C., February 2003.

Muro, Mark, and Robert Puentes, "Investing in a Better Future: A Review of the Fiscal and Competitive Advantages of Smarter Growth Development Patterns," Discussion Paper, Brookings Institution Center of Urban and Metropolitan Policy, Washington, D.C., 2004.

Murphy, Patrick J., *Financing California's Community Colleges*, Public Policy Institute of California, San Francisco, California, 2004.

Myers, Dowell, John Pitkin, and Julie Park, "California's Immigrants Turn the Corner," *Urban Policy Brief*, University of Southern California, Los Angeles, California, March 2004.

Natural Resources Defense Council, *Swimming in Sewage: The Growing Problem of Sewage Pollution and How the Bush Administration Is*

Putting Our Health and Environment at Risk, Washington, D.C., February 2004.

Nelson, Arthur C., and David Peterman, "Does Growth Management Matter: The Effect of Growth Management on Economic Performance," *Journal of Planning Education and Research,* Vol. 19, No. 3, 2000, pp. 277–285.

Neuman, Michael, and Jan Whittington, *Building California's Future: Current Conditions in Infrastructure Planning, Budgeting, and Financing*, Public Policy Institute of California, San Francisco, California, 2000.

Neumark, David, *California's Economic Future and Infrastructure Challenges*, Occasional Paper, Public Policy Institute of California, San Francisco, California, 2005.

O'Rourke, Dara, and Gregg P. Macy, "Community Environmental Policing: Assessing New Strategies of Public Participation in Environmental Regulation," *Journal of Policy Analysis and Management*, Vol. 22, No. 3, 2003, pp. 383–414.

Ohland, Gloria, "The Economic Engine That Couldn't," *L.A. Weekly*, June 9–15, 1995.

Orfield, Myron, "Metropolitics: A Regional Agenda for Community and Stability," The Brookings Institution, Washington, D.C., 1997.

Park, George S., and Robert J. Lempert, *The Class of 2014: Preserving Access to California Higher Education*, RAND Corporation, Santa Monica, California, 1998.

Pastor, Manuel, *Widening the Winners Circle from Global Trade in Southern California,* Pacific Council on International Policy, Los Angeles, California, 2001.

Pastor, Manuel, and Enrico Marcelli, "Men N The Hood: Spatial, Skill, and Social Mismatch for Male Workers in Los Angeles," *Urban Geography*, Vol. 21, No. 6, 2000, pp. 474–496.

Pastor, Manuel, and Deborah Reed, *Understanding Equitable Infrastructure Investment for California,* Occasional Paper, Public Policy Institute of California, San Francisco, California, 2005.

Pastor, Manuel, Peter Dreier, Eugene Grigsby, and Marta López-Garza, *Regions That Work: How Cities and Suburbs Can Grow Together,* University of Minnesota Press, Minneapolis, Minnesota, 2000.

Pastor, Manuel, James Sadd, and John Hipp, "Which Came First? Toxic Facilities, Minority Move-in, and Environmental Justice," *Journal of Urban Affairs,* Vol. 23, No. 1, 2001, pp. 1–21.

Pastor, Manuel, Chris Benner, Martha Matsuoka, Rachel Rosner, and Julie Jacobs, "Community Building, Community Bridging: Linking Neighborhood Improvement Initiatives and the New Regionalism in the San Francisco Bay Area," Center for Justice, Tolerance, and Community, University of California, Santa Cruz, California, 2004, available at http://cjtc.ucsc.edu.

Pastor, Manuel, James Sadd, and Rachel Morello-Frosch, "Waiting to Inhale: The Demographics of Toxic Air Releases in 21st Century California," *Social Science Quarterly,* Vol. 85, No. 2, June 2004.

Pincetl, Stephanie, *Transforming California: A Political History of Land Use and Development*, Johns Hopkins University Press, Baltimore, Maryland, 1999.

Pitkin, John, and Dowell Myers, *California Demographic Futures: Projections of Population to 2030, with Immigrant Generation and Year of Arrival,* Population Dynamics Research Group, School of Policy, Planning, and Development, University of Southern California, Los Angeles, California, 2004 (forthcoming).

PolicyLink, *Investing in a Sustainable Future: An Analysis of ACA 14 and SCA 11*, Oakland, California, July 2003.

PolicyLink, *Building Equitable Communities in California: Framing the Infrastructure Investment Challenges*, Oakland, California, 2005 (forthcoming).

PolicyLink and MALDEF, *Ending School Overcrowding: Building Quality Schools for All California Children*, Oakland, California, 2005 (forthcoming).

Poterba, James, "Is the Gasoline Tax Regressive?" *Tax Policy and the Economy,* MIT Press, Cambridge, Massachusetts, 1991.

Quinn, Timothy, *Managing Water in the 21st Century for People and Fish*, Presentation at the Public Policy Institute of California, San Francisco, California, July 19, 2004.

Raphael, Steven, "The Spatial Mismatch Hypothesis and Black Youth Joblessness: Evidence from the San Francisco Bay Area," *Journal of Urban Economics*, 1997.

Reed, Deborah, *California's Rising Income Inequality: Causes and Concerns*, Public Policy Institute of California, San Francisco, California, 1999.

Reed, Deborah, "Recent Trends in Income and Poverty," *California Counts*, Vol. 5, No. 3, Public Policy Institute of California, San Francisco, California, February 2004.

Reed, Deborah, "Education Resources and Outcomes in California by Race and Ethnicity," *California Counts*, Vol. 6, No. 3, Public Policy Institute of California, San Francisco, California, February 2005.

Reed, Deborah, and Jennifer Cheng, *Racial and Ethnic Wage Gaps in the California Labor Market*, Public Policy Institute of California, San Francisco, California, 2003.

Reed, Deborah, Melissa Glenn Haber, and Laura Mameesh, *The Distribution of Income in California*, Public Policy Institute of California, San Francisco, California, 1996.

Reisner, Marc, *Cadillac Desert: The American West and Its Disappearing Water*, Penguin Books, New York, New York, 1993.

Reyes, Belinda I., ed., *A Portrait of Race and Ethnicity in California: An Assessment of Social and Economic Well-Being*, Public Policy Institute of California, San Francisco, California, 2001.

Rice, Lorien, *Transportation Spending by Low-Income California Households: Lessons for the San Francisco Bay Area,* Public Policy Institute of California, San Francisco, California, July 2004.

River Network, *Exploring the Watershed Approach: Critical Dimensions of State-Local Partnerships; The Four Corners Watershed Innovators Initiative Final Report,* Portland, Oregon, September 1999.

The Road Information Program (TRIP), *America's Rolling Warehouses: The Impact of Increased Trucking on Economic Development, Congestion and Traffic Safety*, Washington, D.C., 2004.

Rogers, Terry, "Guidelines Approved to Cut Polluted Runoff; Local Governments in Charge of Cleanup" *San Diego Union-Tribune*, June 13, 2002.

Rose, Heather, Jon Sonstelie, Ray Reinhard, and Sharmaine Heng, *High Expectations, Modest Means: The Challenge Facing California's Public Schools*, Public Policy Institute of California, San Francisco, California, 2003.

Rueben, Kim S., and Pedro Cerdán, *Fiscal Effects of Voter Approval Requirements on Local Governments*, Public Policy Institute of California, San Francisco, California, January 2003.

Ruffolo, Jennifer, *TMDLs: The Revolution in Water Quality Regulation*, California Research Bureau, Sacramento, California, 1999.

Sacramento Area Council of Governments, *Documentation: Projections for Population, Housing, Employment, and Primary/Secondary Students*, Sacramento, California, May 2001.

Sacramento Area Council of Governments, *A Bold First Step for Mobility in the Sacramento Region: Metropolitan Transportation Plan for 2025*, Sacramento, California, August 2002.

Sadd, James, Tom Boer, Manuel Pastor, and Lori Snyder, "'Every Breath You Take . . .': The Demographics of Toxic Air Releases in Southern California," *Economic Development Quarterly*, Vol. 13, No. 2, 1999, pp. 107–123.

Sanchez, Thomas W., Rich Stolz, and Jacinta S. Ma, *Moving to Equity: Addressing Inequitable Effects of Transportation Policies on Minorities*, Center for Community Change and the Civil Rights Project at Harvard University, Washington, D.C., and Cambridge, Massachusetts, 2003.

San Diego Association of Governments, *Preliminary 2030 Cities/County Forecast*, San Diego, California, April 2003.

Schrag, Peter, *Paradise Lost: California's Experience, America's Future*, W. W. Norton, New York, New York, 1998.

Schultz, T. W., "Capital Formation by Education," *Journal of Political Economy*, Vol. 68, No. 6, December 1960, pp. 571–583.

Schultz, T. W., "Education and Economic Growth," in N. B. Henry, ed., *Social Forces Influencing American Education*, University of Chicago Press, Chicago, Illinois, 1961.

Sears, David O., and Jack Citrin, *Tax Revolt: Something for Nothing in California*, Harvard University Press, Cambridge, Massachusetts, 1982.

Shigley, Paul, "Planning Resumes on Connections Between Riverside, Orange Counties," *California Planning and Development Report*, February 2003.

Shoup, Donald, "Cashing Out Employer-Paid Parking," *Access,* Vol. 2, University of California Transportation Center, University of California, Berkeley, California, Spring 1993, pp. 3–9.

Shoup, Donald, "The High Cost of Free Parking," *Journal of Planning Education and Research*, Vol. 17, 1997, pp. 3–20.

Shoup, Donald, "The Trouble with Minimum Parking Requirements," *Transportation Research, Part A*, Vol. 33, 1999a, pp. 549–574.

Shoup, Donald, "Instead of Free Parking," *Access,* Vol. 15, University of California Transportation Center, University of California, Berkeley, California, 1999b, pp. 8–13.

Shulock, Nancy, *On the Durability of the Master Plan in the 21st Century, or If It's Breaking, Why Isn't Anyone Fixing It?* Institute for Higher Education, California State University, Sacramento, California, February 2004.

Shulock, Nancy, and Colleen Moore, *Diminishing Access to the Baccalaureate through Transfer: The Impact of State Policies and Implications for California*, Policy Issue Report, Institute for Higher Education Leadership and Policy, Sacramento, California, 2004.

Silva, J. Fred, *The California Initiative Process: Background and Perspective,* Public Policy Institute of California, San Francisco, California, 2000.

Small, Kenneth, Clifford Winston, and Jia Yan, *Uncovering the Distribution of Motorists' Preferences for Travel Time and Reliability: Implications for Road Pricing*, University of California Transportation Center, University of California, Berkeley, California, August 1, 2002.

Smelser, Neil J., and Gabriel Almond, eds., *Public Higher Education in California*, University of California Press, Berkeley, California, 1974.

Solow, Robert M., "Technical Change and the Aggregate Production Function," *Review of Economics and Statistics*, Vol. 39, No. 3, August 1957, pp. 312–320.

Sonstelie, Jon, Eric Brunner, and Kenneth Ardon, *For Better or For Worse? School Finance Reform in California*, Public Policy Institute of California, San Francisco, California, 2000.

Southern California Association of Governments, *2000–2030 Regional/County Employment Projections,* Los Angeles, California, September 2002.

Southern California Association of Governments, *Meeting of the Plans and Programs Technical Advisory Committee, August 12, 2003,* 2003a, available at http://scagrtp.migcom.com/docManager/1000000042/TAC_Agenda_081203.pdf, accessed May 2004.

Southern California Association of Governments, *Resolving Regional Challenges,* 2003b, available at http://www.coastalconference.org/pdf/B-Sessions/F2B/SCAG_TCC_October2mergeforPPC.pdf, accessed May 2004.

Southern California Association of Governments, *Destination 2030—Final Draft 2004 Regional Transportation Plan*, Los Angeles, California, 2004.

State of California, *2003 California Five Year Infrastructure Plan,* Sacramento, California, 2004.

Surface Transportation Policy Project, *Transportation Tax Votes in California,* Washington, D.C., 2002.

Tafoya, Sonya M., Hans P. Johnson, and Laura E. Hill, "California's Multiracial Population," *California Counts*, Vol. 6, No. 1, Public Policy Institute of California, San Francisco, California, August 2004.

Taylor, Brian D., "Unjust Equity: An Examination of California's Transportation Development Act," *Transportation Research Record*, No. 1297, Transportation Research Board, National Research Council, Washington, D.C., 1991, pp. 85–92.

Taylor, Brian D., *When Finance Leads Planning: The Influence of Public Finance on Transportation Planning and Policy in California,* Ph.D. Dissertation, University of California, Los Angeles, California, 1992.

Taylor, Brian D., *Statewide Transportation Planning in California: Past Experience and Lessons for the Future,* California Futures Conference Discussion Paper, Institute of Transportation Studies, University of California, Los Angeles, California, November 13, 2000.

Taylor, Brian D., Asha Weinstein, and Martin Wachs, "Reforming Highway Finance: California's Policy Options," *California Policy Options 2001,* School of Public Policy and Social Research, University of California, Los Angeles, California, and UCLA Anderson Forecast, Los Angeles, California, 2001.

Texas Transportation Institute, 2003 *Urban Mobility Study,* College Station, Texas, 2003.

Thorbecke, Erik, and Chutatong Charumilind, "Economic Inequality and Its Socioeconomic Impact," *World Development,* Vol. 30, No. 9, 2002, pp. 1477–1495.

Totten, Glen, *A Briefing on California Issues,* Water Education Foundation, Sacramento, California, March, 2004.

Transportation and Land Use Coalition of the Bay Area, People United for a Better Oakland, and Center for Third World Organizing, *Roadblocks to Health Transportation Barriers to Healthy Communities,* Oakland, California, October 2002.

Transportation California, *House, Senate Pass Eight Month TEA-21 Extension,* n.d., available www.transportationca.com/side/reauth. shtml.

U.S. Bureau of Labor Statistics, "Work at Home in 2001, news release, Washington, D.C., March 1, 2002.

U.S. Census Bureau, Governments Division, Census of Governments, *Compendium of Government Finances* and "Individual Unit File Data Files," 1957–1997; "State by Type of Government Data Files," 2002a, available at www.census.gov/govs/www/estimate02.html.

U.S. Census Bureau, *2002 Census of Governments, Government Organization (Volume 1),* Table 5, Washington, D.C., 2002b.

U.S. Census Bureau, *Census of Population and Housing*, STF-3 (decennial), Washington, D.C.

U.S. Census Bureau, Population Division, *Population Estimates by State*, Washington, D.C., 1957–2003.

U.S. Department of Commerce, *Benchmark Input-Output Accounts of the United States, 1992,* Economics and Statistics Administration, Bureau of Economic Analysis, Washington, D.C., September 1998.

U.S. Department of Transportation, *An Overview of Transportation and Environmental Justice,* Washington, D.C., January 2002.

U.S. Department of Transportation, Bureau of Transportation Statistics, *National Household Travel Surveys*, May 9, 2004, available at http://nhts.ornl.gov/2001/index.shtml.

U.S. Environmental Protection Agency, *1999 Drinking Water Infrastructure Needs Survey*, Washington, D.C., 2001.

U.S. Environmental Protection Agency, *The Clean Water and Drinking Water Infrastructure Gap Analysis*, Washington, D.C., September 2002.

U.S. Environmental Protection Agency, *2000 Clean Watershed Needs Survey*, Washington, D.C., 2003.

U.S. General Accounting Office, *Mass Transit: Bus Rapid Transit Shows Promise*, Washington, D.C., September 2001.

UCLA Anderson Forecasting Project, *The UCLA Anderson Forecast for the Nation and California,* UCLA Anderson Graduate School of Management, Los Angeles, California, June 2002.

UCLA Anderson Forecasting Project, *The UCLA Anderson Forecast for the Nation and California,* UCLA Anderson Graduate School of Management, Los Angeles, California, September 2003.

University Committee of Merced, *Impact of the University of California Campus at Merced on the Regional Economy*, Berkeley Digital Library, 1997, available at elib.cs.berkeley.edu.

University of California, Office of the President, Office of Strategic Communication, *Facts About the University of California: 2004–05 Student Fees*, Oakland, California, May 2004.

Vogel, Nancy, "Calfed Distills New Ideas on Water Use," *Sacramento Bee*, June 25, 1999.

Voith, Richard, "Do Suburbs Need Cities?" *Journal of Regional Science,* Vol. 38, No. 3, 1998, pp. 445–465.

Wachs, Martin, "Critical Issues in Transportation in California," in Xandra Kayden, ed., *California Policy Options 1997*, School of Public Policy and Social Research, University of California, Los Angeles, California, 1997, pp. 55–75.

Wachs, Martin, "Fighting Traffic Congestion with Information Technology," *Issues in Science and Technology*, Fall 2002.

Wachs, Martin, "Local-Option Transportation Taxes: Devolution as Revolution," *State Tax Notes*, September 22, 2003a.

Wachs, Martin, "A Dozen Reasons for Raising Gasoline Taxes," *State Tax Notes*, September 22, 2003b.

Wachs, Martin, and Jennifer Dill, "Regionalism in Transportation and Air Quality: History, Interpretation, and Insights for Regional Governance," in Alan Altshuler, William Morrill, Harold Wolman, and Faith Mitchell, eds., *Governance and Opportunity in Metropolitan America*, National Research Council, National Academy Press, Washington, D.C., 1999.

Water Environment Research Foundation, *New Pipes for Old: A Study of Recent Advances in Sewer Pipe Materials and Technology*, Alexandria, Virginia, 2000.

Water Infrastructure Network, *Clean and Safe Water for the 21st Century*, Washington, D.C., April 2000.

Wolch, Jennifer, Manuel Pastor, and Peter Dreier, *Up Against the Sprawl: Public Policy and the Making of Southern California*, University of Minnesota Press, Minneapolis, Minnesota, 2004.

Wyly, Elvin K., and Daniel J. Hammel, "Islands of Decay in Seas of Renewal: Housing Policy and the Resurgence of Gentrification," *Housing Policy Debate*, Vol. 10, No. 4, 2000, pp. 733–734.

About the Authors

MARK BALDASSARE

Mark Baldassare is Director of Research at PPIC. He also holds the Arjay and Frances Fearing Miller Chair in Public Policy and directs the PPIC Statewide Survey—a large-scale public opinion project designed to develop an in-depth profile of the social, economic, and political forces at work in California elections and in shaping the state's public policies. He is the author of nine books, including *A California State of Mind: The Conflicted Voter in a Changing World*. Before joining PPIC, he was a professor of urban and regional planning at the University of California, Irvine, where he held the Johnson Chair in Civic Governance and initiated and directed the Orange County Annual Survey. He has conducted surveys for the *Los Angeles Times*, the *San Francisco Chronicle*, and the California Business Roundtable. He holds a Ph.D. in sociology from the University of California, Berkeley.

ELISA BARBOUR

Elisa Barbour is a research associate at PPIC. She works on projects related to urban development and local-government fiscal and growth policies. Before coming to PPIC, she worked for community and advocacy organizations and completed research on urban poverty, local labor markets, and workforce-development strategies. She holds a B.A. in political science from Oberlin College and an M.A. in city planning from the University of California, Berkeley.

JONATHAN COHEN

Jonathan Cohen is former Associate Director of the PPIC Statewide Survey and is currently Assistant Director of the ABC News Polling Unit. His research interests include survey methodology, state tax policy, and electoral systems. He is the co-author of the second edition of the *California Latino/Latina Demographic Databook*. He has also written a recent book chapter and magazine articles on electoral politics in California. He holds a B.A. in history from the Johns Hopkins University, a graduate diploma from the Nitze School of Advanced

International Studies, and an M.A. in political science from the
University of California, Berkeley.

SHELLEY DE ALTH

Shelley de Alth is a research associate at PPIC. Before coming to
PPIC, she worked as a research assistant at the President's Council of
Economic Advisers in Washington, D.C., where she studied international
trade policy. Currently, she is working on projects related to education
finance, infrastructure finance, and California state and local budgets.
She holds a B.A. in economics from Dartmouth College.

ELLEN HANAK

Ellen Hanak is a research fellow at PPIC. From 1992 to 2001, she
was a research economist at the Center for Cooperation in International
Agricultural Development, France, and before that held positions at the
President's Council of Economic Advisers and the World Bank. Before
joining PPIC, she focused on the effectiveness of foreign assistance to
developing countries, U.S. trade policy, the impact of agricultural research,
the competitiveness of agricultural supply chains, and food safety. At
PPIC, she has launched a research program in the area of water policy.
She holds a Ph.D. in economics from the University of Maryland.

HANS P. JOHNSON

Hans P. Johnson is a demographer whose research interests include
international and domestic migration, population estimates and
projections, and state and local demography. Before joining PPIC as a
research fellow, he was senior demographer at the California Research
Bureau, where he conducted research for the state legislature and the
governor's office on population issues. He has also worked as a
demographer at the California Department of Finance, specializing in
population projections. He holds a Ph.D. in demography from the
University of California, Berkeley.

PAUL G. LEWIS

Paul G. Lewis is a research fellow and Director of the Governance and
Public Finance Program at PPIC. He has written numerous reports,
journal articles, and other publications on local government, urban
development, and related policy topics and is the author of a book,
Shaping Suburbia: How Political Institutions Organize Urban Development.

He currently serves on the editorial board of *State and Local Government Review*. He holds a Ph.D. in politics from Princeton University.

DAVID NEUMARK

David Neumark is a senior fellow in economics at PPIC and a research associate of the National Bureau of Economic Research. He has published numerous studies on school-to-work, workplace segregation, sex discrimination, the economics of gender and the family, affirmative action, aging, minimum wages, and living wages. He is on the editorial boards of *Contemporary Economic Policy, Economics of Education Review*, and *Industrial Relations*. He has also held positions as professor of economics at Michigan State University, assistant professor of economics at the University of Pennsylvania, and economist at the Federal Reserve Board. He holds a Ph.D. in economics from Harvard University.

MANUEL PASTOR, JR.

Manuel Pastor is Professor of Latin American and Latino Studies and Co-Director of the Center for Justice, Tolerance, and Community at the University of California, Santa Cruz. His research on U.S. urban issues has been published in such journals as *Economic Development Quarterly, Social Science Quarterly, Urban Affairs Review,* and *Urban Geography* and has generally focused on the labor market and social conditions facing low-income urban communities. He is co-author of *Regions That Work: How Cities and Suburbs Can Grow Together* and co-editor of *Up Against the Sprawl: Public Policy and the Making of Southern California*. He speaks frequently on issues of community development, social equity, and regional planning and holds a Ph.D. in economics from the University of Massachusetts, Amherst.

DEBORAH REED

Deborah Reed is a research fellow and Director of the Population Program at PPIC. She is a specialist in labor economics with research interests in labor markets, income distribution, public policy, and poverty. A recipient of fellowships from the Mellon Foundation and Yale University, she has served as a consultant to the World Bank in addition to her teaching and research activities. She holds a Ph.D. in economics from Yale.

KIM RUEBEN

Kim Rueben is a research fellow at PPIC, where she studies school finance and resource equity issues and state and local public finance. She is currently visiting the Tax Policy Center, a joint venture of the Urban Institute and the Brookings Institution, where she is studying the effects on state and local governments of changing the federal deductibility of state and local taxes. She holds a Ph.D. in economics from the Massachusetts Institute of Technology.

Some Related PPIC Publications

California in the New Millennium: The Changing Social and Political Landscape
Mark Baldassare

A California State of Mind: The Conflicted Voter in a Changing World
Mark Baldassare

Metropolitan Growth Planning in California, 1900–2000
Elisa Barbour

The Changing Role of Education in the California Labor Market
Julian R. Betts

California's Infrastructure Policy for the 21st Century: Issues and Opportunities
David E. Dowall

Making Room for the Future: Rebuilding California's Infrastructure
David E. Dowall and Jan Whittington

Who Should Be Allowed to Sell Water in California? Third-Party Issues and the Water Market
Ellen Hanak

Financing California's Community Colleges
Patrick J. Murphy

Building California's Future: Current Conditions in Infrastructure Planning, Budgeting, and Financing
Michael Neuman and Jan Whittington

Federal Formula Grants: "Federal Highway Programs"
Tim Ransdell and Shervin Boloorian

Federal Formula Grants: "Federal Transit Assistance Programs"
Tim Ransdell and Shervin Boloorian

Racial and Ethnic Wage Gaps in the California Labor Market
Deborah Reed and Jennifer Cheng

High Expectations, Modest Means: The Challenge Facing California's Public Schools
Heather Rose, Jon Sonstelie, Ray Reinhard, and Sharmaine Heng

Fiscal Effects of Voter Approval Requirements on Local Governments
Kim S. Rueben and Pedro Cerdán

Urban Development Futures in the San Joaquin Valley
Michael B. Teitz, Charles Dietzel, and William Fulton

"Educational Resources and Outcomes in California, by Race and Ethnicity"
California Counts: Population Trends and Profiles
Volume 6, Number 3, February 2005
Deborah Reed

"How Many Californians? A Review of Population Projections for the State"
California Counts: Population Trends and Profiles
Volume 1, Number 1, October 1999
Hans P. Johnson

PPIC publications may be ordered by phone or from our website
(800) 232-5343 [mainland U.S.]
(415) 291-4400 [outside mainland U.S.]
www.ppic.org